P9-DGE-652

*Critical Essays on*

# KATHERINE MANSFIELD

# CRITICAL ESSAYS
## ON
## BRITISH LITERATURE

Zack Bowen, General Editor
*University of Miami*

*Critical Essays on*

# KATHERINE MANSFIELD

*edited by*

RHODA B. NATHAN

*G. K. Hall & Co. / New York*
*Maxwell Macmillan Canada / Toronto*
*Maxwell Macmillan International / New York Oxford Singapore Sydney*

CHAPIN MEMORIAL LIBRARY
400 14TH AVENUE NORTH
MYRTLE BEACH, SC 29577
(803) 448-3338

823.912
Mansfi

Copyright © 1993 by Rhoda B. Nathan

All rights reserved. No part of this book may be reproduced or transmitted in any form or by any means, electronic or mechanical, including photocopying, recording, or by any information storage and retrieval system, without permission in writing from the Publisher.

| | |
|---|---|
| G. K. Hall & Co. | Maxwell Macmillan Canada, Inc. |
| Macmillan Publishing Company | 1200 Eglinton Avenue East |
| 866 Third Avenue | Suite 200 |
| New York, New York 10022 | Don Mills, Ontario M3C 3N1 |

Library of Congress Cataloging-in-Publication Data

Critical essays on Katherine Mansfield / edited by Rhoda B. Nathan.
    p.   cm. — (Critical essays on British literature)
   Includes bibliographical references and index.
   ISBN 0-8161-8868-8
   1. Mansfield, Katherine, 1888–1923—Criticism and interpretation.
 I. Nathan, Rhoda B.  II. Series.
PR9639.3.M258Z62   1993
823'.912—dc20                        93-2963
                                    CIP

The paper used in this publication meets the minimum requirements of American National Standard for Information Sciences—Permanence of Paper for Printed Library Materials. ANSI Z3948-1984.♾™

10   9   8   7   6   5   4   3   2   1

Printed in the United States of America

# Contents

♦

## THE ARTIST IN CONTEXT

# General Editor's Note

◆

The Critical Essays on British Literature series provides a variety of approaches to both classical and contemporary writers of Britain and Ireland. The formats of the volumes in the series vary with the thematic designs of individual editors, and with the amount and nature of existing reviews, criticism. They are augmented, where appropriate, by original essays by recognized authorities. It is hoped that each volume will be unique in developing a new overall perspective on its particular subject.

Rhoda Nathan's selections of Katherine Mansfield criticism are divided into three sections dealing with her early experience in New Zealand, the art of her stories, and the influences on and of her work. Nathan has introduced each section with a full-length essay of her own, and has included three original essays especially written for this volume.

Zack Bowen
*University of Miami*

# Publisher's Note

◆

Producing a volume that contains both newly commissioned and reprinted material presents the publisher with the challenge of balancing the desire to achieve stylistic consistency with the need to preserve the integrity of works first published elsewhere. In the Critical Essays series, essays commissioned especially for a particular volume are edited to be consistent with G. K. Hall's house style; reprinted essays appear in the style in which they were first published, with only typographical errors corrected. Consequently, shifts in style from one essay to another are the result of our efforts to be faithful to each text as it was originally published.

# Introduction

◆

## Praise and Appraisal: Balancing the Account

### RHODA B. NATHAN

There is an old Talmudic fable about a mature man who had two wives—Old Testament society permitted multiple marriages—one young and one old. The old wife plucked his black hairs as she slept, and the young minx pulled the white hairs as he dreamed in her arms. The final outcome was inevitable: the poor man became totally bald. The tale misses something in translation, which fails to reproduce the idiomatic pungency of the Hebrew, but one gets the point, and is braced for an analogy. The subject is Katherine Mansfield, and, although we are not going to pluck her bald in this volume, she is in fact being somewhat ravaged these days as she dreams her eternal sleep.

Dismissed by some critics in the early years as a Chekhov clone or a minor woman's writer of domestic tales, in recent years Mansfield has increasingly been trotted out as an icon of cults and movements and ideologies she could not have been privy to and to which there is no evidence she could have been sympathetic had they existed in her time. A Mansfield "industry" has indeed sprung up of late, primarily in New Zealand, of course, but in international literary circles as well. In her case, however, unlike the subjects of the Boswell or James "industries," the merchandise eventually begins to thin out and has to be recycled or manufactured. The material is, in the main, speculative: what she

The introduction is an abbreviated version of the Birthday Honors Talk given to celebrate the anniversary of Katherine Mansfield's birth at the Birthplace, 25 Tinakori Road in Wellington on 14 October 1990. The original title was "Praise or Appraisal: Justice to Katherine Mansfield."

might have accomplished had her time not run out; what novels might have sprung from her genius after she had exhausted the genre of the short story.

Mansfield's reputation does not benefit from that kind of wishful critical thinking. After all, Henry Thoreau, whose life was snuffed out at almost as tender an age as Mansfield's, has not seemed to inspire that sort of activity. *Walden,* the Journals, and a handful of brilliantly opinionated essays were enough to guarantee his immortality. Franz Kafka is another similar case in point. Tubercular, neurotic, dead at an early age and as much an exile as Mansfield (a Jew in Prague was as much an outsider as a Kiwi in Europe) he accomplished enough work to guarantee his literary survival. Mansfield's record of publication, analyzed and evaluated in this collection, is enough to assure hers.

In all fairness, one must remember that Mansfield, like so many other artists, was pushed and pulled between supporters and detractors. Her husband, J. Middleton Murry, sanctified and exploited her after her death, while hostile critics such as Frank O'Connor, berated her as wanting "heart." By and large, however, her biographers, from Sylvia Berkman, who lacked salient information but not acumen, to the present day, have done her justice in magisterial biographies. If, like Poe and Whitman, she was poorly served by her contemporary keepers of the flame, her husband and editor first, and her sometime friend Virginia Woolf and her confidant Ida Baker second, such deficiencies have been amply compensated by Vincent O'Sullivan, Antony Alpers, Ian Gordon, and Margaret Scott, among other biographers, scholars, and editors in the ensuing years. Now it is time, as Ian Gordon has suggested, to stop digging up the dirt and probing the "secret life," in order to undertake a serious study of the method of her short stories, because nobody has as yet attempted to do a full-scale analysis of her techniques.

This anthology of source and critical essays, several prepared especially for this collection by New Zealand scholars, is designed to cast fresh light on the life and craft of a writer who has been alternately and sometimes simultaneously undervalued, overinterpreted, and categorized through the years. The essays selected range from Murry's predictably biased, but nonetheless valuable, introduction to the first collection of the short stories, to fresh commentaries on "Bliss," "The Garden Party," and other celebrated and much-debated stories. In choosing the essays for inclusion here, I have kept in mind Mansfield's letters to William Gerhardi (recently purchased by the Turnbull Museum in New Zealand), in which, just a year before her death, she worried that she might be both misunderstood and made "fashionable" to satisfy some itch in her readers that had nothing to do with her creative purposes: "I shall not be fashionable long. They will find me out. . . . I like awfully unfashionable things—and people—I like sitting on doorsteps and talking to the old woman who brings the quinces . . . and listening to the kind of music they play in public squares on warm evenings, and talking to captains of shabby little steamers."

From the evidence of those final letters to the aspiring young novelist whom she had befriended and advised, I conclude that Mansfield would much rather have her stories understood and appreciated than become a cult figure in a movement. Professional to her very bones, she would wish to be honored in terms of her own creative priorities. In one letter she agonized that she might have been thought to be "cruel" to Josephine and Constantia, the sisters in "The Daughters of the Late Colonel." In that spirit, this collection is composed of essays whose purpose is to see to it that she is understood according to her stated intention to convey "the diversity of life" to her readers.

# THE NEW ZEALAND EXPERIENCE

◆

# The Life as Source

## RHODA B. NATHAN

There is scarcely an artist in history whose life is not reflected in some significant way in his work. It is left to the biographer to discover and illuminate the connections between the subject's life and work, keeping in mind the fact that the artist bends, distorts, and reshapes the facts of his life to suit his private vision. In Katherine Mansfield's case, the successive stages of her life are clearly reflected in her fiction. The major events correspond directly with the primary subjects of her stories: the New Zealand childhood; the education and periods of expatriation; the love affairs and uneasy marriages; and finally, the pain, isolation, and increasing "inwardness" generated by the inexorable course of her illness that was to terminate her career and her life at the age of thirty-four.

The writer whom readers know as Katherine Mansfield was born Kathleen Mansfield Beauchamp on October 14, 1888, at 11 Tinakori Road in Wellington, New Zealand.[1] The literary "Katherine"—she abandoned her given name in print at an early age and personally somewhat later in 1910—emerged as early as 1897 when she won a school competition with a story called "A Sea Voyage." Kathleen, nicknamed "Kass" by the members of her family, was the third of six children born to Harold and Annie Burnell Dyer Beauchamp, the first five of whom were daughters and the sixth a boy named Leslie. The only son, a great personal favorite of his father and his writer sister, died at the age of twenty-one during World War I. His death, a grotesque accident, was caused by the inadvertent detonation of a hand-held grenade during a military training session. Leslie, who was holding the grenade, and his sergeant, were both killed. Another Beauchamp child, Gwen, next in line after Kathleen, died in infancy.

With the exception of a cousin named Elizabeth von Arnim, who wrote a best-selling romantic novel called *Elizabeth and her German Garden,* the Beauchamp family was solidly mercantile. Katherine's grandfather, Arthur Beauchamp, began his career as something of a ne'er-do-well, migrating from England to New Zealand after the decline of his family's silversmith business. Failing to secure a parcel of land left him by a wealthy New Zealand relative, Beauchamp then moved on to the Australian goldfields, returning to New

From KATHERINE MANSFIELD by Rhoda B. Nathan. Copyright © 1988 by Rhoda B. Nathan. Reprinted by permission of The Continuum Publishing Company.

Zealand for good when he failed as a prospector. This time he succeeded as a general merchant and laid down the foundation of the family fortune.

In the nineteenth century New Zealand was a pioneering country to which the British came primarily for the purpose of making money. Arthur's son Harold, colonial to the core, prided himself on his rapid rise to material success. Leaving school at fourteen, he joined his father's company and later moved on to a large importing firm where in short order he became a partner. By 1907 he was chairman of the Bank of New Zealand and a wealthy and respected member of the provincial community of Wellington. Knighted later in life for his many civic contributions, he was, even in his earliest manhood, the model of the proper and conventional colonial Englishman who was to feature prominently in a number of guises in his daughter's fiction. Under his authority the Beauchamp family was secure and privileged, and if Katherine and her sisters went to the community school with the postman's and farmers' youngsters, it was only because it was the only educational institution available to her family in that frontier settlement.

Katherine's mother, grandmother, and young maiden aunt also appear frequently in her fiction, presented as the Sheridans and the Burnells in the New Zealand stories. The author did not even bother to alter her mother's own surname, using the maternal "Dyer" and "Burnell" on occasion. In real life she often affixed the names of her family members to friends and lovers, calling her schoolmate Ida Baker "Lesley" after her beloved brother Leslie, and her husband John Middleton Murry "Bogey" after that same brother's pet name. Another family member, her uncle Valentine Waters, and his sons Eric and Barrie, became Jonathan Trout and his two sons Pip and Rags, affectionately drawn but impecunious relatives in "At the Bay." Katherine's parents, by contrast, decorous and deeply devoted to each other, are portrayed over and over in the light of their troubled daughter's shrewd understanding and ambivalent regard for them. Harold, the model for Katherine's recurrent portrait of the "pa man,"[2] was a conservative, didactic, and materialistic man whose tenderness was reserved for his beautiful and elegant wife, Annie, who clearly admired her domineering husband and just as clearly disdained his aggressive energy. She became the model for the detached and frail Linda Burnell of the New Zealand stories, loving her husband but resentful of her repeated maternity and aloof from her many children. Whatever nurturing Katherine enjoyed was at the hands of her maternal grandmother, who cheerfully fulfilled the domestic and familial duties her burdened daughter would not perform. The Mansfield *Journal* is a repository of illustrative recollections such as the note commemorating the birth of the newest ill-fated baby:

> "Her name is Gwen," said the grandmother. "Kiss her.... Now go and kiss mother."... But mother did not want to kiss me. Very languid, leaning against some pillows, she was eating some sago.

The three successive Beauchamp residences, the first and last on Tinakori Road, with a rural Karori interlude, all serve as settings, both real and psychological, for some of the most telling stories of location and dislocation. Moving, with its attendant disorientation, settling in, and readjustment, is a powerful theme in "Prelude" and other stories told from a child's-eye view. The houses themselves, more spacious and substantial with each rise in Harold's fortune, call forth from the author a deep appreciation of their beauty and luxury, as in her detailed description of the Sheridan house in "The Garden Party," as well as a discomfited awareness of the poverty of her neighbors. These mixed emotions of pleasure and guilt generated by her family's privilege are carefully preserved in "The Doll's House." Her family's snobbery of rank and her own sentimental identification with the working classes generate a carefully controlled tone of confusion natural to a young girl who is coming of age and inclined to idealize experience outside her personal limited range and scorn her haven as narrow and unchallenging. All the Beauchamp relations, neighbors, and servants find their way into the New Zealand stories, from her father's handyman Pat Sheehan, the central figure in the celebrated duck-decapitation episode in "Prelude" and in the sketch "About Pat," to the kindly but inelegant Jewish neighbors on Tinakori Road, who, as the fictional Samuel Josephs in "Prelude," help to mind the Burnell children during the family's hectic move to the country.

Personal beauty, parental favoritism, social magnetism, and academic success—the "chips" or commodities on which Katherine's sisters and friends traded in the conventional and class-conscious world of her childhood—were all denied to the young Kass. In a family of attractive and tractable siblings, she was homely, fat, severe, and contentious. The early photographs reveal a sullen face made forbidding by steel-rimmed spectacles and a limp hairdo. A stutterer like the young heroine of "The Little Girl" and "New Dresses," and openly defiant of her parents and teachers, Katherine stood out in a family of docile girls and a favored long-awaited son. Further, the intractable girl exacerbated her position through her uncertain temper and undistinguished record at school, which she herself characterized in later years as a period of idleness.[3] At the Wellington High School, she was described by her headmistress as "surly" and given to untruthfulness. Nevertheless, she showed early evidence of writing talent in her first published short story, "Enna Blake," which even the headmistress praised. In every other way, however, she remained willfully isolated and rebellious, much as Helen, in "New Dresses," is portrayed—rambunctious, troublesome, and appreciated only by those willing to take the trouble to see beneath the surface of her petulance.

The young rebel's first opportunity to escape her confining environment came in 1903, when her parents agreed to have her attend Queens College in London in the company of her two older sisters and her young maiden aunt, Belle Dyer. Katherine was only fourteen. Though she was to return to New

Zealand a number of times thereafter, that date marked the beginning of her intellectual, if not emotional, freedom from her country of origin. While some of her finest stories are rooted there, they are poignant precisely because of that fact of separation, drawing on a long formative period viewed from an unbreachable distance.

Queens College first, and Europe in general, provided the young girl with the nourishment her independent and questing spirit demanded. Her teachers, men of exceptional ability and availability to the small number of girls in residence, acquainted her with the fin de siècle theories and art of Walter Pater and the decadents of the 1890s as well as the literature of Tolstoy and Ibsen. Her *Journal* was peppered with epigrams drawn from Oscar Wilde, for whom she conceived a worshipful admiration, and whose effect is to be seen in stories such as "Marriage à la Mode." Katherine, who was a fair amateur cellist, resumed her music lessons in London, attended concerts, haunted her professors' rooms, and began writing in earnest. She published five stories about her childhood between 1903 and 1905.[4]

Katherine's volatile and intense temperament almost decreed that she should fall in love seriously during this period. Her love affairs, both the trivial and serious commitments, and those realized and unfulfilled, are significant as they contributed to much of the content of the stories that deal with romance, courtship, and marriage. Her own sexual development was ambivalent. While she was completing her secondary schooling at Miss Swainson's School in Wellington, she had fallen in love with an exotic highborn Maori girl. The uncensored second version of her *Journal* reveals her passionate lesbian attraction to the young woman, named Maata Mahukupu:

> I want Maata I want her—and have had her—terribly—this is unclean I know but true. What an extraordinary thing—I feel savagely crude—and almost powerfully enamoured of the child.

Although Maata, known also as Martha Grace, appears to have indulged her aggressive friend, there is no evidence that she reciprocated her feelings. The experience, from Mansfield's point of view, however, is significant, in that she was to touch upon the subject of lesbian love later in some of her stories, most notably in "Bliss," in which Bertha, like Katherine herself, finds herself falling in love with the exotic, remote, and passive Pearl Fulton.

During the period of her infatuation with Maata, Katherine involved herself with a pair of twins who grew up in New Zealand and eventually went to study abroad. She was drawn first to Arnold Trowell, a young cello virtuoso, and, always suggestible, she took up the instrument with the boy's father, Thomas Trowell. Her powerful longing for Arnold was to go largely unfulfilled, and when she returned home she engaged in a lesbian love affair with Edie K. Bendall, a somewhat older woman. When her father finally allowed her to return to London, she turned once again to Arnold, who had remained abroad to study and perform. Finally, in 1908, forced to accept his unequivocal rejection, Katherine transferred her romantic yearnings to his violinist brother Garnet, who returned her feelings. Her letters to Garnet are singularly frank in their sexual allusions. By 1909 she was pregnant by him but abandoned under the deep displeasure of Garnet's father, who persuaded his son to disentangle himself from the high-strung and unconventional girl.

Motivated by the need to find a father for her unborn child, Katherine made an impulsive and loveless marriage with a professional singer named George Bowden, whom she left on her wedding day. The marriage to Bowden, eleven years her senior, was not consummated, and Katherine went to Garnet for an uneasy and ultimately unsuccessful reunion. Her mother, learning the unsavory facts of her daughter's personal life, sailed to London and placed her daughter in a spa in the Bavarian Alps for the duration of her confinement. The group of satires and sketches gathered together under the title *In a German Pension* are based on some of the "cure guests" the young woman met during her enforced lonely exile.

Toward the end of her pregnancy, which was complicated by the first signs of tuberculosis, the disease that would eventually kill her, Katherine gave birth to a premature stillborn child. She stayed on in Germany for a while and gradually entered into a series of love affairs, one with a Polish critic named Floryan Sobienowski, and another with an Austrian journalist identified in the *Journal* only by his initials S. V. When she finally returned to England in January 1910 she went back to the patient Bowden, agreeing to live with him as his wife. The reunion could not have been a success, judging from her portrait of Bowden in the unflattering "Mr. Reginald Peacock's Day," a cynical character study of a vain social-climbing voice teacher. When this experiment proved as dismal as her abortive liaison with Garnet Trowell, she left her husband for good two months later without troubling to file for divorce. Bowden himself took no steps toward securing his freedom until he wished to remarry eight years later.

This was a fateful time for Katherine. According to her devoted friend and lifelong companion, Ida Constance Baker, who wrote a memoir under the initials L. M. (for Lesley Moore, the nom de plume Katherine had designated for her because she thought her own name too ugly, and because the new one reminded her of her dead brother), Katherine was once again pregnant, this time by a man named Francis Heinemann, who probably never knew about his part in the affair, and did not see his lover again for six years and then only when a chance meeting brought them together. As uncelebrated as this love affair was, however, it offered new grist for Katherine's mill, providing the basis for the bitter story, "The Dill Pickle." This time Katherine underwent an abortion.[5] The period marks the onset of her precarious physical condition, for from then on she was never to be entirely well again. She had had an operation for peritonitis of gonococcal origin just prior to the abortion, and was probably rendered infertile from then on. She suffered her first attack of "pleurisy" at that time, although in retrospect it seems more likely the early onset of tuberculosis she contended with. She was to suffer recurrent attacks of rheumatism and a failing heart for the rest of her life, driving her from one cure to another, and from the mountainous sanatoriums of Switzerland to the warm climates of southern Italy and Provence for healing. Stories such as "The Man without a Temperament" record these sad peregrinations with dispassion and fidelity.

After yet another lover, identified in her diary only as "the man," Katherine's impulsive and finally trivial relationships came to an end in 1912.[6] She met John Middleton Murry, who was to play the most significant role in her life until her death, not only as her lover and final husband, but as her mentor, confidant, editor, publicist, and eventual biographer. Murry, an intellectually gifted but weak man, born into a lower economic stratum than Katherine, was invited to move into her flat on Platonic terms two months after they met. When they became lovers a few months after that first arrangement, it was at Katherine's suggestion and seduction. At that time Murry was the editor of an avant-garde literary magazine called *Rhythm,* and had already published Katherine's story "The Woman at the Store" and admired it inordinately before he met its author. Eventually Murry made her his coeditor, and the magazine remained the focus of their joint lives until it failed in July 1913. The distinguished but short-lived monthly ran only a total of fourteen numbers and then struggled along under the title *Blue Review* for three more issues, containing in its final edition pieces by Mansfield, D. H. Lawrence, who was a regular contributor, H. G. Wells, Hugh Walpole, and the poet Rupert Brooke. T. S. Eliot was an occasional contributor during the magazine's lifetime. Katherine persisted in thinking of him as a fiction writer rather than a poet because, as she saw it, "The Love Song of J. Alfred Prufrock" told a story.

Although Katherine and Murry did not marry until six years after they met, by the time they decided to take the step she was already seriously ill with tuberculosis. Their marriage became a migratory affair, with Katherine seeking one haven after another in pursuit of an increasingly elusive restoration to health. The bulk of Murry's time with his wife was marked by increasingly long absences from her, during which periods Katherine journeyed to Cornwall for the sea air, to Ospedalatti and Menton on the Italian Riviera, to Switzerland for purer oxygen, and finally to the Gurdjieff Institute in Fontainebleau, which dispensed a species of faith healing by a hypnotic Russian mystic. The long absences from Murry were punctuated by intense correspondence, marked by longing on her part and frustration on his. Privately he confessed: "She knew, just as well as I, how ill she was; yet she expected our marriage to work the miracle. . . The memory of my wedding to Katherine is a memory of the *anguish,* not the happiness of love."[7]

Although Katherine's illness became the prepossessing concern of her last years when her recurring symptoms no longer allowed her to deny its inexorability, her writing continued to draw attention and recognition. Even

before she signed on as an editor of *Rhythm,* she had received strong encourage-
ment from A. R. Orage, the Fabian editor of the weekly *New Age.* As early as
1910 Orage had published her story, "The Child Who Was Tired," a story
powerfully inspired by, and some say copied from, Chekhov, whose work she
first began to read while she was at the Bavarian pension. In rapid order Orage
published nine more of her stories, and although he was later to write a vicious
denunciation of her when she left him for *Rhythm,* he published six more of her
stories in 1911. Her first book, *In a German Pension,* was well received by the
*Manchester Guardian* and *Athenaeum,* and went into a third printing. The now-
celebrated "Prelude" was laboriously handprinted and bound by Virginia and
Leonard Woolf's Hogarth Press.

In 1919, when Murry moved on to become the editor of *Athenaeum,*
Katherine was appointed to the position of fiction critic for that prestigious
publication, all the time continuing to turn out stories, among them the
highly regarded "Miss Brill" and "Sun and Moon." Her reviews were collected
in a volume called *Novels and Novelists* and were published posthumously by
Murry. Although by 1920 her hold on life was tenuous, one lung having been
destroyed by disease, she wrote the ambitious "Je ne parle pas français," sup-
posedly motivated by her ongoing distaste for the French among whom she
frequently convalesced, and "The Man without a Temperament," a fictional-
ized account of her dependence on the impassive Murry during her frequent
Mediterranean sojourns.

In spite of her declining vitality, Katherine translated Chekhov's letters
from the Russian and wrote poetry under the pseudonym Elizabeth Stanley.
Her growing reputation drew the notice of the influential and wealthy art patrons Sydney and Violet Schiff, who published two stories in their magazine
*Arts and Letters. The Nation* took "The Life of Ma Parker" in 1921, and the *London Mercury* ran "The Daughters of the Late Colonel" in that same year.
Clement Shorter, the editor of *Sphere,* contracted for six stories. The list was a
distinguished one, comprising "Mr. and Mrs. Dove," "An Ideal Family," the
inspired sequel to "Prelude" called "At the Bay," "The Voyage," "The Garden
Party," and "The Doll's House," all completed in 1921. In 1922, her third collection, named for the story that was to become her most widely anthologized
piece of fiction, was published by Constable under the title *"The Garden Party"
and Other Stories,* and underwent a third printing within three months. Such
reputable critics as Rebecca West of the *New Statesman* and Joseph Wood
Krutch in the *Nation* praised her growth as an artist and the polish of her
prose. It is obvious that her disease, which worsened dramatically, failed to
halt her creative pace. In fact, possibly feeling time's winged chariot drawing
near, she completed the story "Taking the Veil" in three hours on January 24,
1922. On July 7 she finished her last complete story, "The Canary," and made
her will on August 14.

From that time, Katherine spent her remaining months seeking new
paths to recovery. At the suggestion of her old friend Orage she began to

investigate the Institute for the Harmonious Development of Man, a center for nondenominational faith healing founded by a hypnotic Caucasian of Greek descent named George Ivanovich Gurdjieff. This self-styled Guru was sufficiently persuasive to have attracted a mixed bag of disciples who had been converted by Gurdjieff's chief spokesman, the journalist P. D. Ouspensky, whose book *Tertium Organum* was the vehicle for the synthesis and dissemination of the Institute's complex philosophy. Despairing of physical cure, Katherine joined the faithful of the Ouspensky circle in the hope of achieving through psychic healing what medical science could not accomplish. In a desperate final move she entered the Institute, which was located in an abandoned Carmelite monastery in the forest of Fontainebleau and died of a massive lung hemorrhage on Tuesday, January 9, 1923. Murry was with her at the time.

The New Zealand expatriate was buried on French soil, as was her beloved brother Leslie. The inscription on her tombstone was taken from Shakespeare's *Henry the Fourth,* part 1, act 2, scene 3: "But I tell you, my Lord fool, out of this nettle, danger, we pluck this flower, safety." Katherine, who created some of her own danger but was surely victimized increasingly by her own unfortunate circumstances, did not in the end succeed in plucking that prized but elusive flower.

## Notes

1. The biographical information in this chapter is drawn, except where otherwise noted, from the two most recent and most meticulously documented studies of the subject's life: Jeffrey Meyers, *Katherine Mansfield: A Biography* (London: Hamish Hamilton, 1978), and Antony Alpers, *The Life of Katherine Mansfield* (New York: Viking, 1980). Mansfield's *Journal, Letters,* and *Scrapbook* have been consulted for authentication along with memoirs, biographies, and letters of her contemporaries.

2. The term "pa man" appears to be a shared Beauchamp family allusion. The original pa man, according to Alpers (p. 7), was Arthur Beauchamp, who was a good-natured but somewhat incompetent bungler. In later years, the term was altered subtly to apply to the more authoritarian and blustering Harold, who, transformed into the fictional character of Stanley Burnell, was nevertheless touchingly vulnerable. Katherine and her brother Leslie used the noun as a description, occasionally referring to some act as "very Pa." In the *Journal* (p. 4) Katherine writes, "What a Pa man!" in response to a poem Dorothy Wordsworth had written about her celebrated brother William's compulsively ordered daily routine.

3. In "Juliet," she is actually describing herself when she writes: "She had been as yet, utterly idle at school, drifted through her classes, picked up a quantity of heterogeneous knowledge—and all the pleading and protestations of her teachers could not induce her to learn that which did not appeal to her."

4. The five stories about childhood written between 1903 and 1905 are "The Pine Tree," "The Sparrows," "You and I" in 1903, "Your Birthday" in 1904, and "About Pat" in 1905.

5. The only mention of this pregnancy appears in *Katherine Mansfield: The Memories of LM* (New York: Taplinger, 1971). Her account reads: "Katherine realized that she was again with child. She wrote repeatedly to the young man and begged him to come and see her, but she never had any reply. . . . So he never knew of the child."

6. Katherine's notoriety for her sexual profligacy was of such a dimension during the years of her love affairs that Virginia Woolf commented when she met her that she had "gone every sort of hog ever since she was seventeen," and had had "every sort of experience."

7. Mary Middleton Murry, *To Keep Faith* (London: Constable, 1958), p. 167. The excerpt is from Murry's diary of March 10, 1954.

# Katherine Mansfield and Her Confessional Stories

## C. A. HANKIN

### 'PRELUDE'

The months which followed Leslie's death were, in Murry's words, 'the happiest time of our life together—one to which we looked back, with love and a certain incredulity, in after years'. It was during this period, at Bandol in the South of France, that Katherine Mansfield wrote the first draft of her longest and most considerable story, 'Prelude'. The immediate inspiration of 'Prelude' was Katherine's desire to 'renew' in her writing the country and the people she and her brother had shared. Yet there is also a sense, too, in which the work represents her attempt to reconstruct in fiction the permanence and security of the home she had repudiated and in real life could not replace. More importantly, the story is an act of extended self-analysis; an attempt to explore in greater depth than ever before (or again) her feelings about life within that home as it had conditioned and shaped her own personality.

Depicting three days in the life of the Burnell family as they move from one house and settle into another on the outskirts of rural Wellington, 'Prelude' is a story whose apparently simple surface is constantly belied by an underlying psychological complexity. Themes that Katherine Mansfield had dealt with separately in her earlier writing are brought together here in a sustained form; and they are centred unequivocally on the interrelationships of the family. What a comparison of 'Prelude' with the much longer first draft (printed separately by Murry as 'The Aloe') reveals is how potentially explosive are the emotional conflicts which run through the work. So intricate is the patterning of 'Prelude' that the obsessive nature of these conflicts is masked and controlled. Almost certainly, it was to achieve patterning and control that Katherine Mansfield eliminated, in her final version, passages which too openly laid bare conflicts that she preferred to convey less directly, through the nuance of association and symbol.

The ordering of 'Prelude' is most obvious in its structural division into twelve episodes during the course of which certain thematic ideas are introduced, brought to a climax, and either resolved or allowed to subside. Unifying these episodes, and providing a natural transition between them, is the

From *Katherine Mansfield and Her Confessional Stories* by C. A. Hankin (London: Macmillan Press Ltd., 1983), 116–135 and 222–34.

repeated appearance of objects or activities which have symbolic meaning. Birds of various kinds are the most pervasive symbols in the story; but almost as important are the plants, trees and flowers of the natural world. As in Katherine Mansfield's previous stories, food and eating carry emotional overtones. Fantasising, moreover, is the single most significant activity indulged in by virtually all the characters: fantasy is at once the medium through which the author explores the minds of her fictional people, and a linking device which helps integrate the various threads of the story.

On the surface, 'Prelude' is a story about life as it occurs in the most unified and secure of circumstances—within the supportive structure of the family. There is the house where each member has his place, the motherly grandmother who sees to the family's domestic needs, and the father who provides for their material welfare. Belying the apparent security of this external framework, indeed demonstrating its fragility, is a disturbing pattern of contraries. Juxtaposed to the orderly existence within the house is the disorder Kezia encounters outside in the natural world; in contrast to the safely humdrum outer lives of the characters are their disturbingly conflict-ridden inner lives; and, as if echoing this division, the world which appears safe and familiar by day assumes hidden, fearful characteristics at night. Even in daytime, there is a strange tendency for things to appear the reverse of what they really are; inanimate objects and plants take on human attributes, while people are seen or treated as if they are mere objects.

Such a reversal of perceptions accords with the duality of feeling and the ambivalence experienced by some of the characters. The ambivalence of Linda Burnell, who loves her husband by day but hates him at night, is shown most explicitly; Beryl Fairfield's ambivalence towards her sister and brother-in-law and towards her friend, Nan Pym, is also conveyed. Indeed, it is through the character of Beryl that Katherine Mansfield chooses to portray the duality of character—the division between the 'true self' and the 'false self'—which serves to emphasise all the other dualisms of the story.

If there is a constant impression of flux in 'Prelude', it is because the narrative moves from the public life of the characters to their private fantasies just as inevitably as the day blends into night. In the fantasies of Linda Burnell, Beryl and Kezia, relationships with the opposite sex are more or less explicit. Central to the public life of the story, and influencing the interrelationships of the entire family, however, are the bonds between mother and daughter. These are complex, for they involve the relationship of Linda and her unmarried sister to their mother, Mrs Fairfield, and that of the three Burnell children to Linda herself as well as to their grandmother.

In the first three episodes, attention is focused upon the subtle interaction of Linda, the young mother, and her daughter, Kezia. Dominating the relationship between these two principal characters (and affecting the emotional movement of the entire story) is Linda's abdication of the role of mother. Almost casually, in the opening paragraph, Katherine Mansfield establishes the abnormality of Linda's feelings as she distinguishes between the 'hold-alls, bags and boxes' which are 'absolute necessities', not to be let out of her sight for one instant, and the two younger children, for whom there is no place in the buggy. '"We shall simply have to leave them. That is all. We shall simply have to cast them off", said Linda Burnell.' Mentally devaluing her children, Linda interchanges in imagination the 'tables and chairs standing on their heads on the front lawn' with Lottie and Kezia, to whom she longed to say, 'Stand on your heads, children, and wait for the storeman.'

Kezia's anxiety at separation from the mother and grandmother who drive off with the favoured older sister, but without her and Lottie, is expressed in her cry, 'I want to kiss my granma good-bye again.' In 'The Aloe' grandmother comforts her with 'It's all right, my darling. Be good.' But in 'Prelude' Katherine Mansfield underlines the child's sense of abandonment by portraying the grandmother as being too absorbed in Linda's needs to reply. Unobtrusively, the working out of psychological cause and effect is conveyed through the succession of events and through the reiteration of certain motifs in different contexts. Thus there is an implicit comparison between the motherliness of Mrs Samuel Josephs, in whose care Kezia and Lottie are left, and Linda's lack of concern for her children. And the rivalry among the many Samuel Josephs children acts as a reminder that, in the Burnell family (as in the Beauchamp family), there are grounds for competition. Only lightly, in 'Prelude', is the existence of discord among the Samuel Josephs children sketched in; in the earlier version, 'The Aloe', there is a more detailed reference to the 'pitched battle' which 'every single one of them started . . . as soon as possible after birth with every single other'.

'Prelude' depicts a tearful Kezia caught up in the other children's aggressiveness during tea, and we learn that 'she did hate boys'. The lengthier description of her stay with the Samuel Josephs family in 'The Aloe' explicitly links her distress at being separated from mother and grandmother with her fear of being left helpless and exposed to physical attack. A comparison of the two versions shows that Katherine Mansfield took pains in 'Prelude' to cover the psychological tracks of her characters. For example, she eliminated from 'Prelude' a description of the Samuel Josephs children as 'jump[ing] out at you from under the tables, through the stair rails, behind the doors, behind the coats in the passage'. In very similar words, however, she describes Kezia's subsequent fearful encounter with 'IT'. Exploring the empty Burnell house after tea, the child imagines in her parents' darkening bedroom that 'IT was just behind her, waiting at the door, at the head of the stairs, at the bottom of the stairs, hiding in the passage, ready to dart out at the back door.'

In 'The Aloe', a sharply drawn scene indicates a relationship between Kezia's haunting fantasy and her fear of physical aggression. After tea, she takes revenge upon her tormentors. Cunningly she devises a 'new game' in which the other children must compete to see who can chew up first the stamen of an arum lily. 'The Samuel Josephs suspected nothing. . . . Savagely they broke off the big white blooms. . . . She flung up her hands with joy as the Samuel Josephs bit, chewed, made dreadful faces, spat, screamed, and rushed to Burnells' garden tap.' Symbolically, the destruction of the 'big white blooms' parallels the little girl's barely conscious fear of being assaulted. By tricking her enemies into devouring the burning, phallic stamens she has turned the tables and successfully warded off attack.

The motif of rushing things is picked up again in the third section of 'Prelude' when Kezia talks to the storeman during the drive home. Here, as he explains the difference between a sheep and a ram, the overtones become more obviously sexual. 'A ram has horns and runs for you', he tells the child. And she answers, 'I hate rushing animals like dogs and parrots. I often dream that animals rush at me—even camels—and while they are rushing, their heads swell e-enormous.'

In 'The Aloe', Linda seems intuitively aware of these secret terrors. She greets the children's belated arrival at the new house with 'Are those the children? . . . Have either of them been maimed for life?' In 'Prelude' the apparently illogical question is omitted. Instead the mother's lack of interest—which also has power to maim—is emphasised. '"Are those the children?" But Linda did not really care; she did not even open her eyes to see.' As she tends the sleepy children, it becomes clear that the grandmother has taken over Linda's maternal responsibilities. Kezia's special relation to her grandmother, whose bed she shares, is suggested but not dwelt upon in 'Prelude'. We are merely told that, when the old woman lay down beside her, 'Kezia thrust her head under the grandmother's arm and gave a little squeak.' The bedtime scene continues in 'The Aloe', however, with Kezia whispering, '"Who am I?" . . . This was an old established ritual to be gone through between them. 'You are my little brown bird", said the Grandmother. Kezia gave a guilty chuckle.' In effect, Kezia's question is an attempt to compensate for her abandonment earlier in the day by asking 'Who am I to you?' The reassurance that she is indeed her grandmother's favoured child is what produces (in view of the sibling rivalry) her guilty chuckle.

Inexorably, the movement of 'Prelude' is towards a series of revelatory scenes in which repression is lifted, and Kezia, Linda and Beryl are brought face to face with their hidden anxieties. There is an inevitability and aesthetic 'rightness' about each revelation; yet so subtle is Katherine Mansfield's introduction and reiteration of key remarks, actions and symbols that tension mounts almost unnoticeably. The details of day-to-day living impart a deceptively matter-of-fact appearance to the surface texture of the narrative, and hardly more obtrusive is the infiltration of objects from the natural world into the characters' dream life. Thus, on the second day of the story, Linda Burnell awakens to the sound of birds whose calls have become part of her dream. The dream unravels and she becomes aware of Stanley dressing; but the bird image merges into her waking thoughts and releases a succession of involuntary disclosures. In the dream, Linda had been walking with her father when he showed her a tiny bird in the grass. Picking it up, she stroked its head. 'But a funny thing happened. As she stroked it began to swell . . . it grew bigger and bigger. . . . It had become a baby with a big naked head and a gaping bird-mouth, opening and shutting.'

The image of the bird which when stroked becomes a baby is one of intercourse and pregnancy. But although Linda's wish, as she looks round her bedroom, that 'she was going away from this house, too . . . driving away from them all in a little buggy', recalls her desertion of the children the previous day, it is not at this stage explicitly related to her dream. Nor is her perception of Stanley as 'a big fat turkey'. From this point on, however, the idea of pregnancy and its ramifications is one which recurs with mounting intensity—even as the bird image acquires symbolic significance for the other characters, too.

Just as the parrots on the wallpaper had seemed alive to Kezia the previous night, so does the poppy on the wallpaper which Linda, still lying in bed in the morning, traces with her finger. Repeating the stroking gesture of her dream, 'she could feel the sticky, silky petals, the stem, hairy like a gooseberry skin, the rough leaf and the tight glazed bud. Things had a habit of coming alive like that.' Then the sight of the washstand jug that 'had a way of sitting in the basin like a fat bird in a round nest' reminds her of the bird dream. Consciously, now, the phallic imagery of the swelling bird and the sticky poppy is elaborated in a menacing sexual fantasy which reads as a more elaborate version of Kezia's 'IT'.

> . . . the strangest part of this coming alive of things was what they did. They listened, they seemed to swell out with some mysterious important content, and when they were full she felt that they smiled. . . . Sometimes . . . she woke and could not lift a finger . . . [because] THEY knew how frightened she was. . . . What Linda always felt was that THEY wanted something of her, and she knew that if she gave herself up and was quiet . . . something would really happen. . . . She seemed to be listening with her wide open watchful eyes, waiting for someone to come who just did not come, watching for something to happen that just did not happen.

The meaning of Linda's dream and of her fantasy is left as oblique for us in 'Prelude' as it is for her. Katherine Mansfield omitted a long passage from 'The Aloe' where a glimpse of Linda's present relationship with her mother, and her past relationship with her father, helps explain her feelings. After Stanley has left for work, the young wife is depicted in 'The Aloe' as regressing to a state of childlike dependency. '. . . playing with her breakfast', Linda refuses even to look at the kitchen and pantries of the new house: 'I don't want to. I don't care', she tells her mother. Needing to remain a child herself,

Linda's rejection of the role of mother is underlined in her refusal to take any part in the feeding of her family.

This portrayal in 'The Aloe' of Linda's immaturity is sharpened by a flashback which projects her retreat from marriage (signified by a constant losing of her wedding ring) against the background of her ideal, non-sexual relationship with her father. As a child, she had been 'his darling, his pet, his playfellow.... He understood her so beautifully and gave her so much love for love that he became a kind of daily miracle to her, and all her faith centred in him.' Sitting on his knee, she used to plan: 'When I am grown up we shall travel everywhere—we shall see the whole world—won't we, Papa? ... And we shan't go as father and daughter.... We'll just go as a couple of boys together—Papa.' Reality destroyed this dream of being both the central figure in her father's life, and a boy, when Stanley Burnell came courting. The year her father died, Linda married.

In such passages Katherine Mansfield analysed fairly explicitly in 'The Aloe' the workings of her characters' minds, spelling out the connections between their past experiences and their present thoughts and actions. When she revised the story as 'Prelude', the explanatory sections were largely eliminated and symbols were left to carry the weight of psychological meaning.

The new house, around which the action of the story takes place and in terms of which the characters are shown defining themselves, is itself a kind of symbol which imposes unity on those who live under its sheltering roof. Sharing the symbolic attributes of the house is Mrs Fairfield, the real mother of the story and the pivotal figure upon whom all the others depend. There is something archetypal about her, as she creates security, order and pattern both in the dwelling and in the emotional lives of its inhabitants. Significantly, she, whose maternal presence must counteract the private anxieties of those in her care, wears at her throat the emblem of 'a silver crescent moon with five little owls seated on it'. Since Linda has refused the responsibilities of motherhood, Mrs Fairfield has, in effect, five daughters: Linda, Beryl and the three little Burnell girls.

Emphasising the implied contrast between the two mothers is Linda's appearance in the kitchen on the first morning at the new house. Of Mrs Fairfield, 'It was hard to believe that she had not been in that kitchen for years; she was so much part of it. She put the crocks away with a sure, precise touch.... When she had finished, everything in the kitchen had become part of a series of patterns.' While the older woman is invariably concerned with the preparation and serving of food, Linda shows hardly more interest in eating than she does in satisfying the needs of others. On the first night in the new house, the young wife sits apart and refuses the meaty chops which Stanley and Beryl devour with gusto. In 'Prelude' (as in 'The Aloe') she merely picks at the breakfast her mother prepares, asking childishly, 'Beryl, do you want half my gingerbread?'

While Linda, in the orderly kitchen reflects that 'There was something comforting in the sight of her [mother] that . . . she could never do without', and refuses to 'go into the garden and give an eye to [her] children', Kezia, outside in the garden, is exploring the disorder of the natural world beyond the house. Kezia's sensibility is linked with that of her mother by the pattern of symbolism. Her secret terror, 'IT', is paralleled by Linda's fantasised 'THEY'; the rushing animals and parrots she so dislikes because 'their heads swell e-enormous' become in her mother's dream life the swelling bird, the poppy with the 'fat bursting bud' and the 'things' which 'swell out with some mysterious important content'. Sharing an emotional dependence on Mrs Fairfield—sharing, in effect, the same mother—both Linda and Kezia want freedom their first morning at the new house. Earlier, Linda had wished to escape from the bonds of family life; now Kezia escapes her bossy older sister and wanders off alone into the 'spread tangled garden' where 'she did not believe that she would ever not get lost'.

The inherent duality of the story is evident in the symbolism of the garden. Divided by the drive leading up to the house, the garden has two sides with many little paths on either side. 'On one side they all led into a tangle of tall dark trees and strange bushes . . . that buzzed with flies . . . this was the frightening side, and no garden at all.' In contrast, on the other side 'there was a high box border and the paths had box edges and all of them led into a deeper and deeper tangle of flowers.' With its tangle of tall, masculine trees, the frightening side of the garden suggests the uncontrolled fantasy worlds of Kezia and her mother; the other side, with its ordered box borders and profusion of sweet smelling flowers, corresponds to the security and reassurance that Mrs Fairfield provides.

With their connotations of order and disorder, the opposing sides of the garden suggest the divided human psyche, alternately overwhelmed by private fantasy but also participating in the public life of the family; seeking independence and separateness on the one hand yet dependent upon a nurturing maternal presence on the other. The island 'that lay in the middle of the drive, dividing the drive into two arms that met in front of the house' is like a bridge between the two sides.

Significantly, the mother and child, who are at once separate and the same, experience their only moment of direct communication as they stand in front of the island, gazing at the aloe tree which is the central symbol of the story. Asked 'Mother, what is it?', Linda 'looked up at the fat swelling plant with its cruel leaves and fleshy stem'. The mother, with a smile and half-shut eyes, tells her daughter that the plant is an aloe, which flowers only once every hundred years. Linda's smile suggests a secret empathy with the aloe. By an act of displacement, Kezia's 'Mother, what is it?' registers in her mind as 'Mother, what are you?' Partly answering the question is the description of the aloe. Linda's obsession with pregnancy is reflected in the 'fat swelling' of the plant. Its leaves are 'split and broken . . . cruel'. Similarly Linda herself is broken, apathetic and uninterested in life around her, cruel in her rejection of the children. As the plant clings with 'claws' to the earth it grew from, so she clings selfishly to her mother; and, like the aloe with its 'blind' stem and leaves which seem to be 'hiding something', Linda half-shuts her eyes. She too is hiding something.

There is a suggestion, in this depiction of Linda's first encounter with the aloe tree, that while looking at it she has experienced a degree of self-understanding. With dramatic inevitability 'Prelude' progresses towards an exposure of what is psychologically hidden, towards the crystallisation, by means of a catalytic symbol, of the characters' only partly understood anxieties. On the third and final day of the story, Kezia, Linda and Beryl, in a moment of revelation, confront their innermost selves. Kezia's secret fears are the first to come to a head. Her dislike of the teasing Samuel Josephs boys, and the similarity of her fantasies to those of Linda's, indicate that her anxieties (perhaps transmitted from her mother) are based upon a fear of sexual attack. And, indeed, the game which the three little girls play with their boy cousins Pip and Rags Trout is a childish imitation of adult sexuality. 'Mrs Smith' tells 'Mrs Jones' about the new baby which 'came so suddenly that I haven't had time to make her any clothes, yet. So I left her. . . .' Lottie, significantly, doesn't want to play 'hospitals' with the boys 'because last time Pip had squeezed something down her throat and it hurt awfully'.

The climax occurs for Kezia when Pat, the handyman, offers to show the children 'how the kings of Ireland chop the head off a duck'. As the headless duck begins to waddle 'Kezia suddenly rushed at Pat and flung her arms round his legs. . . . "Put head back! Put head back!" she screamed.' If the child's reaction is overcharged, it is because she (like the female characters of Katherine Mansfield's earlier stories who unconsciously empathised with the suffering of another) has put herself in the place of the headless duck. Her distress at being 'abandoned' by her mother, at being teased by the Samuel Josephs boys, at encountering the fearful, imaginary 'IT', has merged, together with her unpleasant thoughts of rushing animals with swelling heads, into the one overwhelming horror of the decapitation. Yet the shock is purgative. Now that the vaguely dreaded physical attack has been vicariously experienced, her anxiety diminishes.

Light relief from this tense scene comes when the focus shifts to Alice, the servant girl. The element of fantasy, which is so prominent in the working out of the story's psychological themes, recurs in the portrayal of Alice. For her, however, fantasy is a source not of terror but of comforting mastery. In 'Prelude' the episode where Alice peruses her dream book in the kitchen and then composes a series of imaginary conversations in which she mentally gets even with the haughty Beryl is followed directly by a depiction of the whole family eating the duck at dinner. But in 'The Aloe' there is an intervening scene in which Mrs Fairfield and her daughters—the married Doady Trout, Linda and Beryl—are depicted sewing together. Here Katherine Mansfield probes at greater length the phenomenon of fantasy-living. Like other long excisions from 'Prelude', this passage is important for the light it throws on the author's original conception of her characters' psychology, as well as on the aspects of family life which preoccupied her.

Fantasising or day-dreaming is common to Kezia, Linda, Beryl and Doady. All four youthful characters are sharply differentiated; yet their sharing of certain traits suggests that, besides being members of the same family, they may also represent different stages in the emotional development of the author's own troubled personality. For Kezia and Linda, fantasising is an almost involuntary activity, one in which some external object or event causes repressed anxieties to rise to the surface of their minds. But for Beryl and Doady it is a conscious indulgence which allows them to escape from daily routine and gratify, at least in imagination, their unfulfilled wishes. Doady Trout, the bored suburban housewife who lives on the sofa wondering 'why it was that she was so certain that life had something terrible for her . . . until by and by she made up perfect novels with herself for the heroine, all of them ending with some shocking catastrophe', is remarkably similar to the adolescent author of 'Juliet'. Katherine Mansfield might almost be parodying her own early creation when she depicts the Dickensian sentimentality of Doady's imaginings: 'Her child would be born dead, or she saw the nurse going in to Richard, her husband, and saying: "Your child lives *but*"—and here the nurse pointed one finger upwards like the illustration of Agnes in *David Copperfield*—"your wife is no more."'

It is significant that Doady's destructive fantasies are implicitly attributed to envy. More often than not, the imagined tragedy would befall not Doady herself but some member of her family. As if envious of the Burnells, she imagines their new house on fire and her mother appearing for a moment at the window before 'a sickening crash'. While she keeps such daydreams a 'profound secret', the jealousy that she feels for Linda is less easily concealed. When Linda laughs off her spiteful suggestion that the new house 'will be very damp in the winter', the smouldering rivalry between the three sisters bursts into the open. 'What can you expect from Linda', says Doady bitterly. 'She laughs at everything—everything.' Beryl, who 'felt her anger like a little serpent dart out of her bosom and strike at Linda', joins in the attack:

'Why do you always pretend to be so indifferent to everything?' she said. 'You pretend you don't care where you live, or if you see anybody or not, or what happens to the children or even what happens to you. You can't be sincere and yet you keep it up—you've kept it up for years. In fact'—and she gave a little laugh of joy and relief to be so rid of the serpent, she felt positively delighted—'I can't even remember when it started now'.

Perhaps because they revealed too much, Katherine Mansfield eliminated from 'Prelude' the two 'Aloe' scenes in which she had explicitly depicted sibling rivalry. Yet competition for possession of the mother-figure is clearly a motivating factor in the psychology of her female characters. Beryl and Doady, in 'The Aloe', are shown resenting Linda's retreat from adulthood and her virtual monopoly of their mother. It is Linda herself, however, who in this earlier version of 'Prelude' is made to suggest the relationship between her own behaviour and Kezia's emotional well-being. As if supporting Beryl's accusations, Linda appears to recognise Kezia's separation anxiety, and cruelly reinforce it. 'Your Mother doesn't care, Kezia, whether you ever set eyes on her again. She doesn't care if you starve. You are all going to be sent to the Home for Waifs and Strays to-morrow', she cynically teases.

In 'The Aloe' there is an easing of emotional tension—and a preparation for the next episode—as the sewing scene closes with another reference to birds. To her son's question, 'Mum . . . which would you rather be if you had to—a duck or a fowl?', Doady replies, 'I'd rather be a fowl—much rather.' Katherine Mansfield eliminates from 'Prelude' any such open correlation between a human being and a duck. Such a correlation, however, is psychologically central to the scene at dinner that night when Stanley Burnell carves the duck whose killing has so shocked Kezia. Stanley's enjoyment of the roast duck emphasises his carnal appetite. In contrast to his wife, who is uninterested in eating, Stanley (like the *German Pension* males) is invariably associated with food. Portrayed on the first evening eating a chop and 'picking his strong white teeth', he returns from work on the second day devouring a bag of cherries, 'three or four at a time, chucking the stones over the side of the buggy'. His present to Linda that night is 'a bottle of oysters and a pineapple'. As if there is for him an unconscious association between food and procreation, the sight of his children at supper reminded him of the son he wanted; and he 'tightened his arm round Linda's shoulder'.

As he carves the duck at dinner on the third day, Stanley openly refers to it as a child: 'this must have been one of those birds whose mother played to it in infancy upon the German flute. And the sweet strains of the dulcet instrument acted with such effect upon the infant mind.' Thus by subtle association Kezia's traumatic experience earlier that day is linked with her father's attitude to food—and with Linda's response to her husband. For, as if she understands the underlying symbolism of the carving scene, Linda sits apart after the meal. Her mounting emotional tension expresses itself in an unspoken warning to two moths: 'Fly away before it is too late. Fly out again.'

This, then, is the setting for the climactic scene in which Linda, contemplating the aloe tree, admits to consciousness her own deepest feelings. All the imagery of the story—birds, plants, food, swelling head and grotesquely human inanimate objects—has been leading up to this moment. As she gazes up at the aloe in the moonlight, Linda's rejection of the children, her longing for escape, and her clinging to Mrs Fairfield, all coalesce as aspects of her polarised feelings for Stanley. On the previous day, she had envied the impenetrability and maleness of the tree. Now, when the moon is full and 'the house, the garden, the old woman and Linda' are all 'bathed in dazzling light', mother and daughter seem to be enclosed in a world exclusively their own; and the budding aloe appears as a feminine symbol, a ship.

> 'Do you feel it, too', said Linda, and she spoke to her mother with the special voice that women use at night to each other as though they spoke in their sleep or from some hollow cave—'Don't you feel that it is coming toward us?' She dreamed that she was caught up out of the cold water into the ship with the lifted oars and budding mast. . . . Ah, she heard herself cry: 'Faster! Faster!' to those who were rowing.

The empathy of mother and daughter contrasts with the emotional gulf between Stanley and Linda. Full moon, house and garden are all feminine symbols; but the aloe-as-ship represents the womb itself. Only there, between mother and unborn child, could there be communication 'at night . . . in their sleep . . . from some hollow cave'. Like the island on which the aloe grows, the earth to which it clings, the ship symbolises the prenatal world which protects and nourishes; and it is to the safety and nothingness of that world that Linda wishes to return. 'Nobody would dare to come near the ship or to follow after', she thinks as she looks at the 'long sharp thorns that edged the aloe leaves. . . . Not even my Newfoundland dog . . . that I'm so fond of in the daytime.'

The dualities which so pervade 'Prelude' are brought sharply into focus as Linda confronts the difference between her day-time and night-time feelings for Stanley:

> He was too strong for her; she had always hated things that rush at her, from a child. There were times when he was frightening—really frightening. When she just had not screamed at the top of her voice: 'You are killing me.' And at those times she had longed to say the most coarse, hateful things . . .
>
> 'You know I'm very delicate. You know as well as I do that my heart is affected, and the doctor has told you I may die any moment. I have had three great lumps of children already . . .'
>
> Yes, yes, it was true. . . . For all her love and respect and admiration she hated him. . . . It had never been so plain to her as it was at this moment. There were all her feelings for him, sharp and defined, one as true as the other. And there was this other, this hatred, just as real as the rest.

The scene is central in that, as Linda comes to understand and admit openly the meaning of her fantasies, the separate threads of the story are drawn together. Her secret happiness at casting off the children is symptomatic of a stronger, but hitherto suppressed, desire to be free of the sexual role imposed by marriage to Stanley. Haunted by fears of sexual intercourse and childbearing, and transmitting these to Kezia through her rejection of motherhood,

Linda seeks refuge in regression to a state of asexual, childlike dependence upon her mother. But a return to childhood, in the sense that Linda really desires it, is possible only in death; as if recognising this, her attitude is essentially nihilistic: 'And why this mania . . . to keep alive at all? . . . What am I guarding myself for so preciously? I shall go on having children and Stanley will go on making money. . . .' Like the aloe, which earlier seemed 'becalmed in the air', Linda is herself becalmed. Forced to accept a life that leads nowhere, with only fantasies of escape as an outlet, hers is a kind of living death.

Linda's admission of her divided feelings about Stanley throws into relief all the other patterns of opposites in 'Prelude'. Philosophically central to the story is the idea that objects and people can appear in two different and contrasting guises. As opposed to the way things really are, there is the way they seem when viewed through the distorting lens of fantasy. Fantasy, in its ability to transmute reality, is like the coloured-glass window Kezia peeped through at the empty house. First she saw a blue lawn, then a yellow. When a yellow 'Chinese' Lottie came into view, she wondered, 'Was that really Lottie? Kezia was not quite sure until she had looked through the ordinary window.' In the same way, such objects from the natural world as birds form part of the narrative's realistic backdrop when viewed through ordinary glass; when viewed through the coloured glass of fantasy they become children—children waiting to be born, demanding attention, or vulnerable to potentially aggressive males.

Fantasy causes food, too, to take on ambiguous connotations. Greedily devoured by Stanley, it conjures up the threatening sexual love that Linda fears. But, when given by a mother as nourishment to her children, food symbolises love in its life-sustaining capacity. By the same token, however, the deliberate withholding of love (as Linda withholds love from her children) is a symbolic act of murder.

For all the understanding with which Linda Burnell's plight is depicted, the symbolism of 'Prelude' unequivocally damns her for being an unloving mother. The focus shifts, in the final episode, from the close family group of grandmother, parents and child to Linda's unmarried sister, Beryl. Beryl's prominence in the closing section, and her characterisation, have puzzled some critics. Sylvia Berkman believes that Katherine Mansfield 'had some difficulty in presenting a successfully integrated character', and that this trouble arose because she '"made up" more of Beryl Fairfield than of any other character in the story'.

It is the author's adolescent writing which provides the key to Beryl's characterisation and importance. Both physically and emotionally, there is a remarkable similarity between Beryl and the heroine of 'Juliet'. This suggests that Beryl is, if anything, less 'made up' than any other character in 'Prelude'. Katherine Mansfield, like other writers of her generation, repeatedly cast herself as a central character in her fiction. Her private difficulty in 'Prelude' is that she is at once recreating the tensions she had felt among her own family—and attempting to reconstruct her life within the confines of that family. Because her life had been divided into two distinct phases—her years as a child before she left for school in England, and her later brief residence in New Zealand as a young woman—she needed two separate characters to represent both versions of herself. In Kezia she created an idealised version of herself as a child; onto the figure of the real Aunt Belle who lived in the Beauchamp household she grafted aspects of her own rebellious young womanhood.

Given the psychological coherence of 'Prelude', it is peculiarly fitting that the story which opens with the temporary—but painful—physical desertion of the child by her mother, and which goes on to account for that desertion in terms of Linda's inner conflicts, should be rounded off with a portrayal of the far-reaching effects of emotional insecurity on the adult Kezia-as-Beryl. What is emphasised in this closing episode is Beryl's hopeless inner division.

Beryl, like Linda, fantasises about her own sexuality. Seeing in marriage a solution to her unfulfilled life, she imagines on the first night at the new house that a young man is outside watching her undress. When, in a sexually suggestive gesture, he offers her a bouquet and 'thrust his head among the bright waxy flowers, sly and laughing', she cries, 'No, no', and embarks on a less frightening daydream. Beryl, like Linda, is the victim of sexual ambivalence; and her behaviour is marked by conscious play-acting. Fundamentally narcissistic, she is reminiscent of Juliet (and other early Mansfield heroines) in her substitution of self-adoration for mature love. Thus, on the evening of the second day, she plays the guitar and thinks, 'If I were outside the window and looked in and saw myself I really would be rather struck.' In the absence of an external admirer, she enjoys her own beauty in the mirror. The final scene of 'Prelude' depicts Beryl once more gazing at her reflection. 'Yes, my dear,' she tells the mirror face, 'there is no doubt about it, you really are a lovely little thing.'

There is barely a hint in 'Prelude' that the young woman's self-admiration is a substitute for the adoration of her friend, Nan, to whom she has been writing. Katherine Mansfield excised a passage in 'The Aloe' which conveys fairly explicitly the repressed lesbian relationship between the two. At boarding school, it had been the fashion for the girls to brush Beryl's lovely hair.

> But nobody brushed it as beautifully as Nan Fry. . . . She shook it out, she yielded it up to Nannie's adoring hands. Slowly she brushed, with long, caressing strokes. . . . She would say with a kind of moaning passion . . . 'It's more beautiful than ever, B. It really is lovelier than last time.' . . . She seemed to send herself to sleep with the movement and the gentle sound. . . . But nearly always these brushings came to an unpleasant ending. Nannie did something silly. Quite suddenly she would snatch up Beryl's hair and bury her face in it, and kiss it, or clasp her hands round Beryl's head and press it back against her firm breast, sobbing: 'You are so beautiful!' . . .

And at these moments Beryl had such a feeling of horror, such a violent thrill of physical dislike for Nan Fry. . . . She didn't even try to suppress her contempt and her disgust. . . . Nan Fry seemed to understand this. . . . And the *more* curious thing was that Beryl let her brush her hair again, and let this happen again . . . and again there was this silly scene between them . . . never referred to in the day time.

This flashback into Beryl's past throws light on both her narcissism and her role-playing. Secretly she enjoys Nan's caresses; but shame and anxiety about indulging in 'forbidden' behaviour force her to repudiate both Nan and the self which accepts such love. Struggling to deny her lesbian impulses, then, she mentally separates her personality into a day and a night self. The night self she calls her 'false self' and blames for her unhappiness. If there is an uncertainty in Beryl's characterisation, it is because the vital information about her guilty relationship with Nan has been dropped from 'Prelude'. Shown bitterly castigating her falseness, and the self which is 'silly and spiteful and vain', the admission that she shows off to visitors and flirts with Stanley hardly accounts for the intensity of her condemnation.

Not only does 'The Aloe' indicate the real reason for Beryl's self-castigation; it also reveals the importance Katherine Mansfield attached to her character's sense of inner division. The idea of a false or second self is one which recurs in her writing. More openly than in any other story, she analyses in 'The Aloe' the phenomenon of the 'false self'—in terms suggesting Dr Jekyll's possession by Mr Hyde:

> The Beryl who wrote that letter might have been leaning over her shoulder and guiding her hand—so separate was she: and yet in a way, perhaps she was more real than the other, the real Beryl. She had been getting stronger and stronger for a long while.
> There had been a time when the real Beryl had just made use of the false one to get her out of awkward positions—to glide her over hateful moments. . . . But that was long ago. The unreal Beryl was greedy and jealous of the real one. Gradually she took more and stayed longer. Gradually she came more quickly, and now the real Beryl was hardly certain sometimes if she were there or not.

A note on the manuscript of 'The Aloe' indicates that Katherine Mansfield had an actual double in mind. 'What is it that I'm getting at?' she asked herself. 'It is really Beryl's *Sosie*. The fact that for a long time now, she hasn't been even able to control her second self: it's her second self who now controls her.' Beryl's second, or false, self in 'Prelude' is no worse than a naughty child; that described in 'The Aloe' is sinister, because uncontrollable. Through the metaphor of the double, Katherine Mansfield is trying to convey the extent to which Beryl has assumed a defensive mask to hide her guilt and insecurity. The psychological price for this protection is a continuing sense of unreality.

The author's comment on the 'Aloe' manuscript—'I want to get at all this *through* her.... To suddenly merge her into herself'—implies that she wanted Beryl to break through her repression, to confront herself and in a moment of self-revelation to admit the unpleasant truth. In 'Prelude' Beryl is indeed accorded, like Linda, a climactic flash of insight. This occurs when she looks at herself once more in the mirror, not to admire but to ask, 'what had that creature in the glass to do with her?' But with Beryl repression is only partially lifted, the problem of sexual ambivalence only partly faced. As if to underline this, our last glimpse of Beryl is of her asking a series of questions that can only be answered in the negative: 'Shall I ever be that [real] Beryl for ever? Shall I? How can I? And was there ever a time when I did not have a false self?'

Beryl is shown to have no true identity; and in the closing lines of the story her character almost merges with that of Kezia, her younger self. Kezia, remaining in the room after she has called Beryl to lunch, metaphorically enacts the answer to her aunt's anguished questions. As if she were continuing the dialogue between the two selves, she admonishes the calico cat she has placed on the dressing-table with a cream-jar lid over its ear: 'Now look at yourself.' When the cat falls to the floor, with the undamaged lid, the child is overcome with guilt for a crime imagined—not committed. Her tip-toeing from the room, 'far too quickly and airily', is symbolic of the inner confusion which will continue to torture Beryl and which bodes ill for Kezia as well.

At the heart of 'Prelude' is a pessimism about the ability of human beings to control their fate. Although Linda can bring into the open her true feelings about Stanley, she has no power to alter her circumstances. Beryl can neither face up to her self as she really is, nor effect any change in her own personality. If 'Prelude' is one of Katherine Mansfield's greatest stories, it is partly because she creates a group of characters so psychologically believable they might be living people. Delicately investigating the nature of character, she represents the mysterious processes of the inner life to suggest how personality is determined by events far back in childhood. As Katherine Mansfield portrays them, human beings—especially women—are doubly beset: they are at the mercy both of external circumstances and of the internal conflicts that fester beneath their conscious minds. Bringing these to the surface can be a cathartic experience which affords some relief. Yet people have little power to change what they are. And, for the dilemma of the emotionally ambivalent women whose social destiny is marriage, Katherine Mansfield can provide no answer.

## 'AT THE BAY'

The major work of Katherine Mansfield's last years—indeed, arguably her greatest story—is 'At the Bay'. Frank O'Connor, one of her more severe critics, has given his verdict that 'At the Bay' and 'Prelude' are Katherine Mansfield's 'masterpieces and in their own way comparable with Proust's breakthrough into the subconscious world'.

Apart from the length of these works, which makes them more nearly novellas than short stories, and their unusually large cast of characters, they are different thematically from her other stories. The loneliness and emotional apartness which separates one human being from another is in some way central to virtually every story she wrote; and it is central also in 'Prelude' and 'At the Bay'. But in these longer works there is an attempt to counteract existential loneliness by presenting characters as they live together within the companionable structure of the family and, in 'At the Bay', of the universe. As a consequence, the narratives operate on two different levels. There is the surface level, which shows us the comings and goings of family members in the course of an ordinary day; and there is a deeper level which, probing the isolation of individual minds, constantly questions (by implication) the security offered by the family. 'At the Bay' is both gentler and profounder than 'Prelude' because here Katherine Mansfield achieves a philosophic resolution to the emotional contradictions of family life.

In another sense, too, these stories stand apart from her other writing. Both were written in response to the certain knowledge of death. Distraught by her brother's death in 1915, Katherine quickly linked his fate with her own death, which she felt must follow. 'Prelude' became a conscious act of reparation, an attempt to expunge the bitterness she harboured towards her family. By the time she came to write 'At the Bay' in 1921, the death she had wished so dramatically for herself was looming closer. One doctor had finally admitted that her case was hopeless, and she wrote in her journal, 'Why am I haunted every single day of my life by the nearness of death and its inevitability?' As a healthy young writer, Katherine Mansfield had savoured death in countless romantic, literary gestures. Dying in 1921, she wanted to celebrate life. 'What can one say of the afternoons? Of the evening? The rose, the gold on the mountains, the quick mounting shadows?' she wondered in her journal. 'But the late evening is the time—of times. . . . To write something that will be worthy of that rising moon, that pale light.' With its affirmation of the oneness of the world of nature and the world of man, 'At the Bay' is surely that story. For what Katherine Mansfield needed to plumb now was not so much the mysterious depths of human relationships: it was the mysterious ebb and flow of life itself. The death which she faced alone had to be seen in the wider, universal perspective of the death—and renewal—of all natural forms. Thus individual suffering, individual regret, give way in this story to a greater but shared pain at the knowledge of life's shortness.

The relationship of death to life is therefore central to the thematic structure of 'At the Bay', and critics have given it due weight. They have perceived other thematic patterns in the work as well. Saralyn Daly emphasises an inherent contrast between the principles of order and disorder; Marvin Magalaner

stresses the significance of freedom versus imprisonment. But, while Magalaner finds that 'as an artistic representation of what life is about ['At the Bay']
is masterful', he says that it 'lacks the complexity of imagery and association of
"Prelude"'. For him, 'the relevance of each episode to the others is not always
clear . . . for the good reason that it is not there except in a nebulous, hazy fashion'.

The problem with understanding and evaluating 'At the Bay' is that no
critic has fully explored the rich thematic texture of the narrative, or the
wealth of imagery which gives it both power and coherence. Indeed, to analyse
the story closely is to see that everything *is* relevant and interconnected and
that, if anything, 'At the Bay' is a more complex work than 'Prelude'. In the
latter, Katherine Mansfield was primarily concerned with the emotional tensions underlying family life. In 'At the Bay' these tensions are still present,
but intertwined with them is an anxiety about death.

What has partly confused readers of these two major stories is Katherine
Mansfield's continual refinement of a technique reflecting her early immersion
in symbolism. In her adolescent 'Vignettes' she had struggled to find ways at
once to represent and disguise 'the forbidden'; when she came to write the
*German Pension* stories she gave both objects and actions symbolic meaning
that was sometimes obtrusive; but by the time she wrote her last, great New
Zealand stories she had learned to handle symbolism so delicately that it virtually defies detection. In 'At the Bay' there are no such concrete and identifi-
able symbols as the swelling bird and the thorny aloe tree. Her technique here
is a logical extension of her earlier methods, but it is different. With the utmost subtlety she endows the impersonal forces of nature with some of the
psychological attributes which in 'Prelude' were invested in male and female
characters, especially in Linda and Stanley Burnell. The most prominent vehi-
cles of symbolic meaning in 'At the Bay' are the pervasive motifs of the sun as
it marks the time, and the sea. Associated with the fiery heat of the sun is
forceful masculinity; the sea, which both gives and destroys life, is linked with
women in her various guises.

While the cast of characters in 'At the Bay' is almost the same as in 'Prelude', the emphasis has changed, then. Although Linda and Jonathan Trout
dream of what might have been, and Beryl at night again conjures up a lover,
Katherine Mansfield does not attempt to explore deeply the frightening fantasies of individual minds. The characters' thoughts are revealed to us, but not
the workings of their subconscious. And so the symbols which in 'Prelude' expose the subconscious are no longer prominent. Instead, Katherine Mansfield
weaves into her narrative motifs whose universality suggests something very
like the Jungian collective unconscious.

As if representing this, the omniscient author quietly uncovers for us the
world of nature in its least observed moods, interprets the universal significance of these moods, and shows us the instinctive closeness of human beings
to their natural surroundings. 'Very early morning. The sun was not yet risen',

the story opens. The voice of the author describing the natural world blends into the background of the narrative. Part of the background also, and at the same time central to the meaning of almost every episode, are the motifs of the sun and the sea.

Inseparable from the sun in its movement through the sky is the idea of time. Time is a structural device which emphasises the limitation of the action to one day and unifies the separate sections of the work. But it also conveys a sense of the unity of all living beings. Time is integral to the author's thematic concern with life's shortness; and it thus bears a weight of meaning which is primarily philosophical. The sun, on the other hand, is frequently associated with psychological themes. Both the patterning of incidents and the attitudes of the characters suggest a correlation between the power and potential destructiveness of the sun, and masculinity. Significantly, Stanley Burnell's daily movements parallel the sun's: he rises with the sun and returns home when the sun sets. And, just as the presence of the sun is felt in virtually every episode of the story, so does the figure of Stanley Burnell, whether present or absent, command more attention than any other character.

The complexity of meaning and patterning in 'At the Bay' derives partly from the portrayal of some characters' instinctive avoidance of the sun (and heat) and others' conscious association with these forces. Mrs Harry Kember's perverse unnaturalness is characterised by her deliberate and excessive exposure to the sun's heat. Unlike the wholesome and motherly Mrs Fairfield, who protects herself with 'a black hat tied under the chin', Mrs Harry Kember has allowed herself to become 'burnt out and withered. . . . When she was not playing bridge . . . she spent her time lying in the full glare of the sun. She could stand any amount of it; she never had enough. All the same, it did not seem to warm her.' Always known by her husband's forename, 'Harry', Mrs Kember appears to have identified herself with the male element: childless, lacking in femininity, insinuatingly lesbian, she seems to Beryl 'like a horrible caricature of her husband'.

Unlike Mrs Kember, the little Burnell girls go down to the beach wearing sunbonnets; and their mother, in episode VI, is depicted remaining out of the sun in the shady garden. Linda's exposure to the male element in the form of Stanley Burnell (with whom living was like being 'in a house that couldn't be cured of the habit of catching on fire') has left her broken and chilled. Linda, in her fruitfulness, should seem the opposite of Mrs Kember: the archetype of natural woman. But she is not. She is a mother who 'did not love her children. . . . No, it was as though a cold breath had chilled her through and through on each of those awful journeys; she had no warmth left to give them.'

The sun of which Linda will have no part—just as she wants no part of her husband's life-giving potency—is in the next episode depicted as oppressive. 'The sun beat down, beat down hot and fiery on the fine sand, baking the . . . pebbles. It sucked up the little drop of water . . . it bleached the pink convolvulus . . . At this point in the narrative, when the sun is at its hottest and most destructive and Kezia and her grandmother are taking their siesta, the theme of death is raised openly. The fate of Uncle William, who, the old woman says, 'went to the mines, and . . . got a sunstroke there and died', underlines the sun's power to kill and maim. As the afternoon wears on and the sun's heat diminishes, the intensity of emotion associated with it abates. Even so, the association between heat and masculinity lingers on in episode VIII when Alice, the servant girl, who carries 'a very dashed-looking sunshade', walks out to visit Mrs Stubbs, the local storekeeper. Mrs Stubbs, with her long bacon knife and her photographs of herself beside such suggestively phallic objects as a Grecian pillar, a giant fern tree and a towering mountain, is another woman with the attributes of a man. Her primus stove exudes heat and, as she talks cheerfully of Mr Stubbs's death, Alice uneasily wishes that she was back home.

The symbolic connotations of the sun in 'At the Bay' have escaped critical notice, but the complementary motif of the sea has not. Saralyn Daly points out that the sea dominates the entire story, although she does not probe its symbolic meaning. Marvin Magalaner recognises such a meaning and suggests that 'the Jungian idea of water as an ever-moving feminine flow, the archetype of fecund woman . . . may be applicable here'. Water, he says, 'bears a heavy weight of historical, mythical, and psychological meaning'. But he chooses not to pursue the idea of the sea-as-woman. Instead he links the sea-as-life with the theme of freedom versus escape.

One difficulty in coming to grips with the weight of meaning carried by the sea in 'At the Bay' is that this motif, like that of the sun, embodies meanings that are both philosophical and psychological. Philosophically, the time–sun motif is associated with the theme of death; the sea carries the contrary mythic resonance of birth. In the opening paragraph, the voice of the author describing the gradual awakening of life at the bay hints at the mysteries of creation: 'Perhaps if you had waked up in the middle of the night you might have seen a big fish flicking in at the window and gone again.' The reassuring, mythic overtones of this section give way to something different, however, when Stanley Burnell and Jonathan Trout come out for their morning swim. Possessive of the water, Stanley in his resentment of Jonathan's presence there first acts as if the sea were feminine: part wife, part mother. To be immersed in its depths is to partake of its life-giving qualities—to be reborn and revitalised. But to remain too long in its womblike embrace (as does Jonathan) is dangerous.

There is a sense, then, in which the sea in 'At the Bay' is symbolically invested with some of the psychological attributes of woman, especially in her role of mother. In 'Prelude' there were two mothers: Mrs Fairfield, whose presence was reassuring and unifying, and Linda, the reluctant mother, whose rejection of her role provoked anxiety and divisiveness in the family. While both mothers are present in the later story, their functions have subtly changed. The sea, not Mrs Fairfield, is the presiding mother-deity, the unifying force around which all the characters gather; and the sea (or water) acquires also the negative attributes of Linda in her rejecting, emotionally destructive moods. It is significant that water is especially inimical to men. Both Stanley and Jonathan are left unfulfilled—'cheated'—by their early morning swim. After Stanley leaves for work, Alice underlines the dangers that water holds for the opposite sex. Exclaiming, 'Oh, these men', she holds the teapot 'under the water even after it had stopped bubbling, as if it too was a man and drowning was too good for them'. The idea of water as destructive to men is later picked up comically when Mrs Stubbs reveals to Alice the cause of her husband's death: 'it was dropsy that carried him off at the larst. Many's the time they drawn one and a half pints from 'im at the 'ospital.'

The pervasive motifs of the sun and sea (or water) provide a unifying framework for 'At the Bay' and very subtly reinforce the emotional tensions in the work. If the sun's heat has the strength and potential destructiveness of a man, water, the opposing element, has a woman's power to deny as well as to bestow life. Revealed with deceptive casualness, an inherent hostility of female towards male imparts emotional relevance to the separate episodes. The first hint of such an antagonism is provided in the opening section by Florrie, the female cat. 'What a coarse, revolting creature!' she thinks as the male sheepdog passes by. In episode III, after the blustering, bullying Stanley Burnell has left the house, there is a sense of conspiracy among the women: 'Oh, the relief, the difference it made to have the man out of the house. Their very voices were changed as they called to one another; they sounded warm and loving and as if they shared a secret.' As if aware of this feeling, Stanley overreacts to the loss of his walking-stick: 'The heartlessness of women! The way they took it for granted it was your job to slave away for them.' Alice's thought that drowning is too good for a man sums up the latent hostility of this early-morning scene—the only scene where all the family are shown together.

Later, at the beach in mid-morning, the battle between the sexes is portrayed openly. The Samuel Josephs boys and girls continually have to be restrained from fighting one another; and we learn that Mrs Harry Kember is so alienated from her husband that 'some of the women at the Bay privately thought he'd commit a murder one day'. Halfway through the story the theme of sexual hostility reaches an emotional climax. Linda, sitting meditatively apart from the others, makes the admission (paralleling her admission of sexual hatred for Stanley in 'Prelude') that the time not spent in calming her husband and listening to his story is 'spent in the dread of having children . . . that was her real grudge against life'. Nor is the theme dropped at this point. In a lighter vein, Mrs Stubbs that afternoon revels in her freedom from married life, enigmatically calling the death of her husband 'a judgmint'. And the frightened turning away of a woman from a man's sexual advances dominates the ending of the story. Beryl, in the closing episode of 'At the Bay', wrenches herself free from Mr Harry Kember. Frozen with horror by his 'bright, blind, terrifying smile', she runs from him calling, 'You are vile, vile.'

In 'At the Bay', as in 'Prelude', there is another side to a woman's resentment and fear of male sexuality: a mother's rejection of her children. Linda's dread of having children is conveyed quite explicitly in the central episode of 'At the Bay'. She decides that it is 'useless pretending' to love her children and that, as for the baby boy, 'he was mother's, or Beryl's, or anybody's who wanted him.' Linda's unexpected surge of feeling for the smiling infant does not cancel out her earlier expressions of indifference towards her children, and Kezia seems instinctively to understand her mother's attitude. As in 'Prelude', she turns to the grandmother for maternal care and is fearful at the prospect of abandonment. 'You couldn't leave me. You couldn't not be there', she agonises, at the thought of her grandmother's death.

It is not only Kezia who exhibits a degree of emotional insecurity, however. Nearly all other members of the family demonstrate, in one way or another, that they, too, yearn for love and suffer from anxiety about separation. Lottie, for instance, is afraid that the two older sisters will hurry to the beach leaving her behind; at the end of the day the children playing in the wash-house are fearful that the grown-ups have forgotten—or abandoned them. 'No, not really forgotten. That was what their smile meant. They had decided to leave them there all by themselves.' But the grown-ups themselves are emotionally anxious. There is Jonathan Trout, who goes about with 'a look like hunger in his black eyes' and whimsically asks Linda for 'a little love, a little kindness'. Beryl, in the closing scene, wants a lover because 'it's so frightfully difficult when you've nobody'. Perhaps Stanley, more than all the adults, suffers from his dependence on being loved and a sense that his needs are constantly thwarted. Trying to punish his wife for her lack of concern over him, he calls out as he goes to work, 'No time to say good-bye!' But Linda, as if she had never noticed, replies to his request for forgiveness at the end of the day with a cutting 'what must I forgive you for?'

There is, then, a clear psychological patterning in 'At the Bay' which is reinforced by the motifs of the sun and the sea. Less important thematically, yet helping connect the different episodes of the story, is Katherine Mansfield's use of animal imagery. In 'Prelude', the repeated bird motif had emphasised a common bond among the female characters: their childbearing function and its ramifications in their emotional lives. Animal imagery in 'At the Bay' serves several purposes. It adds to the impression that human beings are hardly separable from the natural world in which they live; it introduces a note of humour into the story; and, more significantly, it links the characters and conveys some essential aspects of their personalities. Thus the likening of Mrs Harry Kember with her 'strange neighing laugh' first to a horse and later, when she swims, to a turtle and a rat, underlines her physical perverseness. In this grotesque presentation of the woman there is an implied condemnation of the mannish lesbian who would poison some such vulnerable person as Beryl. The quite different comparison of Alice and Mrs Stubbs to cats is a humorous way of suggesting the common ground they share, and it is a means of reducing the anxiety caused by the appearance of yet another masculine woman in the form of Mrs Stubbs. Animal imagery has sexually ambiguous overtones when Linda, musing in the garden during the morning, fleetingly thinks of her husband as looking like 'a trapped beast'. At the end of the day Jonathan Trout walks with Linda in the same garden and philosophically likens himself to an insect, feeble in its entrapment.

A more light-hearted use of animal imagery occurs in episode IX which is devoted to the children. Earlier, the grandmother's affectionate understanding of Kezia's personality had been expressed when she called her 'my squirrel' and 'my wild pony'. Playing animal snap in the wash-house, the children assume animal names which suggest their own characters. Pip, the dominant boy cousin, identifies himself with the strong, masculine bull; Rags, who follows his brother obediently, becomes a sheep; Lottie, whose personality is still fluid, changes from a donkey (which she behaves like) to a dog, whose part she cannot play. Isabel, a conceited boaster, appropriately becomes a crowing rooster; and Kezia, who is sensitive but able to hit back, is given the role of a bee with power to sting.

The qualities of a masterpiece resist definition. 'At the Bay' is especially difficult to explicate because the story which appears so simple on the surface is in fact extraordinarily complex. Thematically, it encompasses a whole range of feelings about human life. Woven into the texture of the narrative is a sense of the psychological conflicts between men and women, parents and children. These are the problems of youth, and in the natural course of things give way to the pressing problem of age: anxiety about death. Katherine Mansfield's achievement in this story is to weave into one tapestry the preoccupations of youth and age, and so to balance psychological truths against philosophical truths that they seem indistinguishable. Thus life, death and sexuality are intertwined; and the same motifs which convey a mystical sense of man's continuing life in the endless round of creation are linked with a woman's fear of the hazardous process of giving birth.

But it is not just with the beginning and end of life that the author is philosophically concerned: it is with how best to use the interval between birth and death. There is a choice, Katherine Mansfield implies, between safety and danger: between existing in a kind of inertia or waking sleep (and failing to realise one's potential); and extending life's boundaries through exploration or active discovery.

The contrast between inertia and exploration, like that between death and life, is conveyed through a sequence of motifs which runs through the entire narrative. References to sleep recur in the first half of 'At the Bay'. In the opening section we hear the soothing sounds of 'the sleepy sea'; then the reemergence of human life is signalled when 'the first sleeper turned over and lifted a drowsy head'. Taking his morning swim with Stanley, Jonathan Trout is preoccupied with the 'extraordinary dream' he had last night. Later in the morning, Mr Harry Kember with his 'slow, sleepy smile' is compared to 'a man walking in his sleep', while his wife is shown lifting 'her sleepy face . . . above the water'. In the garden, Linda Burnell 'dreamed the morning away', the baby boy 'sound asleep' at her side. Not until episode VII when Kezia and her grandmother are taking their siesta together, does the motif of sleep give way to the more sombre one of death.

Katherine Mansfield conveys her sense that exploration, with all its dangers, is preferable to inertia—indeed, necessary, if life is to be experienced to the full—through the characters themselves. In the second episode she implicitly compares the attitudes to life of Stanley and Jonathan Trout. Stanley, who exults as he enters the sea that he was 'first man in as usual! He'd beaten them all again', reacts like an explorer beaten to his goal when he discovers that Jonathan is already swimming. In contrast to Stanley's energy and competitiveness is the other man's lassitude, his preference to 'take things easy, not to fight against the ebb and flow of life, but to give way to it'. The suggestion that life is something to be explored, and that there are discoveries to be made, recurs in the fourth episode. The little Burnell girls look like 'minute puzzled explorers' as they hurry to join their boy cousins searching for 'treasure' in the sand. 'Look what I've discovered', cries Pip.

In the following episode Beryl, on another part of the beach, explores a new and potentially dangerous relationship with Mrs Harry Kember while Linda, lying inactive under the manuka tree, muses about her youthful dreams of exploring with her father 'up a river in China'. Marriage has limited her opportunities, forced on her a different role: 'It was always Stanley who was in the thick of the danger. Her whole time was spent in rescuing him.' As the day wears on, the motif of exploration persists. Kezia's uncle William 'went to the mines' in Australia in search of adventure. On a smaller scale, Alice, timidly venturing along a deserted road to visit Mrs Stubbs, is testing out something new. And later the children playing in the darkening wash-house continue their exploration of life's possibilities: 'You were frightened to look in the corners . . . and yet you had to look with all your might.' Similarly frightened but courageous, Beryl, in the final episode, follows through to its conclusion her thought, 'If I go on living here . . . anything may happen to me.' Foregoing the safety of her bedroom, she responds to Harry Kember's mocking challenge, 'you're not frightened, are you? You're not frightened?' by stepping out into the darkness to meet him.

Linda's discussion with Jonathan Trout in episode X brings this theme to a climax and draws together the different threads of the story. 'I've only one night or one day, and there's this vast dangerous garden, waiting out there, undiscovered, unexplored', he laments. Jonathan acquiesces in his entrapment: 'Weak ... weak. No stamina', he confesses. Linda shares with her brother-in-law a sense of life's shortness, a frustration at the ties of marriage and a passivity which precludes change. But his admission of inertia and defeat is for her an emotional turning-point—and a moment of discovery. The circumstances of Linda's life prevent her from extending the limits of her physical existence, from exploring space: yet she is able to make discoveries of another kind. In the morning she had discovered in spite of herself a new feeling for her baby boy; now, as Jonathan bemoans his helplessness, she inwardly compares him with her husband. The recognition that Jonathan is 'not resolute, not gallant, not careless' causes her to see Stanley in an altered light. She makes her second major affirmation that day when he returns home from work. 'Enfolded in that familiar, eager, strong embrace', Linda rediscovers her love for him as she smiles at, and accepts, his foibles.

Such an affirmation of life is essential to the resolution of the philosophical problem which is raised in 'At the Bay'. The question, 'Why be born at all?' is implicit in Linda's meditation in the garden that morning. All through the narrative, however, the interpreting voice of the author suggests her own answer to the problem of life's dualisms—to the fact that human beings must live with the knowledge of their own inevitable end; that they are divided between a longing to explore the dimensions of life, and a fear to leave the known and familiar; that they aspire to freedom from family ties yet are emotionally dependent on each other; and that some are forced to accept sexual roles that they would rather be without.

Katherine Mansfield's answer, so subtly conveyed that it is hardly noticeable, is that there is a 'mysterious fitness' and unity in the natural order. Involving the reader with her inclusive 'you', she so merges the world of nature and the human world that they are barely distinguishable. In the mythic opening section where 'you could not see where [the hills] ended and the paddocks and bungalows began', the sea, the little streams and the vegetation not only seem timeless: they seem consciously alive. The awakening animal and human life partakes of nature's timelessness. With his 'velvet trousers tied under the knee', the old shepherd might be appearing from an earlier century, while his sheep which 'seemed to be always on the same piece of ground' are virtually interchangeable with the 'ghostly flocks and herds' which answer them from under the sea.

As we watch the mists lift on yet another morning, we sense an implied reassurance that everything is constantly reborn, that nothing really dies. Another such reassurance about the continuity of life in nature occurs midway through the story. In episode VII, when human beings have withdrawn from the sun's heat, the natural world is again seen to reassert its own life. The voice of the author compares the weed-hung rocks to 'shaggy beasts come down to the water to drink' and each pool to 'a lake with pink and blue houses clustered on the shores'. The voice asks, 'Who made that sound? What was going on down there?'

Against the backdrop of this interchangeable, perpetual life there is an intrinsic rightness to the grandmother's acceptance that death 'happens to all of us sooner or later'. The philosophical problem of death is raised for the third and last time in episode X, when Jonathan and Linda talk in the garden. Earlier in the day, Linda had reflected on the cruel paradox that the petals which 'shone as if each was the careful work of a loving hand' were destined to be wasted. Now, the voice of the author seems to merge with Linda's thoughts in one possible, negative explanation of the wastage inherent in creation: the beams in the sky 'remind you that up there sits Jehovah, the jealous God, the Almighty. . . . You remember that at His coming the whole earth will shake into one ruined graveyard.' And yet all the time counteracting this notion of a tyrannical, Old Testament God is the beauty of nature: the 'rose-coloured clouds', the blue sky overhead which faded and 'turned a pale gold', and the beams which finally seem to Linda 'infinitely joyful and loving'.

From Tolstoy, Katherine Mansfield copied into her journal in 1921, 'Life is everything. Life is God. All is changing and moving and that motion is God.' Imperceptibily, in 'At the Bay', she resolves the paradox of life and death by fusing a Wordsworthian concept of the oneness of nature and man with her perception that nature itself shares in the attributes of a loving Christian God. And so at the end of this story which juxtaposes a woman's dread of childbearing with the necessity for birth and renewal, we are prepared to return to the beginning—and the continuance of life: 'A cloud, small, serene, floated across the moon . . . and the sound of the sea was a vague murmur, as though it waked out of a dark dream.'

# How Kathleen Beauchamp Was Kidnapped

## Lydia Wevers

In a letter to *Zealandia* published in October 1889, a reader asked, 'Why is colonial literature, "the formative power of true Colonialism", called an abortion . . . To create a national entity we must give heed to our latent character and not what is alien.'[1]

My starting point in this paper is this description of colonial literature as the 'formative power of true Colonialism'. In representing literature as the empowering location of colonial identity, this letter indicates a complex concern amongst colonial readers and writers about what colonial literature might be, and how it might distinctively characterise itself.

On the one hand the term 'colonial' is an unacceptable expression of cultural separation, as in this letter published in 1890:

> Do not let us have a purely Colonial literature; it cannot be a good thing to fetter us to the narrow circle of the Colonies . . . We do not want yet a Colonial style any more than we want a Colonial accent, and our noblest aim is to belong to English, not Colonial, literature.[2]

On the other, 'colonial' becomes the signifier of specific difference located in the 'life' and 'character' of narrative, so it is a cultural separation both necessary and positive, as in this book review:

> This book is described on the title page as a colonial tale. The scene, it is true, is laid in the colonies—first in Oamaru and Dunedin, and afterwards in Melbourne—and to this extent it is a colonial tale; but there is nothing distinctively colonial in either the characters or the incidents. It seems a pity to use thus indiscriminately the term 'colonial' which should only be applied to tales that illustrate some phase of colonial life or character.[3]

In this paper I want to consider the colonial short story as a signifier of colonial discourse, and as one of the places where the term 'colonial' is intended to represent a distinctive cultural identity defined by difference and separation from the originating culture. I want also to suggest the ways in which this discourse is expressed in the 'colonial' stories of Katherine Mansfield, most particularly 'The Woman at the Store', but also 'How Pearl Button was Kidnapped' and

Reprinted from *Women's Studies Journal* 4:2 (December 1988):5–17.

'Millie'. My title, 'How Kathleen Beauchamp was Kidnapped' can serve as a signifier to the writer KM might have been had she stayed in her colonial dress, and resisted appropriation by Europe.

Colonial writing is a discourse of exteriority. In order to suggest the distinctiveness of their representation of the colonial, colonial writers rely heavily on a visible external expression of difference, typically that of clothing, landscape and stereotype, and on a narrative structure authorised by the inclusion of or dependence on incidents which derive from documented or anecdotal history. In New Zealand these range from goldmining and tribal conflict to the conditions of material existence in a still wild and unEnglish landscape. The writer wishing to register 'colonial' as a distinctive term typically concentrates on external characteristics as a sign of the successfully separated colonial self, identified with and by the context of otherness, by appearing in colonial dress both literally and metaphorically. Association of dress and place is explicit. 'Teddy had worn pinafores in Australia, wide collars in England, and dungarees from one end of New Zealand to the other.'[4]

In the story by G.B. Lancaster, Teddy is not, however, confined simply to wearing dungarees as the expression of true colonialism; he is also 'strong in the knowledge gained as indubitable owner of a nine-by-fourteen sod *whare*, and a two thousand acre run many miles down the river'.[5] Teddy's dungarees dress him for his possession of land, and his specifically colonial identification is associated both with his ownership of a sod whare and a large piece of land, and with his occupation—he works on his land, this is what legitimates his possession of it, and why the knowledge of his property gives him strength. Teddy's ownership of land is represented not as appropriation by Teddy, but as the assimilation of Teddy to his context; his sod whare and his run by the river dress him as distinctively colonial, just as his dungarees do. Property as knowledge and ownership as strength are characteristic tropes in colonial fiction. By emphasising a visible external characterisation associating work and identity, the colonial writer is able to represent appropriation as assimilation, and economic dominance as legitimated ownership.

If 'colonial' comes to mean a cultural identity externally recognisable by its work and the place in which that work is done, then what is frequently distinguished as 'alien' in colonial fiction is not the other, the subject people who define colonial as a racial and racist identification, but the culturally separated self represented for example as the New Chum, in whom the boundary of difference is constructed as a difference in *knowledge*—the knowledge of place and of the work associated with it that allows the colonial to become overtly assimilated to the place which colonial work is appropriating and 'civilising'.

'Colonial' identity therefore, as fiction writes it, is suggested by characteristics expressed as external—clothing, context, landscape—which represent a form of knowledge that separates the colonial subject from his or her self of origin. Colonialism is thus the recognition of a selfhood distinctive from, but still within, a culture that defines it. However, too great a cultural separation in colonial identity becomes problematic. Colonial writers are, on the whole, anxious to claim an essential unity of human nature at the same time as they mark off the visible distinctiveness of the colonial as local colour. The judge of a 1900 Prize Story Competition held by the *New Zealand Illustrated Magazine* remarked that:

> there is one great danger however, in applying this canon of art (that essentials and externals must be distinctly local) into which writers much greater than competitors fall, and that is the constant tendency to sacrifice to it all genuine human interest and to stifle the appeal that their works should make to human nature generally; the writer of a New Zealand story must not ignore that touch of nature which makes the whole world kin.[6]

Making the whole world kin is a very useful way of removing problems in colonial identity. As long as the non-essential difference which constitutes local colour is simply external variation which defines colonialism as a form of knowledge, problematic differences such as race or gender are absorbed into the kinship of human nature, and the boundary of knowledge that distinguishes the colonial from his self of origin need not argue any essential transformation. So colonial fictive modes prefer to suggest essential human unities, while emphasising the specific cultural differences expressed in the colonial subject. A review of Blanche Baughan's collection of verse *Shingle Short* praises it for being essentially 'colonial in conception and in inspiration', which means that it employs 'rugged' language, and the life depicted is 'true in every detail' but the tone is 'clean and lofty'.[7] But if 'colonial' writing illustrates too wide a gap between the colonial subject and acceptable convention in the originating culture, then colonial writing, in attempting realism and a specific characterisation of difference, is at fault. Clara Cheeseman, author of an article titled 'Colonials in Fiction', published in the *New Zealand Illustrated Magazine* in 1903, expressed concern that the literary representation of colonial life was so extreme as to devalue the colonial in his place of origin:

> The saddest and most unflattering accounts of colonial life are to be found in the books written by those who ought to know it best. A lecturer or literary man— I forget the name—went Home after a lengthened tour of the colonies, and spoke with severity of the drunkenness and profanity of Australians; their gambling and horse-racing habits, the vulgarity of ordinary conversation and so forth. A storm of indignation burst about his ears. To justify himself he points to their own novels. 'Read these,' he said, in effect, 'and see if I am mistaken.'
>
> And, indeed, there are few colonial stories which are quite free from this taint. The same might be said of many which have been written by New Zealanders. Altogether, colonial people have much need to pray that they may not be taken at their own valuation.[8]

This problem is particularly acute in the case of woman writers, for whom the terms 'woman' and 'writer' already suggest a cultural gap, which is only increased by the addition of 'colonial':

> Many women invent situations which they ought to be ashamed of, and write down language which surely they would not have the hardihood to read aloud. Sometimes this is done through ignorance, or under the mistaken impression that they are making their writings forcible. And so they are in one sense—too forcible. Everyone admires strength but we do not want to be struck with a sledgehammer.[9]

This sledgehammering colonial woman may be seen in the bush, but must not appear on the page. However, these anxieties about literary decorum indicate a real problem inherent in the colonial self and what it represents. If the true depiction of colonial scenes requires that the colonial adopt not just the visible differentiation of dress, work location and rugged language, but also an essential transformation of morality, a moral otherness, identity becomes problematic. To be culturally distinctive, the term 'colonial' must indicate some separation from the culture from which the colonial derives. Colonial fiction suggests this separation in the location of external difference; but narrative structures increasingly suggest the difficulty of containing change and separation as exterior. The ways in which the predominant types of narrative fiction work at defining colonial identity suggest its developing complication.

Colonial short fiction falls characteristically into particular narrative forms. First, and least troublesome, is the yarn or tale which authenticates its distinctiveness by dependence on historical event. It typically asserts cultural dominance either as labour and administration, the civilising work of clearing the land, in which the signifying other is the landscape; or by reference to events which characterise the locality as other, such as goldmining, or sometimes war; or, less problematically, by humorous incidents arising from the exigencies of material life in a recently built settlement. The 'voice' of the yarn is always male; in its language and anecdotal narrative structure it is the least problematic representation of colonial identity as visible, stereotypic, and non-essential difference. Here is Bill the bullock-driver from 'A Yarn from our Township' (1901) dressed in the speech and garments of cultural identity, discovering his woodpile has been stolen:

> He was a square-set, obstinate-looking man dressed in dungaree pants, crimson shirt and leggings. His coat was tied around his neck by the sleeves, and from his blucher boots to his flabby felt hat he was coated with mud and steaming with moisture—a hairy man with a beard that looked as if it would turn grey with the shock, if it happened to meet by accident with a comb or a brush.
>
> 'Not a bit. Not a-coruscated ebullition of adjectives-bit! Not even enough to light a fire with! Well I'm blowed!'[10]

Yarns and tales represent their origin as 'real' experience; but another preferred colonial mode, the ghost or mystery story, represents its origin in experience that is explicitly other—outside empirical knowledge, located outside conventional social structures. Indeed, in a story called 'The Mystery of Black Grange' (1900), in which a beautiful woman is imprisoned in a remote building in the Kaipara, the place of her imprisonment is described as being outside British law: 'Look at country, mister, British law 'ud get lost an' starved in it.'[11]

Colonial ghost stories typically represent the presence of otherness which positions the culturally separated colonial self not as place or work, but as supernatural and Maori. The Maori as other is the object in a fantasy about inexplicable primitive power, seen from a culture stressing empirical knowledge and rationality. Close association with this power by the colonial subject is usually destructive; rather, the power of colonial knowledge is asserted by dramatising an ambivalent desire for the other which is then denied. It is not overt colonial identity which is problematic in ghost stories, but the nature of the other, a racial stereotype which is, in Homi Bhabha's terms, both phobia and fetish.[12] In expressing ambivalent desire as part of the colonial experience of other, rejection of the object becomes a cultural assertion of superior rationality. A characteristic example is the end of "The Disappearance of Letham Crouch' (1901):

> McCrea hesitated a moment, and then put down his pipe very deliberately.
>
> 'If he was mad,' he said slowly, 'it was a queer case. The Maori part of him was sane enough. It seemed to me as if the personality of the Maori, who had died in the whare, had eaten its way into him through his environment in some way.'
>
> 'Bosh' said McShane, and I got no further information of any value out of either of them.[13]

Of the 86 stories submitted for the *New Zealand Illustrated Magazine's* Prize Story Competition in 1900, 90 percent were love stories. If short fiction has a predominant colonial mode it is romance melodrama, a fictional form of pronounced conventionality in which the surface narrative structure becomes a kind of dressing—the superimposing of a familiar pattern on an unfamiliar environment. There may be distinctive externally recognisable colonial figures in the love story; but in its articulation of desire, and its formulation of the object of desire as ultimately, after trial, attainable, it reiterates and affirms the colonial preference for the essential unities of human nature; it quite literally makes the whole world kin.

But the love story can also be read as a signifier of colonial preoccupations. Its fictional nexus is typically the interaction of love and money, or less often the interaction of love and race, so the subject/object relationship in a love story articulates the successful satisfaction/completion of desire as the appropriation or rightful possession of wealth or land, or, conversely, the subject's frustrated desire for wealth or land. When the object of desire is also Maori, as is not infrequent, the fictional model of the love story is able to absorb or rewrite racial difference as though it is a natural appropriation; the subject's successful desiring of the object legitimates possession. When both subject and object are Maori, as is also often the case, then the love story becomes a cultural appropriation, rewriting the other as a familiar narrative of essentialism. 'The Last of the Ngatiahutus' by Roderick MacDonald (1900) is an example: 'A conflict between love and duty—such a one as is experienced by men and women, both brown and white, savage and civilised, all the world over—was taking place in the mind of the stern young warrior.'[14] In this way colonial love stories are a model for the legitimate appropriation of the object of desire, and the writing out of racial, cultural, and gender difference (men and women, brown and white, savage and civilised) in favour of essentialist unities here expressed as love and duty.

However, colonial romances also typically express an uneasiness about cultural separation in the subject, indicated either through the eruption of violence into the story, or by the frequent discovery that the colonial lover's self-representation is duplicitous, that he is not the man he claims to be—he is not single, but married, or his claim to fortune is misrepresented. The visible distinctiveness of the colonial may misrepresent the social and cultural identity left behind in England, and so the external clues by which identity announces itself become liable to misrepresentation. Or, as in the following example, a ludicrous mismatch of self-representation and social convention re-invents identity and its representation, and so begins to destabilise social convention. In a story by Clara Cheeseman first published in 1878, 'Married for his Money', the object of desire—in this case a young man who has inherited a fortune—is dressed for the part:

> Mr Simpelson had, since the arrival of his fortune, indulged in a style of dress resembling that often affected by lucky diggers, and other suddenly-enriched mortals. Although it was only eleven in the forenoon, he was in full evening costume; his black suit was of superfine cloth, his new boots creaked with every step he took. The jewelry that the misguided young man wore would have realised a small fortune; coral and gold studs, and sleeve links, a gold watch with a guard that was nearly thick and strong enough to be used as a dog chain, and from which were suspended various ornaments, while six rings, studded with enormous gems, adorned his fingers.[15]

Mr Simpelson quite literally clanks with the external announcement of identity; it is one thing to represent yourself as the successful coloniser of wealth, another to wear it all on your person.

In colonial love stories the surface narrative of events frequently signals anxiety about the uncontrollable gap between the colonial and the self from which he has separated in order to become distinctively identified as colonial. It is a cultural separation which the colonising subject always implies, and which includes the difficulty of containing both subject and colonised object unambiguously within the conventions of the appropriating culture. Colonial romance, dressing itself distinctively in the externals of cultural identity, employs a narrative structure which locates that identity as itself problematic; as existing within a colonial discourse of appropriation and possession, and as part of a subject/object relationship which often suggests that the experience of the other is morally transforming and destabilising.

'The Woman at the Store', the first of Mansfield's 'colonial' stories submitted to *Rhythm* in 1912 and 1913, announces its distinctive colonial location in characteristically external terms—the heat, the wind, the tussock grass, pumice dust, horses, physical discomfort, manuka bushes.

Jo and Hin are seen, are recognised, by their clothing which announces visible identity: a blue galatea shirt, corduroy trousers and riding boots, a wideawake, blue duck trousers. What they wear and what they eat—fly biscuits and apricots by the side of a swampy creek—represent them as colonial, assimilated, identified with place and occupation. They have in view a conventional object which reaffirms the gender and fictional identity of the subjects—a woman with blue eyes and yellow hair 'who'll promise you something else before she shakes hands with you'.

But as soon as Mansfield has established the recognisable conventions of colonial self-representation, she begins at once to subvert them, drawing explicit attention to the unease and anxiety about cultural identity which the colonial romance/melodrama attempts to contain. The woman at the whare greets the travellers (Jo bursts into song at seeing her) with a rifle; her welcome is ambivalent and her representation as an object of desire is ludicrous, a 'figure of fun':

I smiled at the thought of how Hin had pulled Jo's leg about her. Certainly her eyes were blue, and what hair she had was yellow, but ugly. She was a figure of fun. Looking at her, you felt there was nothing but sticks and wires under that pinafore—her front teeth were knocked out, she had red, pulpy hands and she wore on her feet a pair of dirty Bluchers.

'I'll go and turn out the horses,' said Jim. 'Got any embrocation? Poi's rubbed herself to hell!'

'Arf a mo!' The woman stood silent a moment, her nostrils expanding as she breathed. Then she shouted violently, 'I'd rather you didn't stop . . . you *can't* and there's the end of it. I don't let out that paddock any more. You'll have to go on; I ain't got nothing!'

The woman's external representation of gender, her pinafore, her yellow hair, her child, seems to be nothing but external: as an object of desire she exists only in fantasy, under her pinafore 'you felt there was nothing but sticks and wires'. Metaphorically and descriptively the woman is identified externally with her territory; she is the woman at the store, like Teddy with his two thousand acre run; but *as* a woman, and the desired object in a romance, she is little more than an animated pinafore who's 'gone a bit off 'er dot'.

The place inhabited by the woman at the store is distinctively and externally characterised. Visible within it are the signs of cultural separation; English periodicals are plastered to the walls, but the inside of the whare is a place of work, of material discomfort, of flies and smells, and a coloured print of Richard Seddon. This large room, papered with the out-of-date pages of another self, is filled with the utensils and broken down objects of working existence, the work of the coloniser by which she is identified and which entitles her to possession—but significantly, as a wife, possession limited to the occupation of this room. Like the pinafore, it is a form of dressing that represents her as colonial woman, an exterior identity. The narrator, sitting on the table waiting for the embrocation for Hin's horse, becomes conscious of a quality of the landscape, 'a curious half-hour when everything appears grotesque—it frightens—as though the savage spirit of the country walked abroad and sneered at what it saw. Sitting alone in the hideous room, I grew afraid.'

It is in the 'hideous' room that the narrator becomes conscious of the other who is not the woman with the yellow hair, though she is still the ambivalent object of desire, but the savage spirit that inhabits the countryside which the colonial subjects of the story are passing through, and which the woman at the store is occupying with her work, her scone-baking and her ironing. And as the narrative events of the story proceed, the visible cultural identity of the woman at the store is seen to have as much substance as her pinafore; it is a kind of dressing concealing her transformation into other, unknown, phobia; her appropriation by the savage spirit of the country.

The barmaid, pretty as a wax doll, who knew 125 different ways of kissing, isn't the same woman any more; the coloniser has been colonised; and woman as object has been doubly displaced from her conventional identifications as an object of desire, a wax doll, to sticks and wires and to murderer. She is identified by her action as other, savage, no longer object but subject, no longer woman but unwoman, whose identification as other is confirmed by her child representing herself in her drawings which are the 'creation of a lunatic with a lunatic's cleverness'.

'The Woman at the Store' represents itself as a distinctively colonial melodrama, and then subverts the discourse signified by its fictional model. Not only does Mansfield subvert romance by representing the object of desire as a fantasy of purely external gender identity, of dress. Romance as a conventional structure of the attainment and possession of desire, and thus as a colonial discourse of legitimate appropriation and possession, is subverted by the transformation of the object into other, into savage; from 125 ways of kissing she has learned one way to kill. But in the story, it is only Hin and the narrator who become, through the child's drawings, aware of the gap between the woman who has murdered her husband, the secret the child must never tell, and the woman dressed in her best, her white calico dressing jacket and her black skirt, who plays kissing feet under the table. Fictionally, the reader is positioned with the narrator and Hin in the store room, sitting on two sacks of potatoes, as it were, behind the dressing up, behind the pinafore, behind the room with its door shut where Jo and the woman with yellow hair have gone for the night, seeing, not in speech or act, but in the child's drawing the sticks and wires of the other. Meanwhile, in the shut room, the social and fictional conventions of romance continue. Jo, at any rate, attains the object of desire.

Mansfield positions her narrative exactly at the point at which the separations of colonial identity are most evident. Here the double view, of the woman who is both object and other, destabilises and inverts the cultural identity of the colonial subject, and the gender stereotype of the woman. The woman at the store has become someone, or something, that Hin and the narrator are not expecting; the cultural separation of her selfhood which is represented as the wax doll barmaid who has become the woman in the bush with a rifle has resulted in an identity that is distinctive in its colonialism, but also distinctive in its moral otherness. She is herself colonised/appropriated, become savage, undesirable.

Mansfield further complicates this by destabilising the assumption of narrative type that opens the story. Jo and Hin are identified conventionally as visibly and externally colonial men, but the narrative voice, it is suggested, is that of a woman. The child watches 'her' bathing, but apart from the pronoun, other clues to the narrator's gender are marginal.[16] She is not asserted as a woman; rather the pronoun 'her' shatters the assumption that it is three men who ride into the story, and so it functions as a separation of the reader's understanding of the colonial subject. Mansfield subverts the gender difference implied in the structure of subject/object, and places the narrator outside the identification of type which is writing the story within a distinct colonial mode. She successfully deconstructs all her narrative categories, and the text becomes the site of uncertainty and questioning. The narrator is effectively placed outside the categories of cultural identity, subject and gender which allow us to 'read' the story; thus she acts as a subversive commentary on the kind of colonial discourse her narrative signifies. If the narrator cannot be constructed, can the narrative?

Mansfield's subversion of convention, structure and discourse acts in her colonial stories generally to rewrite the preoccupations of colonial self-representation. As in "The Woman at the Store', 'Millie' establishes colonial distinctiveness in external location; Millie is the woman alone in a hot dry landscape, the sun 'like a burning mirror', the boys gone to hound down the young English johnny who'd been on the station learning farming. The young English johnny is a New Chum. Like the picture on Millie's bedroom wall,

'Garden Party at Windsor Castle', he is foreign. Millie, looking at the towers
of Windsor Castle, flying three Union Jacks, and in the middle of the picture
the old Queen, 'like a tea cosy with a head on top of it', rejects it in favour of a
large photograph of her and Sid taken on their wedding day, fern trees and a
waterfall behind them and Mount Cook in the distance. To Millie, Windsor
Castle with its social structures is foreign, other, it has too much side. She rejects what she is culturally separated from, and justifiably so; for the rejected
other, in the person of the young English johnny, is also morally other, a murderer, representing an extreme.

> As Sid said, if he wasn't strung up where would they all be? A man like that
> doesn't stop at one go. There was blood all over the barn. And Willie Cox said
> he was that knocked out he picked a cigarette up out of the blood and smoke it.

When Millie realises the murderer is in her wood pile, stops seeing him as the
representative of all that she is opposed to and thus defined by, and recognises
in him a sick child, she determines to save him from the men who are now
beasts, until he escapes later in the night and in becoming the object of the
hunt, positions Millie with the hunters.

It is tempting to see in 'Millie' Mansfield playing with a recurrent colonial narrative like 'The Drover's Wife': the woman alone in the landscape,
threatened by the other to whom she is object, the other who represents an extreme of social and moral opposition. 'Millie' plays with and shifts the notions
of otherness which constitute the narrative location of the story by reversing
and complicating the social and human relationship of the woman and the boy
who threatens her: he arouses painful motherly feeling in Millie, and, though
a murderer, is clearly of a higher social class, more obviously 'civilised' than
she. Yet at the same time the story affirms their cultural separation which finally determines how Millie reacts to him. Her colonial identity is established
by her opposition to Windsor Castle and the Union Jacks and the young English johnny, human and child though he is. Essential human unity is abandoned. 'She rushed into the road—she laughed and shrieked and danced in the
dust, jigging the lantern. "A-ah! Arter 'im Sid! A-a-ah! ketch him Willie. Go
it! Go it! A-ah Sid! Shoot 'im down. Shoot 'im!"'

In 'How Pearl Button was Kidnapped', Mansfield plays with racial otherness in what is also a preoccupying motif of colonial fiction, the lost or kidnapped child. If colonial romance signifies a discourse of racial and territorial
appropriation, then the colonial fear of being in turn appropriated is typically
represented in a displacement onto women, the women who go mad in the
bush, or children, the children appropriated by the other, either as landscape
or as human. But when Pearl Button with her yellow curls goes with the two
fat Maori women to a meeting house, and then to the beach, imprisoned in her
clothes and in her social conventions, her narrative movement out into landscape and into a knowledge of racial and cultural difference is a liberation from

the constriction of being the colonial subject, caught in a House of Boxes.

Mansfield's colonial stories show her ability to adapt colonial dress and then subvert it, so that the anxieties expressed in colonial narrative modes and structures—about identity, about cultural separation, and about appropriation both by and of the colonial subject—become the location of her texts. As always, Mansfield's stories are where questions are asked, where what it is to be colonial is re-invented, re-written and re-understood.

## Notes

1. John C. Thompson, Letter to *Zealandia* No. 4, October 1889:236.

2. W.R. Haselden, 'Novel Reading' *Zealandia* No. 6, December 1890:387.

3. W.A. Sim, Review of *The Mystery of the Forecastle* by R.V. McPherson. *Zealandia* No. 3, September 1889:151.

4. G.B. Lancaster 'God Keep Ye Merrie Gentlemen', *New Zealand Illustrated Magazine* December 1901:168.

5. G.B. Lancaster ibid.

6. Some Remarks on the Recent Prize Story Competition by One of the Judges, *New Zealand Illustrated Magazine* February 1901:344.

7. Anonymous review of B.E. Baughan, *Shingle Short and Other Versus, Current Thought* Vol. 1 No. 1, September 1908:18–19.

8. Clara Cheeseman, 'Colonials in Fiction', *New Zealand Illustrated Magazine* January 1903:275–6.

9. Clara Cheeseman ibid.

10. Colin C. Biernacki, 'A Yarn from our Township', *New Zealand Illustrated Magazine* May 1901:595.

11. Elma Vronberg, 'The Mystery of Black Grange', *New Zealand Illustrated Magazine* October 1900:18.

12. Homi K. Bhabha, 'The Other Question: difference, discrimination and the discourse of colonialism', in *Literature Poetics and Theory*, ed. Barker *et al.*, Methuen 1986:148–172.

13. Chas. Owen, 'The Disappearance of Letham Crouch', *New Zealand Illustrated Magazine* July 1901:781.

14. Roderick McDonald, 'The Last of the Ngatiahutus', *New Zealand Illustrated Magazine* August 1900:824.

15. Clara Cheeseman, 'Married for His Money', reprinted in *Happy Endings,* ed. E. Webby and L. Wevers, Allen and Unwin 1987:59.

16. In the text of this story published in *Rhythm* Vol. I No. 41912, the child avoids a pronoun and uses 'that one' (p. 16); but in the version of the story printed in *Something Childish and Other Stories,* 1924, the pronoun 'her' is used, in a sentence previously attributed to the narrator, but in the later version to the child (p. 68).

# Reading with the Taint of the Pioneer:
# Katherine Mansfield and Settler Criticism

## BRIDGET ORR

Some anniversaries are easier to celebrate than others—the centenary of Katherine Mansfield's birth in Wellington in 1888 doubtless presented the cultural affairs officer of the New Zealand High Commission in London with much less of a problem than the upcoming reckoning with a hundred and fifty years of pakeha kawanatanga in Aotearoa established by the Treaty of Waitangi in 1840. One index of this perhaps is the fact that the High Commission has hired the same P.R. consultant who works on the Sisyphean task of increasing U.K. access for New Zealand dairy products to manage the publicity surrounding our national birthday party. The Katherine Mansfield centenary produced exhibitions, conferences, panel discussions and magazine articles; whereas the Waitangi 'celebrations' are likely to produce widespread protests. However the two events do have more in common than the distinction I have invoked between an unproblematic cultural site on the one hand and the conflictual terrain of racial politics on the other. Both are occasions which demand and have produced accounts of national identity—what constitutes 'New Zealand'—based on an interpretation of contentious texts. Mansfield's role as the first if not now the only peacock in the New Zealand literary garden, coupled with her expatriate status predictably provoked a critical discussion still at least in part concerned with the question of what is local and what European in her writing: is she really one of us or just the one who got away?

The authoritative answer to that question, most recently articulated by Vincent O'Sullivan in his inaugural address at Victoria University usually attributes the formal inventiveness of her texts to her metropolitan-modernist sensibility, treating the colonial materials which form the basis of her most famous stories as primary products of the imagination alone, deep-frozen content which like the rest of the best from home was most profitably reconstituted and consumed abroad.[1] Regardless of how the issue of Mansfield's 'New Zealandness' is decided however, the insistence of the question bears witness to the pervasiveness of origin-hunting (to use Jonathan Lamb's apt phrase) in local cultural criticism.[2] The political nature of the stake involved in how the Treaty of Waitangi, 'New Zealand's' founding text, is read,

From *Landfall: A New Zealand Quarterly*, 43:4 (December 1989), 447–61.

is pretty clear; this essay will explore the politics of various readings of Mansfield, our first author. I want to suggest that the series of binary oppositions with which New Zealand critics work—examples being colonial/metropolitan, regional/modernist and subjectivist-feminine/provincial-masculist—function to shore up a unitary notion of national identity which Mansfield's 'life' and writing continually unravel. Further, the settler critics' occlusion of Mansfield's 'colonial difference' is repeated in recent metropolitan feminist accounts which focus on her specifically feminine contribution to the modernist project. Rather than Kath Romancefield, the doomed bohemian femme fatale on the fringes of Bloomsbury, site of feminine identification and masculine fantasy, I'm interested in a version of Mansfield which reconstructs her not just as the 'little colonial' but as a member of a colonising elite. Self-described as a woman with the taint of the pioneer in her blood, this writer produced texts marked by those fracturing discursive strategies which Homi Bhabha identifies as specifically colonial and names hybridity and mimicry.[3] Symptomatic of an identity multiply determined and divided by race as well as gender, class and sexual preference, not just the generally ignored settler thematics but also Mansfield's technical innovations—the internal ventriloquism and fragmented narrative structure of her stories—register the irreducible significance of her position as a colonial subject, one peculiarly well-suited, as Galsworthy put it, 'to reach and bring before us the in-between spaces and things and thoughts.'

Cherry Hankin's treatment of Mansfield's writing as female confession aside, the most influential New Zealand critical assessments of the stories in the last two decades have been provided by C.K. Stead and Vincent O'Sullivan. In 'Katherine Mansfield: the Art of the Fiction' Stead argues that once disengaged from the cloying clutches of John Middleton Murry and New Zealand critical nationalism, Mansfield's central theme emerges as 'the male seen as the destroyer of the female in a sexual relationship', while her formal originality and the quality of her imagination 'places her among the moderns and makes her contemporary with Pound and Eliot.'[4] Exile, loneliness and a 'distantiated' relationship with metropolitan convention are adduced as conditions crucial to the free exercise and development of that 'imagination'; but the modernist in exile loses, for Stead, any specificity as a New Zealander:

One brief experiment consists of three stories which are interesting because they indicate a whole line of development she denied herself by becoming a European writer. 'Millie', 'Ole Underwood' and 'The Woman at the Store' are New Zealand stories quite different to the evocations of middle-class childhood for which she is best known. They are stories of raw colonial life, conventionally shaped toward a dénouement. They anticipate a whole genre of New Zealand fiction; and they lead Elizabeth Bowen to ask whether Katherine Mansfield might not, under different circumstances, have become a regional writer.[5]

Stead's erection of an antithesis between colonial and European writing and his relegation of the bulk of Mansfield's texts to the latter category enables him to bracket her regionalist stories as an insignificant element of her literary production. He implies that there were only three such pieces, although in fact Ian Gordon's collection of the New Zealand stories, *Undiscovered Country,* includes no less than ten of what are referred to as 'Scenes from Colonial Life'; and far from being a 'brief experiment' early in her career, fictions like these were produced by Mansfield as late as 1922. In addition to this minimising of Mansfield's role as regionalist, there's a peculiar slide in Stead's attempt to define the nature of the distinction between the two kinds of stories she produced. He establishes a 'raw' New Zealand as the necessary basis for the production of straightforward realist narrative, but this ground of 'colonial life' just slips away in his account of the later stories which are deemed to be evocative of an unspecified but presumably English existence, defined primarily in terms of class. This distinction between the 'harsh regional manner' best adapted to depicting the 'savage spirit' of 'New Zealand reality' and the 'perfumed' writing of the later stories in which New Zealand is only a 'faint wash', a neutralised background, is made more explicit in his recent review of Claire Tomalin's biography: in this piece he suggests that stories like 'Prelude' and 'At the Bay'

> civilise the colony. They are rather genteel middle-class stories. Their lesser characters—Alice, the servant girl, and Mrs Stubbs, for example—belong more to the comic underplots of 19th century English fiction than to a New Zealand reality.[6]

What's at stake here for Stead (son-of-Sargeson)? The polarities he establishes enable him to define a raw colonial New Zealand engaged in a unitary human struggle with nature from which the internal social divisions signalled by class distinctions, and aesthetic complexity, are banished to the metropolis. The settler myth of New Zealand as a homogenous egalitarian society born in 1840 is left intact; if you read 'At the Bay' as a story 'designed to put an English middle-class reader at ease, saying Relax. You're not on foreign soil. This is fictionland' you not only can't account for the specificity of Mansfield's treatment of class in Wellington at the turn of the century, you won't be able to see that racial difference is at issue in 'Prelude' or 'Kezia and Tui'. These mutually reinforcing misreadings of text and context, which implicitly bracket Mansfield's evocation of a complex and conflicted colonial society in the later stories, turn on the assumption that regional realism is the only really adequate way in which New Zealand 'reality' could be represented. Such an assumption installs Sargeson as the true father of New Zealand letters, and Mansfield's production of regional texts is seen as proleptic only, a false start—she 'anticipated' or 'foreshadowed' a whole genre of New Zealand fiction but the true origin, oddly enough, comes later.

Predictably perhaps, in 1978 she is however announced to be the source for an 'other' kind of New Zealand fiction: in an article entitled 'The Inside Story: Helen Shaw, Russell Haley and the Other Tradition', Lawrence Jones argues that Mansfield initiated a 'predominantly feminine subjective' kind of writing which serves as a counter-tradition to 'mainstream realism'.[7] This account again begs the question of Mansfield's generative relation to realist fiction: moreover, its vaguely feminist counter-narrative reinforces a tendency widely apparent in Mansfield criticism to exclude considerations of class and race as determinants of her writing by privileging gender as an analytic category. Kath Romancefield, the dark lady of Menton, reappears as the mother of formally reflexive, self-conscious private fiction cut off from the public or social world. As with Stead's emphasis on metropolitan and formal originality, the effect of this definition is to produce dehistoricised readings of the stories, which are assumed to be radically other to the 'common phenomenal world'. Jones' account thus reinforces the claims of a predominantly masculine regional realism to represent New Zealand in history.

Vincent O'Sullivan's accounts of Mansfield's work include 'The Magnetic Chain: Notes and Approaches to K.M.' published in 1975 and *Finding the Pattern, Solving the Problem: Katherine Mansfield the New Zealand European,* published in 1989.[8] The earlier essay points to Mansfield's symbolist affiliations and expands the terms of discussion of the sexual dimensions of her work by emphasising the evidence of her lesbianism. Interestingly, two of the passages which O'Sullivan cites in illustration of the latter, one from an unpublished story called 'Summer Idylle' and the other from Mansfield's notebook, both involve Maori women:

Do other people of my own age feel as I do I wonder so absolutely powerful *licentious.* So almost physically ill—I alone in this silent clock filled room have become powerfully—I want Maata I want her—and I have had her—terribly—this is unclean I know but true. What an extraordinary thing—I feel savagely crude—and almost powerfully enamoured of the child I had thought that a thing of the Past-Heigh Ho!!!!!!!!!! My mind is like a Russian novel—

Marina, a part-Maori girl, tells her friend a legend concerning fern trees. '"They are cruel even as I might wish to be to thee, little Hinemoa." She looked at Hinemoa with half-shut eyes, her upper lip caught back, showing her teeth, but Hinemoa caught her hand. "Don't be the same," she pleaded.'

This is a feature of Mansfield which any perspective must include.[9]

The identification here between sexuality and racial difference is surely equally worthy of attention: but as in the recent essay, a piece which explicitly raises the issue of colonial identity, O'Sullivan refers to Mansfield's writing about and identification with Maori women only to empty out any cultural specificity in the allusions.[10] In *Finding the Pattern, Solving the Problem* Maata the half-caste, the putative heroine of a short story called 'Strife' and an un-

completed novel, is elided with Mansfield in order to figure the pure displacement which O'Sullivan regards as the latter's final position. He argues that
Mansfield's experience as an expatriate colonial exposed to the Great War in
close-up eventually rendered her the archetypal alienated subject of moder-
nity, embodying:

> rejection of the centre, rejection of the borders as well, the sense of discompo-
> sure *anywhere,* the constant play of feeling absent and present at the same time
> in almost any place.[11]

In his elegant delineation of what he calls the 'Medea principle' O'Sullivan
initially acknowledges the crucial role of racial and sexual difference in the
constitution of colonial subjectivity, and then in a move not unusual among
commentators on modernist writers in exile, he shreds Mansfield's accretion of
a complex identity by erecting her into a deracinated universal 'twentieth century voice', a figure whose transcendent status thus renders questions about
what is 'New Zealand' in her writing 'limited and parochial.'[12] The critical
consensus on which his remarks depend—whereby the alienated existence and
fractured texts of modernist writers are regarded as exemplary of a peculiarly
modern subjectivity—has however been undermined by the work of a variety
of feminist and Marxist critics.[13] Even more pertinent is the revisionist project
of colonial discourse analysis. In a recent essay entitled 'Modernism and Imperialism' Fredric Jameson argues that:

> . . . the structure of imperialism not only produced its specific literature and left
> palpable traces on the content of other metropolitan literary works of the period
> but also made its mark on the inner forces and structures of that new mutation
> in literary and artistic language to which the term modernism is loosely ap-
> plied.[14]

He suggests that the imperial subject's inevitable ignorance of colonial others,
essential though they are to the constitution of metropolitan identity, produced a meaning loss marked on the one hand by the production of barbarous
others from rival imperial states (the Germans for example, figuring as Huns)
and contained on the other by the development of a style capable of representing a newly disordered sense of space. In a discussion of *Howards End* which is
extremely suggestive in relation to Mansfield, Jameson shows how Forster's
evocation of a Utopian social community presided over by a 'very dear person',
a woman, is counter pointed with the urban sprawl of the city dominated
by—

> . . . another type whom nature favours—the Imperial. Healthy, ever in motion,
> it hopes to inherit the earth. It breeds as quickly as the yeoman, and as soundly;
> strong is the temptation to acclaim it as a super-yeoman, who carries his coun-
> try's virtue overseas. But the imperial is not what he seems. He is a destroyer.[15]

Mansfield's sustained contrast between the hearty patriarchs of the Burnell and Sheridan families and the business world they inhabit, and the female communities of Karori and Days Bay presided over by the gentle grandmothers spring immediately to mind. Further, Jameson's attempt to articulate the dislocation of imperial subjectivity and sense of space through a definition of modernist 'style' as the substitution of a reconstituted spatial or perceptual 'meaning' for an inevitably absent transcendental signifier provides a suggestive way of accounting for the co-existence of fragmentation and intensity in the evocation of the phenomenal world in Mansfield's writing. Finally however, it seems to me that attending to Mansfield's peculiar position as a colonial from a settler society, a figure somewhere between Jameson's imperial subject and the colonised other, problematises his schema in so far as in her writing, the 'persons of the colonised' are not structurally occluded: for in a settled colony with policies of racial assimilation, the other is with/in you.

Jameson's binary opposition between imperial subject and colonial other excludes the creole, the figure whose narrativisation in Rhys' *Wide Sargasso Sea* Gayatri Spivak uses to critique the imperialist axiomatics latent both in Charlotte Bronte's *Jane Eyre* and in first world feminist accounts of the novel.[16] In my view, Kate Fullbrook's recent discerning study of Mansfield, which participates in the feminist reassessment of modernism referred to above, is substantially weakened by its blindness to the 'colonial difference' of Mansfield's writing. Fullbrook, who made a trenchant critique of K.M.'s appropriation by New Zealand official culture during the centenary celebrations, seems committed to what Spivak describes as a 'basically isolationist admiration for the literature of the female subject in Europe.' She has provided by far the most convincing account of the relation between Mansfield's refusal to privilege sexuality as the unifying principle of identity and the writer's evocation of subjectivity as 'multiple, shifting and nonconsecutive' in symbolist prose. However, by so privileging Mansfield's feminism as the crucial determinant of her style, she not only diminishes the role of class but dismisses the colonial dimension of her identity almost entirely:

> The Journal . . . marks her early rejection of what she saw as the unreal and undesirable security of her colonial background (though Katherine Mansfield transposed its resources of brashness, self-confidence and privilege to the artistic sphere).[17]

Mansfield's 'colonial background' was a much more mixed heritage and much more crucial in her attempts to deconstruct socially prescribed notions of the self than Fullbrook's account suggests. The New Zealand in which she grew up was still in the most elementary stages of national 'self-definition'; Mansfield's father, Harold Beauchamp, for example, sat on a Royal Commission throughout 1901 to hear submissions on the question of whether the colony should join the Australian Commonwealth or remain independent. Educated opinion wrestled with the problem of whether New Zealand should expand further into Polynesia or simply attempt to retain its identity as the little England of the South Pacific. The desire to remain 'British' clashed with the assumption that the Maori would be simply absorbed into the white population, eventually rendering most New Zealanders a 'golden hue.' These contradictions are marked in general accounts of the country:

> In fact, the New Zealander is very proud of his British origin, and very glad to resemble as closely as possible the stock from which he has sprung. He identifies himself very closely with British thought and British feeling . . .
>
> . . . when asked to join the Australian Federation, the people of New Zealand steadfastly refused . . . On the other hand, the Government of New Zealand has always displayed a readiness to absorb any of the Pacific islands, however distant they may be. How far this tendency may be indulged, depends, of course, on the Imperial Government. Should limits be imposed upon New Zealand ambition in that direction, there still remains for New Zealanders their other ambition to be gratified—that of remaining the 'Britons of the South Seas'.[18]
>
> Claimed to be an off-shoot of the Caucasian race, the Maoris share a common stock with Europeans. No such gap exists between the brown and white man as between black and white. It needs only a few generations of intermarriage to obliterate distinctive Maori characteristics . . . In that happy way will be solved the racial question in New Zealand.[19]

The triumphalist tone of this prose notwithstanding, these passages betray a considerable uncertainty over both the external and internal boundaries of national identity. The New Zealander is to be either a mimic man (the Briton of the South Seas) or a hybrid, quite literally absorbing the Polynesian other.

In Mansfield's writing these contradictions are registered in a sense of the inauthenticity of the colonial:

> Here too, I meet Prodgers—it is splendid to see once again real English people—I am so sick and tired of the third-rate article—give me the Maori and the tourist but nothing in-between![20]

The confident identification with the 'real English' expressed by the eighteen year old in the Ureweras gives way however when Mansfield was established in London: 'Who am I to be certain that I understand? There's always Karori to shout after me.' Far from being an unproblematic source of brash self-confidence, New Zealand identity produced radical self-doubt:

> I am the little colonial walking in a London garden patch—allowed to look perhaps, but not to linger. If I lie on the grass, they positively shout at me: 'Look at her, lying on our grass, pretending she lives here, pretending this is her garden, and that tall back of a house, with windows open and the coloured curtains lifting, is her house. She is a stranger—an alien. She is nothing but a little girl sit-

ting on the Tinakori hills and dreaming: "I went to London and married an Englishman and we lived in a tall grave house, with red geraniums and white daisies in the garden at the back."'[21] .

These remarks are frequently quoted: the pathos of their evocation of the colonial as childlike fantasist providing a particularly attractive locus of identification for other New Zealanders. Less often discussed however is a series of texts in which colonial anxiety is played out in an un-familiar key. In the autumn of 1916 Mansfield went to the Cafe Royal near Piccadilly Circus with Mark Gertler and S.S. Koteliansky. The next day, Gertler sent an account of events there to Lady Ottoline Morrell. Antony Alpers summarises the account and quotes from Gertler's letter as follows:

> Gertler's letter described how he and Kot and Katherine (a Polish Jew, a Ukrainian Jew, and a Colonial) finding the cafe packed, were obliged to sit at a table already occupied by a coloured man, 'an Indian perhaps, but a weak type,' whom they hardly noticed. After a time a 'Long Thin White Herring of a Woman with a Terrific High Bunch of Crimson Hair' came to join him, and then a coloured man made a third:

> 'We immediately hated all three of them. Soon to our astonishment they began to talk "Intellectually"—they were University Blacks—using "perfect" English, very long words, carefully chosen. They talked about Dostoevsky, Russia, the New Age, all in a very advanced manner. All this irritated us enough. But imagine our Hatred and Horror when the red headed piece of dried Dung produced a Volume of Lawrence's poems and commenced to discuss Lawrence with the other, in this perfect English and carefully picked, long words! We had been ragging them all the time, but now we knew something drastic must be done. We sat and thought. Suddenly Katherine leant towards them and with a sweet smile said "*Will* you let me have that Book a moment?" "Certainly" they all beamed back—even more sweetly. Imagine their horror and utter amazement when Katherine without a word more, Rose from the table, Book and all, we following most calmly—most calmly we walked out of the Cafe!!!'[22]

Mansfield's imperious appropriation of the high cultural text—the 'Book'— from its black readers performed two tasks: at the same time that the gesture confirmed her position as a fit owner/interpreter of 'advanced' intellectual property, it marked her distance from other more visibly marginal colonial subjects. The violence of the gesture—not to mention Gertler's language— register the threat to the imperial subject presented by the unsettling mimicry of the 'hybrid'. In Bhabha's account, colonial mimicry is a function of the desire to produce a 'reformed, recognisable other as a subject of difference that is almost the same, but not quite'—Anglicised but not English, 'not quite/not-white'.[23] However, because mimicry continually produces a difference, a slippage or excess, which registers as recalcitrance or inappropriateness, it problematises colonial authority. Then the paranoid structure of colonial desire transforms the mimic man's slight divergence into an almost total difference which is menacing. Thus in Gertler's account, the unsettling speech of 'University Blacks'—'perfect English, very long words, carefully chosen'—which implicitly claimed a discursive equality on the cultural terrain of the Cafe Royal's advanced patrons provokes a slide from the depiction of a 'Long Thin White Herring of a Woman' to 'the red-headed piece of dried Dung'. It is the minute differences in a speech which also suggested identity rather than the visible difference of skin colour which provoked Mansfield, Gertler and Koteliansky, themselves metropolitan 'parodists', into asserting a violent imperial authority over the Lawrentian text.

This scene and the contextual materials with which Alpers frames it represent Mansfield's colonial anxiety in a racist key which has received much less attention than the pathos of her own self-representations or the romanticism of her accounts of the Maori. It should not, however, be read as the final awful truth 'underlying' the other writing. Her position was thoroughly ambivalent and her social performances in particular appear ambiguous: dressing up as a Maori as is reported of her early years in London could be a simple exploitation of the exoticism of her background but can also plausibly be read as a way of projecting her sense of difference in a metropolitan context. Her written response to Lady Ottoline Morrell's inquiry about the Cafe Royal incident is suggestively evasive: she wishes she could 'dress up, alone in the studio here— Tie up my head in a turban, make myself fat . . . act Lady Mary Wortley Montague.'[24] There is no attempt to justify her behaviour; instead, she 'explains herself' to Morrell by figuring herself in the Oriental disguise of a blue-stocking famous for her travels in the East. The passage suggests that Mansfield can only account for her behaviour through reference to a sense of herself as characterised, like the 'coloured gentlemen' she has abused, by an exotic, if here comic (but also slightly disgusting) mobility of identity.

There are numerous 'regionalist' stories which narrativise the process by which such unstable selves are produced and come to crisis in the context of a settler society: 'The Wind Blows', 'Old Tar' and 'The Woman at the Store' being obvious examples. But the 'perfumed' stories 'of middle-class childhood' also define the soul-making of their protagonists in terms of a dense web of social relations in which a very particularised sense of racial difference plays its part along with the family and class distinctions.[25] 'Kezia and Tui', a story excluded from Alpers' definitive edition of the fiction, provides an exemplary instance of this process.[26] The story charts Kezia's shifts in mood, from her angry reveries at school, through a soothing encounter with her grandmother in her parents' garden, to a visit with a Maori family, the Beads, an episode followed by a final epiphanic moment of self-consolidation under the stars. A feminist reading would take account of the way in which the story establishes Kezia in angry opposition to her father: at school she broods 'That was the first time I've ever stood up to him . . . I wonder if everything will be different now,' and comforts herself by thinking about her grandmother's supportive love:

She saw herself sitting on the Grandmother's lap and leaning against the Grandmother's bodice . . . that was what she wanted.[27]

The two female pairs of characters—Kezia and her grandmother and Tui and Mrs Bead—exchange gifts of food which signify the warm mutuality of their relations while Kezia's father is by contrast figured in terms of the greedy consumption Mansfield often uses to image male appetite:

She remembered suddenly the way he sucked in his moustache when he drank and the long hairs he had on his hands, and the noises he made when he had indigestion. . .

Mr Fairfield is associated with the repetitive and oppressive routine of institutionalised learning while her grandmother is metonymically connected with lyric poetry and the soothing natural world of the garden:

Suddenly the sad tune and the trees moving so gently made her feel quite calm. She looked down at the withered sweet pea that drooped from her blouse. She saw herself sitting on the grandmother's lap. . .

The story concludes when Kezia, having freed herself from anxiety over her father, enjoys an epiphanic moment in the garden before having to return to the ordered domesticity of the Fairfield household. The moral might seem to be that loving and playful female interchanges can repair the damage wrought by patriarchal power.

That's only half the story, however. The visit to the Beads—whose surname invokes the valueless tokens with which colonists notoriously acquired land (fair fields?) from 'the natives'—positions Kezia very differently. The first sections of the story evoke Kezia's consciousness using free indirect discourse, creating a considerable sense of intimacy for the reader. During the visit to the Beads however, a much greater sense of distance is established by the use of dialogue rather than the narration of an internal monologue. Further, in contrast to her revulsion from her father's brutality or her rather passive invocations of love from her grandmother (couched in terms of pansies and pets), Kezia twice exhibits the same sexually inflected aggression associated with Mr Fairfield:

'Hello Mrs Bead,' said Kezia. She buried her head in the Maori woman's neck and put her teeth in a roll of soft fat. Mrs Bead pulled Kezia between her knees and had a good look at her.

'Pour a jug of water on my head, Mummy. O Kezia, don't listen to her.'
'Pooh! it's nothing new,' said Kezia. 'You're always lying. I'll pour the water over your head.' She rolled up her sleeves and deluged Tui, who gave little moaning cries.

The aggression with which these physical intimacies are described marks them as erotic in a scene in which Kezia, who 'hasn't got any front at all' and is 'hard, hard, hard' assumes a masculine position. She explicitly defines herself against Tui's sexual ambition and 'romantic mood', rejecting the suggestion that she accompany Tui to Sydney in pursuit of a husband and explaining that she plans a pastoral future with her grandmother. Kezia's refusal to participate in Tui's cultivation of her femininity can't be read simply as a rejection of an identity rigidly ordered by gender, for her behaviour with the Beads is already sexualised. Its aggressively masculine form (reminiscent of Mansfield's account of her relations with Maata in the notebook) is clearly linked to racial difference. Kezia's scorn for Tui's desire to 'marry a rich Englishman and have five boys with beautiful blue eyes' (an ambition not so foreign to other 'little colonials') and for the unsuccessful redecoration of her 'shabby, untidy little room' with pink sateen bows and an old skirt is inflected by the appearance elsewhere in the text of familiar figures of 'native' insufficiency, laziness, incompetence and mendacity. Thus the evocation of the disorderly hedonism of the Bead household, with its weedy garden and gifts of coconut cake which 'hasn't riz at all and is a little damp in the middle' reinscribes debasing tropes of racial difference which its casual depiction of a free female exchange might seem initially to transcend.

Tui and her mother are presented as unsuccessful mimics, speaking the degraded language of magazine romance and mismanaging a 'piggy little house' which lacks any masculine presence. But Kezia's world of home and school, the former governed by her father, the latter saturated by the banalities of imperialist dogma ('She . . . recited "How Horatius kept the Bridge" like a little girl in a dream') suggests that any escape from the institutional structures which define the material lives and desires of every character is likely to be fraught and temporary. The language which provokes and frames Kezia's reveries is as eviscerated in its way as Tui's: the suggestive verse from the book the two girls share at school is banal in a literary key. None of the characters has more than brief access to a sense of self and a speech which is full, whole or authentic. The hybridity of colonial discourse cuts both ways.

Excluded from the most widely circulating editions of Mansfield's work, 'Kezia and Tui' is unlikely to be read much. While the current definitions of the writer as feminist symbolist and European modernist stand, attention to the story's economical evocation of female identities encoded in a very specific semiotics of race is probably going to be limited. Currently the story is most likely to be encountered by the reader who co-operates with Ian Gordon's attempt to construct the missing great New Zealand novel out of Mansfield's native remains in *Undiscovered Country*. But it seems interesting that New Zealand's first author, in contrast to the great narrators of other emergent states, problematises rather than consolidates identity in fictions of peculiar polyvalency. Insofar as the Treaty of Waitangi is also conspicuously a hybrid text, we might do worse than practise our reading skills on Katherine Mansfield.

## Notes

1. Vincent O'Sullivan. *Finding the Pattern, Solving the Problem: Katherine Mansfield the New Zealand European.* (Wellington: Victoria University Press, 1989).

2. Jonathan Lamb, 'Risks of Myth: the Politics of New Zealand Literary Journalism', *Meanjin,* 46, no. 3 (September 1987), pp. 377–384, and 'Problems of Originality: or, Beware of Pakehas baring guilts', *Landfall,* 159 (September 1986), pp. 352–358.

3. My remarks here draw on a series of articles by Bhabha, including: 'Signs Taken for Wonders: Questions of Ambivalence and Authority under a Tree Outside Delhi, May 1817', *Critical Inquiry,* 12, (1985), pp. 144–65; 'The Other Question—The Stereotype and Colonial Discourse', *Screen,* 24 (1983), pp. 18–36 and 'Of Mimicry and Man: The Ambivalence of Colonial Discourse', *October,* 28, pp. 125–33.

4. C.K. Stead, 'Katherine Mansfield: the Art of the "Fiction"', *In the Glass Case: Essays on New Zealand Literature* (Auckland: Auckland University Press-Oxford University Press, 1981), pp. 29–46.

5. *In the Glass Case,* p. 32.

6. C.K. Stead, 'Mrs Bowdenhood', *London Review of Books,* 26 November, 1987, pp. 24–26.

7. Lawrence Jones, 'The Inside Story: Helen Shaw, Russell Haley and the Other Tradition', *Islands,* 31–32 (1981), pp. 120–135.

8. The first essay was published in *Landfall,* 114 (June 1975), pp. 95–131: the second by Victoria University Press, Wellington, 1989.

9. Vincent O'Sullivan, 'The Magnetic Chain: Notes and Approaches to K.M.', *Landfall* 114, June 1975, p. 118 and 119–120.

10. I understand Professor O'Sullivan gave a further paper focusing on 'Maata' at the Centennial Conference in Wellington. As I have been unable to read this essay as yet, my remarks are pertinent only to the positions expressed in the two works cited.

11. *Finding the Pattern, Solving the Problem,* p. 5.

12. George Steiner's *Extraterritorial* (1978), Terry Eagleton's *Exiles and Emigres* (1970) and Andrew Gurr's *Writers in Exile* (1981) all share this assumption. I would like to acknowledge the help of Nikas Papastergiadis for guiding me through the literature on exile.

13. Feminist revisionism takes the form both of rereading female writers already admitted into the modernist canon and of exploring the contribution made by currently more marginal figures such as Stein, Richardson and H.D.. Marxian accounts have been influenced recently by the development of colonial discourse theory: c.f. for example, Terry Eagleton's 'Nationalism: Irony and Commitment', Field Day Pamphlet, 13 (Derry, 1988) and Fredric Jameson's 'Modernism and Its Repressed or, Robbe-Grillet as Anti-Colonialist' (1976) in *The Ideologies of Theory,* Vol. 1. (London: Routledge, 1988).

14. Fredric Jameson, 'Modernism and Imperialism', Field Day Pamphlet 14, (Derry, 1988) pp. 5–6.

15. Jameson citing Forster, ibid., p. 17.

16. Gayatri Chakravorty Spivak, 'Three Women's Texts and a Critique of Imperialism', *Critical Inquiry,* 12 (1985), pp. 243–61.

17. Kate Fullbrook, *Katherine Mansfield* (Brighton: Harvester Press, 1986), p. 21.

18. E. Arnold, *The New Zealand Colony* (London, 1910), p. 130.

19. J. Colwell, *A Century in the Pacific* (London, 1918), p. 149.

20. Katherine Mansfield, *The Urewera Notebook,* ed. Ian A. Gordon (Oxford, Oxford University Press, 1978), p. 61.

21. Quoted by Ian Gordon in the introduction to *Undiscovered Country,* p. x.

22. Antony Alpers, *The Life of Katherine Mansfield* (1980: rpt. Oxford: Oxford University Press, 1987), p. 216.

23. 'Of Mimicry and Man', p. 126.

24. Katherine Mansfield, *The Collected Letters of Katherine Mansfield,* Vol.1, ed. Vincent O'Sullivan and Margaret Scott (Oxford: Clarendon Press 1984), p. 280.

25. The division later imposed on the two sorts of New Zealand stories doesn't seem to have been so clear to Mansfield herself. In October 13 she wrote to her sister:

> My dear, I wrote a story called 'Old Tar' the other day, about Makra Hill, and sent it to the Westminster who accepted it . . . Don't leave the paper on the Karori road or I shall be taken up for libel. They have asked for some more New Zealand work so I am going to write one on the Karori School. (*Letters,* Vol.1, p. 132).
> —'The Doll's House' is presumably the other 'Karori' story indicated.

26. On the question of Mansfield's publishing history, as on many others, I am grateful for the guidance offered me by Sophie Tomlinson.

27. All quotations are from 'Kezia and Tui' (1916), in *Undiscovered Country: The New Zealand Stories of Katherine Mansfield* ed. Ian A. Gordon (London: Longmans, 1974) pp. 167–171.

# Katherine Mansfield: the Wellington Years, a Reassessment

## IAN A. GORDON

Katherine Mansfield lived in Wellington for a total of sixteen years, just under half her lifetime. She was born there, and she was sent to three Wellington schools, each a step up the social and educational ladder. Her father, Harold Beauchamp, ambitious for his daughters and well able to provide for them, made a decision to further the process by placing them in a school in England. From April 1903 till July 1906, KM[1] and her two older sisters lived as boarders in Queen's College, Harley Street, London. They returned to Wellington at the end of that year.

KM in 1906 was no schoolgirl. She was a young woman of eighteen of considerable determination, equipped with the skills, the experiences, and the tastes that had been rapidly developed in these four formative years in London. She had become a competent musician (in love, too, with a young professional musician), a keen concert-goer. She knew the London art galleries; she had been to the opera and to those new performances (for which the word 'cinema' had not yet been invented); she could write with some competence both French and German; she was widely read in English, totally immersed in the literature of the 'decadent' nineties. She had even written a section of a novel. Whether it was to be her cello or the manuscript of *Juliet* that would lead to the next step, she had not yet decided. But one thing she did know, when she returned to Wellington in 1906, that she would not be there for long, in this small, distant, colonial town. She exerted pressure on her family to allow her to return to London. It took her a year and a half before she finally departed, in July 1908. Her writing career—and her later reputation—were still in the future.

This bald account of the external facts is well known. It has all the makings of the standardized story of the young writer of promise who breaks with family and home to struggle towards accomplishment and ultimate recognition. It is, with greater detail, what emerges from the accounts written by all her main biographers. But when one sets this quite conventionally patterned narrative (youthful rebellion justified by adult achievement) against KM's own major work in fiction, we are—or should be—left with a certain disquiet.

Reprinted from Katherine Mansfield, *The Urewera Notebook,* ed. with an introduction by Ian A. Gordon (Oxford: Oxford University Press, 1978), 11–30.

If she disliked her birthplace so much, why is it the centre of all her best work? If she rebelled against her Victorian family, why is that family—lovingly remembered—at the core of all her great stories? If the external facts represent the truth, why did she not go on later to write, as other writers of the time did, works that display the painful stresses of Victorian family life, as Gosse did in *Father and Son* and Butler in *The Way of All Flesh*? Why did she, instead, (as she wrote to a friend in 1921) 'try to make family life so gorgeous—not hatred and cold linoleum—but warmth and hydrangeas'?[2]

The life has been told many times. Only three biographers have written of her with scholarly care, R. E. Mantz (1933), S. Berkman (1951), and A. Alpers (1953).[3] The picture that emerges from all three of KM, in her year and a half in Wellington between 1906 and mid-1908, is consistent. She is a moody and disgruntled adolescent at odds with her family. 'Dark thoughts crowded upon her' . . . 'dark moods of restlessness' . . . 'pressure of unhappiness' . . . (Mantz); 'exiled in the wilderness' . . . 'in moody reverie' . . . 'her heart was sick with despair' . . . 'fever of unrest' . . . 'in this season of rebellion' . . . (Berkman); 'outrageous scenes' . . . 'bitterness in her heart' . . . 'to the parents . . . a problem and a social embarrassment' . . . . (Alpers). These phrases are a fair representation of the KM of the Wellington years presented by her three most careful biographers. Where, in all this misery, did she find the 'warmth and hydrangeas'?

In view of what evidence was available to them, I do not think the biographers could have come to any other conclusion. It was a reasonable enough inference at the time. Till the late fifties, the 'facts' of her life and attitude could be deduced only from five of her printed books, the *Journal* published in 1927 (and later expanded in 1954), the *Scrapbook* published in 1939, the two volumes of *Letters* published in 1928, and the *Letters to John Middleton Murry* published in 1951. KM had no hand in any of these publications.[4] All five volumes were posthumous, all edited by KM's husband Murry. All were utterly 'authentic' in the sense that—apart from Murry's commentaries—every word in them was written by KM.

They are also utterly unreliable, because (without recourse to the documents from which they have been drawn) one cannot be certain on any page that it has been accurately transcribed, or that what one reads is the whole of what KM wrote, or that what is presented is presented in a sequence that KM herself would have determined. This uncertainty extends even to the edition of the *Journal* of 1954, in spite of the reassurance on the title-page: 'Definitive Edition'.

The evidence for this unreliability is now available, in KM's own papers and notebooks. She wrote, during her lifetime, considerable material which she did not publish. She kept it in notebooks, diaries, sheets torn from writing-pads (pinned together to ensure their sequence), single sheets of paper. The earliest extant notebook was begun in 1903, when she was fourteen; the latest, shortly before her death in 1923. The material is varied. On occasion, she bought a printed pocket diary—and the entries tend to be quite perfunctory 'diary' entries (tapering off towards February). The separate sheets may contain drafts of stories, brief 'story' ideas, poems (sometimes her own, sometimes a copy of verses that had attracted her), 'personal' observations on life and literature (which may or may not be dated). The notebooks have seldom any internal unity of material and certainly no absolute internal 'order'. They are simply her rough working notes. She will make entries at several points in a notebook, filling in the intervening pages at later dates. She will begin a notebook—and then turn it upside-down and 'begin' it again from the 'back'. She will, on occasion, return to an old notebook, re-read it, and add further observations.

The contents of these notebooks can be almost anything: 'diary' entries; clothing lists; household accounts; shopping lists; her sizes in gloves and shoes; brief jottings of 'ideas' for stories; stories in draft form; draft letters (which may or may not have been re-copied and posted); isolated sentences and isolated paragraphs worked up to the 'finished' form in which they appear in her printed works; personal observations on places and people (dated and undated); pages where she is simply thinking aloud; critical observations on her current reading; again and again (usually in the final pages of a diary or notebook) meticulously kept balance-sheets of income and expenditure, entered up with quite professional skill.

KM clearly set great store by this accumulation. Six notebooks were filled before she left New Zealand in 1908. They travelled with her. 'I'm taking', she wrote her sister Vera on 19 June 1908 just before her departure, 'only half a dozen books and my photographs'.[5] The 'books' were her own notebooks. They travelled with her constantly. I have the distinct impression that in all her many shifts from house to house, from country to country—New Zealand, England, France, Italy, Switzerland—her growing pile of notebooks, diaries, and manuscripts went with her, raw material for creation.

In his preface to the 1927 *Journal,* Murry stated categorically that she had destroyed her early 'huge complaining diaries'. He consequently opened the 1927 version of the journal at 1914. I find his undocumented assertion unconvincing. By 1933 Murry had clearly uncovered some of her notebooks written earlier than 1914, and these were disclosed to Mantz, since she used fragments of them in her *Life* of that year. There is also no confirmation, anywhere in KM's own writings, of such wholesale destruction. The passage Murry cites as his sole evidence is an apostrophe to her dead brother ('To whom did I always write when I kept these huge complaining diaries?'[6]) and it says nothing of destruction—indeed 'kept' (for all its ambivalent meaning) suggests the opposite. The appearance in the late fifties of a whole group of pre-1914 notebooks (one of them the subject of this edition) now casts additional doubts on

Murry's statement. KM, even when she was re-reading what made her angry or miserable, was a great hoarder of her own papers. 'We can't afford to waste such an expenditure of feeling', she wrote in 1921 to Dorothy Brett.[7] She felt the same about her papers, especially if they contained her past. She could not afford to waste them, with the result that we have them today.

After the death of KM, Murry issued two posthumous volumes of her stories, *The Doves' Nest* (1923) and *Something Childish* (1924). He then turned to the vast accumulation of her notebooks and sheets of paper which he had inherited, and from this—with quite superb editorial skill—he quarried the 1927 *Journal*. The *Journal of Katherine Mansfield* was a best-seller. It remains a remarkable book. But Murry's editorial methods make this beautiful and pious memorial of a dead wife an insecure basis for biography. He discarded, suppressed, edited, and manipulated. He ran together (without indication) 'diary' entries and passages of KM's fiction; dropped in—at what seemed 'appropriate' places—poems which KM had copied out on single undated sheets and which she had no thought of using to reinforce any 'diary' entry. He discarded everything that did not fit in with his presentation of the idealized portrait of a rare spirit.

He discarded her downright enjoyment of New Zealand on her return. He discarded early entries on her 'passion' for the woman artist EKB. He discarded her tough-mindedness; her shrewdness with money; her carefully kept accounts and balance-sheets; her single-minded (on occasion, even ruthless) determination; her jealous bitchiness when she suspected him of having an affair with Dorothy Brett; her very explicit account of *her* affair with the French novelist Francis Carco.[8] His selected and re-arranged material offered instead a romanticized, insubstantial persona who, he wrote, 'seemed to adjust herself to life as a flower adjusts itself to the earth and the sun'.[9]

This central figure of the 1927 *Journal* greatly appealed to the reading public of the day, and it has had a profound influence on later biographical and critical studies. It was not the KM known to her contemporaries. Where in the *Journal* is the KM whom Carrington reported to Lytton Strachey as having 'danced ragtime' at Garsington?[10] Where is the 'forcible and utterly unscrupulous character' recorded by Virginia Woolf?[11] This latter portrait is coloured by openly admitted jealously. But it cannot be ignored—and it can be found in KM's own notebooks. Lytton Strachey knew her well; had tea with her at Gower Street; acted with her at Garsington; even (for a time) 'she took my fancy a great deal';[12] then changed his mind when he found there was steel behind her mysterious charms. When the 1927 *Journal* appeared, he found it 'incomprehensible'. With his usual combination of spitefulness and acute insight he put his finger infallibly on its contrived falsity. The implications of his comments are inescapable—'I see Murry lets it out that it was written for publication—which no doubt explains a great deal. But why that foul-mouthed, virulent, brazen-faced broomstick of a creature should have got herself up as a pad of rose-scented cotton wool is beyond me.'[13] Strachey in 1927 had no way of knowing that the masquerade was one in which his old acting-partner KM had no part.

Murry some years later made a further incursion into the paper accumulation he had inherited, transcribing enough to fill another volume, which he entitled the *Scrapbook* (1939). Finally, in 1954, he assembled a revised version of the 1927 journal material; added on considerable portions of the 1939 scrapbook material, and expanded this collection by incorporating a group of 'fragments' (his description)[14] from the pre-1914 notebooks. They are only fragments because of his editorial decision to print fragments from what were well-filled notebooks. This new collection became the 'Definitive Edition' of the *Journal,* published in 1954. In his new preface, he stated that he had restored passages 'suppressed in the original edition'. But his instincts remained: to trim; to excise; to reshape. The notebooks of KM's Wellington years made their first appearance in 1954 heavily edited and consequently distorted. The 1954 *Journal* is as unsecure a basis as the 1927 version on which KM's biographers had been unwittingly compelled to build.

KM's entire accumulation of notebooks and papers became for the first time available on Murry's death in 1957. They were bought at auction by the New Zealand Government and are now in the Alexander Turnbull Library in Wellington. Simultaneously, the library acquired her letters to Murry. The collection was later expanded, notably by the acquisition of his letters to her, of a number of her letters to her contemporaries, and of a considerable group of Beauchamp family documents. From this collection, several early 'Unpublished Writings of Katherine Mansfield' have been printed in the *Turnbull Library Record,* transcribed and edited by Mrs Margaret Scott. The Turnbull collection has brought a new dimension to Mansfield studies. It is now possible to study, from her own drafts and corrections, something of her method of composition. Above all, a more real KM has emerged from behind the partly fictional persona of the *Journal.*

The present edition of what I have called the 'Urewera notebook' presents an aspect, so far unrecorded, of KM's New Zealand experience. It is transcribed from what she called a 'Rough Note Book',[15] which she began in Wellington in November 1907 and carried to England in 1908, continuing to write it up in London till the end of that year, concluding it in Belgium in April 1909. KM, in November and December 1907, was one of a party which made an extensive camping trip through the North Island of New Zealand. The first half of the notebook was written during the trip. It forms a detached and self-contained episode.

Murry made no use of the notebook in the 1927 *Journal.* In the 1954 version he presented (pp. 22–33) a considerably truncated version of KM's notes on the trip. His text is marred by numerous misreadings (admittedly of a very difficult manuscript, often written on a moving waggon) but also by considerable suppressions and large excisions which result in inevitable falsification. I do not think the falsification is deliberate. Murry in this notebook encountered a KM he had never known, describing a country he had never visited, in a handwriting that even he could only partially decipher. His shortened version of 1954 (only the first part of the trip is attempted), with its misreadings of some words of strategic importance in the narrative, firmly established the conception of KM as an unhappy young woman on her return to New Zealand, miserably trailing her way through a 'loathsome trip' and finding in Rotorua a 'little Hell'. It is no wonder that despair, bitterness and misery have been built on this foundation.

The full text reveals an astonishingly different KM, alertly recording the landscape, visiting bustling sheep-yards, fascinated by the Maoris (especially the Tuhoe people of the only recently penetrated Urewera country), recording their language with accuracy (even to the extent of using phonetic script), apart from a few days of sickness (brought on by Rotorua's rotten-egg smell) vigorously enjoying herself ('we laugh with joy all day'), sitting on a rock beside the rapids of the Waikato River imagining that she and her companions are Wagnerian Rhine Maidens, climbing down a ladder under the Huka Falls and finding the experience reminds her of a London production of Tannhaüser, luxuriating in the hot mineral pools ('happy—blissfully happy'), finding in the landscape parallels in her reading of H. G. Wells, Walt Whitman and Maeterlinck, eating rounds of bread and jam and drinking great pannikins of tea, revelling in life in a tent ('we are like children here all happiness'), walking mile after mile uphill to lighten the load on the horses, writing it all up every night in the tent and (on occasion) as she sat on top of the luggage in the baggage-waggon—and bouncing back from the Urewera adventure to put on, for the benefit of her friend Edie Bendall (EKB), comic imitations of her travelling companions and of fat old Maori women[16]—and then firmly setting down in the notebook her clear-cut and organized programme for her next move—she even enjoyed Rotorua's 'little Hill'—'Hell' was a Murry misreading.

The Urewera notebook is a key text for an understanding of the young KM. She was no disgruntled adolescent, but a young, vigorous, independent-minded woman who saw in the travelling and camping adventure an opportunity to expand her experience and to explore a technique of observation and reportage. Her notebook is not a diary. It is a writer's notebook, analogous to an artist's sketchbook. She records, not the day-by-day minutiae of camp life, but landscapes, characters met by the way, incidents, emotional reactions. The writing, though in sketchbook form, is deliberate and careful, at times showing significant signs of stylistic revision. Some of it—for a writer of nineteen—I find impressive. Witness her sympathetic portrait of young Johanna, the guide's niece (a 'Mansfield character' in embryo), her reaction to the Urewera bush ('gigantic and tragic even in the bright sunlight'), and the brilliant little steel-engraving of the Maori group at Taupo.

* * *

She returned from the camping trip to Wellington in mid-December 1907, confident and full of plans. She left for England six months later. All accounts of KM depict these six months as a time of unhappiness—'bitter and painful months' (Mantz); 'through late winter and spring she suffered' (Berkman, forgetting or unaware that January and February are, in New Zealand, high summer); 'a fevered mind' . . . 'hysteria' (Alpers). What had happened to the confident and 'blissfully happy' young woman of the Urewera notebook?

Had she, in fact, altered at all? The evidence for an unhappy half-year of self-pity proves, on close examination, to be both minimal and dubious. It consists of two bare items. Ida Baker (LM), her ever-attentive companion in England and Europe, had a memory (nearly half a century old) of a letter she had once received from KM. The letter had long since disappeared. On this basis, Alpers reconstructs a family quarrel as the source of her hysteria. He takes the sensible precaution of prefacing his reconstruction of the scene with the word 'conjecturally'.[17]

The only other evidence ultimately resolves itself into three brief 'diary' entries totalling twelve lines (10 February, 18 March, 1 May 1908) first printed in the Mantz Life.[18] These have been faithfully re-cited in all subsequent studies. Even Murry, collecting material for the 1954 Journal, covered these critical six months by reprinted brief excerpts already printed by Mantz and he made no attempt to supplement them with KM's considerable notebook entries for 1908. There was thus established in 1933 what one might call the 'Mantz portrait', from which all subsequent portraits are derivatives, the KM of the 'bitter and painful months' of 1908. The Mantz portrait has been accepted without examination. It does not match the documents.

KM's notebooks for the period (from which Mantz selected only a few apparently self-dramatizing lines) run to many pages. They are a collection of personal notes, extensive pieces of fiction, sometimes an amalgam of both. The material requires the most careful assessment in context if it is to be used for biographical inferences. The 'heroine' of any particular page is as likely to be a fictional creation, or a literary experiment in the rendering of possible moods, as a self-portrait. These notebooks must be read in the context of documentation that was either not available or, if available, was not fully read and used in the nineteen-thirties. Once again, a very different KM emerges.

The Mantz portrait of KM, the distraught sufferer of the years 1907–8, on which all subsequent versions have been based, has as little foundation as the rare spirit of the Journal. The full text of KM's letters of the time, her early notebooks, the testimony of her Wellington contemporaries of her own social group, family documents, school records—almost none of which were accessible until recently—present a quite different picture. KM remained the confident young woman of the Urewera notebook.

When she returned to Wellington, she settled down to a regular routine. She spent hours alone, writing. That is what one expects of a writer. She had by now been published several times in Australia; and the journalist Tom L.

Mills (whom Beauchamp had called in to advise her and who was now on a provincial newspaper) printed more of her contributions in his weekly literary supplement.[19] She went on with her preparations for the life ahead; set herself a stiff course of reading at the General Assembly Library; and abandoned her cello for a training more appropriate to a writer. 'My plans', she wrote to her sister Vera, 'they are work and struggle and learn and try and lead a full life and get this great heap of MSS off my hands.'[20]

This is hardly the programme of an unhappy literary recluse. 'Lead a full life'? She threw herself into the life around her—swam in the Thorndon Baths[21] went walking with her fourteen-year-old brother ('I never dreamt of loving a child as I love this boy');[22] went to the theatre with her family ('to the *Three Little Maids* last night');[23] holidayed with her sister Chaddie at Day's Bay;[24] played billiards at the home of the Prime Minister Sir Joseph Ward (Rubi Seddon, daughter of a Prime Minister, was in the party);[25] attended with Tom Seddon (Rubi's brother) a debate at the university college (to the indignation of the women on the committee who considered that Tom should have squired a properly matriculated student);[26] enjoyed—and coolly rejected—*five* offers of marriage (her italics);[27] engaged in the summertime tennis parties at the family home at 47 Fitzherbert Terrace;[28] danced with the young men of her social group in Wellington with open enjoyment ('I think I am more popular than any girl here at dances');[29] It was, of course, no more than a continuation of the life she had been leading before the camping trip, when the family gave a dance for her nineteenth birthday and showered her with gifts ('Mother gave her greenstone ear-rings, Father two sweet Liberty broaches').[30] It was a life, in the social circle in which she had been brought up, of quite orthodox normality.

The only element in the life of this lively and attractive young woman of nineteen that was neither normal nor orthodox was her steely determination. She was still determined to return and write in London and determined to persuade Harold Beauchamp that her plan was feasible. With only a few sketches and stories in print, she was already on the way to becoming a young professional, coolly observing her material in terms of how it could be utilized and rendered in fiction. After one quite casual (and innocuous) conversation with a visiting musician, she wrote in one of her notebooks 'I'm glad about the whole affair. I shall pervert it—and make it fascinating'. (This comment, excised from the 1954 printed version of the *Journal*,[31] well illustrates the dangers of a simplistic use of her writing as biographical data.) In the same notebook, she records of one of her many Wellington admirers 'I am so eternally thankful that I did not allow J——to kiss me ... I used him merely for copy'.[32] The KM that Virginia Woolf came to know was already in the making. It would not be long before she got her own way in Wellington.

KM went on with her writing—and her planning. Her next move was shrewdly practical. Several of the young men she danced with were taking degrees at the recently founded university college. She, too, could have matriculated. But she had different priorities, and in the autumn quarter of 1908 she went back to school. Her fourth Wellington school, the Wellington Technical School, taught plumbing and engineering to the tradesmen of the town; for the leisured ladies of KM's circle (like Tom Seddon's sister May) it offered painting, sculpture, repoussé metal-work. KM did not join the leisured ladies. She paid her guinea (along with some of Wellington's future commercial leaders) to enrol as a student of 'Commercial Subjects', and spent her mornings on typing and book-keeping.[33] It was all calculated, deliberate and organized. She described her programme—that of a hard-working student—to Vera: 'I go to the Technical School every day—Library till five—then a walk—and in the evening I read *and* write'.[34] KM was deliberately, I think, adding some useful skills for the future—later she handled her little Corona typewriter[35] with effect and (a banker's daughter) she always kept careful and balanced accounts.[36] She was also, I think, in the early part of 1908, impressing on her father that she was well able to look after herself.

Beauchamp had, originally, been reluctant to agree to KM's plan to return, on her own, to London. Indeed he had come to regret sending the girls overseas for their schooling. He found he had lost his daughters,[37] and he did not repeat the experiment with the two younger children. Mrs Beauchamp came up with a more acceptable alternative—a flat in London and £300 a year for the three young women.[38] But KM's older sisters had other plans for their future.

Finally, it was all decided. 'There could be no question of standing in her light', Beauchamp wrote in his *Reminiscences*.[39] He settled on her an allowance for the rest of her life.[40] There was a round of farewell parties, culminating in a grand affair at the residence of Sir Joseph Ward, the Prime Minister; and then KM, 'more popular than any girl here at dances', left it all behind. She sailed in July. The Urewera notebook was in her luggage. Some years later, she set it all down, in a story called 'The Scholarship'—the eager anticipation of going 'off to Europe' mingling with regret at leaving the 'darling, darling little town'.[41] She never forgot (how could she?) Wellington and the warmth and hydrangeas of Fitzherbert Terrace. In 1921 it became the setting for one of her most moving stories, *An Ideal Family*.

When KM arrived in London, in the autumn of 1908, the New Zealand notebooks were for a time laid aside. She had her old associates to link up with and a very different kind of full life to occupy her attention. She had also her writing; but in the competitive London scene, the 'little colonial' (her own phrase)[42] made at first slow headway, only a few oddments finding their way into print. In the early months of 1910, within two years from her arrival, she had made the breakthrough with a story in the *New Age*. Thereafter, she was a regular contributor, and till early in 1912 it published her tartly satirical stories with settings familiar from her recent experiences in England, Belgium and Bavaria. The Bavarian stories, collected in 1911, became her first published volume, *In A German Pension,* twice reprinted and enthusiastically re-viewed. This led to a request for a story from an unknown young editor, John Middleton Murry, who had recently started a periodical *Rhythm.* He found her contribution (a 'bitter fairy story') not easy to understand and asked for some-thing different.[43] Though neither knew it, a turning-point had come in their lives.

KM had already, in her search for themes, made a secret return to Wellington. 'A Birthday' (printed in the *New Age* in May 1911) stands apart from the ill-humour that runs through the other stories in *In A German Pen-sion.* Only the names are German. Setting and theme come from her Welling-ton memories, and the house of Andreas Binzer is recognizably the house of the opening pages of 'Prelude'. It is no accident that it is the one story in *In A German Pension* that radiates warmth. If Murry wanted something different from what she had been publishing in the *New Age,* she knew where to find it; and she provided *Rhythm* and its successor the *Blue Review* during 1912 and 1913 with a series of New Zealand stories: 'New Dresses' and 'The Little Girl', based on memories of her family; 'Ole Underwood' from her memory of a Wellington street character; 'The Woman at the Store', 'Millie', and 'How Pearl Button was Kidnapped' based on the Urewera notebook.

She began with the Urewera notebook. Murry received from her the story 'The Woman at the Store' and he printed it in his spring issue of 1912. So close is the dependence of one text on the other, she must have had the Urew-era notebook open before her as she was writing 'The Woman at the Store'. The plot is simple: three travellers, one of them a girl, after riding over the plains, plan to set up their tent for the night by a lonely whare inhabited by a woman and her small daughter. The father is absent ('away shearing'). The child reveals, by a drawing, that the woman has murdered her husband. All the elements of the story and much of the language is derived directly from the Urewera notebook. The landscape is that covered twice by KM and her party on their camping trip, the great pumice plain between Rangitaiki and the Waipunga River. For the central characters, the woman and child, KM has combined two of her recorded impressions, her suspicions of marital discord at the Rangitaiki Hotel (see pp. 46 and 86) and the 'garrulous' woman with 'great boots' and the 'farm child' encountered the following evening (see p. 86). The setting is composite—KM has moved the Rangitaiki store a day's march to the east.

The language of the story follows closely the language of the notebook; sometimes it is identical. The 'heat' and the 'chuffing' horses, the 'shrilling' larks, the collocation of tussock and orchid and manuka, the rider's 'blue duck' trousers, the whare's 'horsehair sofa', the 'swampy creek', the absent man who is 'away shearing', the 'pair of dirty Bluchers', the narrator bathing in the creek, the boiling billy, all are in the notebook in virtually the same words. Whole phrases and incidents are transferred. The Rangitaiki hotel people in the notebook 'give us fresh bread'; in the story the woman offers to 'knock up a few extry scones'. The notebook's 'We are like children here all happiness' becomes in the story 'We behaved like two children . . . laughed and shouted to each other'. The violent thunderstorm of the notebook becomes, in the story, an integral part of the plot.

To Murry 'The Woman at the Store' was by far the best thing *Rhythm* had printed. The plotted story with a surprise ending was a form that KM rapidly grew out of; but it remains an effective piece of writing, its solid authenticity derived from KM's notes of 1907.

KM turned to the notebook once again later in the year, to write a quite different kind of story 'How Pearl Button was Kidnapped', which appeared in *Rhythm* in September 1912. This is a 'fairy story' with obvious allegorical overtones. Pearl is taken from her House of Boxes by two 'dark women' who mother her and she spends an idyllic day with 'other people of the same colour as they were' till she is discovered and returned to the House of Boxes. It is a reaction against the brittle sophistication of the *New Age,* a plea for warmth and simplicity. The flax basket of ferns, the rugs, the feather mats, the Maori interior are all derived from the notebook. KM is drawing on her notes on Umuroa and on Te Whaiti (where she had been presented with a 'Maori kit' or flax basket) and on her memories of the warm welcome the 1907 party had received from the Maori guide and his family. The following year KM provided Murry with one further 'backblock' story 'Millie', printed in June 1913 in *Rhythm*'s successor the *Blue Review.* It is a reworking of the violence of 'The Woman at the Store'. The landscape and setting are once more derived from the notebook.

With 'Millie' the Urewera notebook had exhausted its immediate usefulness and no further stories were directly based on her old camping record. The experience remained part of her. I do not think it accidental that when she came in 1922 to draw up her will, making sure that all would be left tidy behind her, the words that came to her were 'I desire to leave as few traces of my camping ground as possible'. For her it was no mere conventional turn of words.

I doubt if she opened the notebook after 1913. But phrases and images and incidents recorded there lay stored in her memory. 'At the Bay' is full of such memories. It opens with a single phrase—'Very early morning'. 'Everyone' is asleep. Only the narrator is awake. This diary-like opening phrase and the ensuing collocation of bush/dew/snapping of twigs forms an image that finds its ultimate source in these early morning scenes (everyone but KM asleep) recorded several times in the notebook.

The day after the trip concluded, KM wrote a poem in the notebook: the theme was the fragility of the flowers of the manuka—and of human life. This poem, never revised and probably forgotten, is the buried source of the sixth section of 'At the Bay', where Linda is covered by the falling flowers of the manuka, symbols of everything that is 'wasted, wasted'. (A more detailed discussion can be found in the text.)

One image haunted her for years. In the opening pages of the notebook she recorded the felled and burnt-over bush seen through the train window—masses of charred logs 'like strange fantastic beasts'. She returned to the image several times. Among her papers there is an unrhymed poem, in which the masses of logs have become rocks—'like some herd of shabby beasts'. She marked this sheet 'revise', and elsewhere in her papers there is a revision: the unrhymed poem has been rewritten as prose; the beasts, which had been 'fantastic' and then 'shabby', have now become 'shaggy'. Finally, in 1921, fourteen years after she first set down the phrase in the Urewera notebook, it all came right in the precise and meticulous imagery of 'At the Bay'—'Over there on the weed-hung rocks that looked at low tide like shaggy beasts come down to the water to drink . . .'.

Is it any wonder that the Urewera notebook survived? The *New Age* had cast its young writer in a single role, provider of brittle and 'bitter' sketches, firmly rejecting her attempts to break away from the formula that had been established for her.[44] Murry's quite casual invitation to write something different led her back to the notebook which she had brought with her from Wellington. In a few years it was going to lead to the great New Zealand stories of her maturity.

## Notes

1. All writers on Katherine Mansfield face the purely technical problem of what to call her. The constant repetition of 'Katherine Mansfield' becomes somewhat long-winded. The 'Miss Mansfield' or the 'Mansfield' of some writers carries misleading connotations. In my *Undiscovered Country* (London, 1974), I called her 'Katherine', which one reviewer found too paternal. I have settled here for 'KM', a form she frequently used in her manuscripts.

2. KM to A. E. Rice, printed in *Adam International Review,* London, no. 300, p. 93.

3. R. E. Mantz (and J. Middleton Murry), *The Life of Katherine Mansfield*, London, 1933; S. Berkman, *Katherine Mansfield,* New Haven, 1951; A. Alpers, *Katherine Mansfield A Biography,* New York, 1953.

4. *Journal of Katherine Mansfield,* 1927; *Journal of Katherine Mansfield,* Definitive Edition, 1954; *The Letters of Katherine Mansfield,* 2 vols., 1928; *The Scrapbook of Katherine Mansfield,* 1939; *Letters to John Middleton Murry,* 1951. All volumes were published in London and edited by John Middleton Murry.

5. KM to Vera. Turnbull MS.

6. *Journal,* 1954, p. 96.

7. *Letters,* 1928, vol. ii, p. 96.

8. Murry's treatment of KM's papers has been analysed in some detail in: Ian A. Gordon, 'The Editing of Katherine Mansfield's Journal and Scrapbook', *Landfall,* Christchurch, New Zealand, March 1959, pp. 62–9; Philip Waldron, 'Katherine Mansfield's Journal', *Twentieth Century Literature,* Hempstead, N.Y., January 1974, pp. 11–18.

9. *Journal,* 1927, Introduction by John Middleton Murry, p. xv.

10. *Carrington: Letters and Extracts from her Diaries,* ed. D. Garnett, London, 1970, p. 41.

11. Virginia Woolf to Vanessa Bell, 11 February 1917: *The Question of Things Happening, The Letters of Virginia Woolf,* London, 1976, vol. ii, p. 144.

12. Michael Holroyd, *Lytton Strachey, The Years of Achievement,* London, 1968, p. 112.

13. *Ibid.,* p. 538.

14. *Journal,* 1954, Preface by Murry, p. x. 'The fragments from 1904 to 1912 ... appeared to have escaped destruction by pure accident'. They were filled notebooks, not fragments; and they survived because KM retained them.

15. Turnbull MS. accession no. 97306.

16. Account by Mrs G. G. Robieson (Edie Bendall) 1946. Morris MS. (in possession of Mrs Susan Graham, Auckland, New Zealand).

17. Alpers, p. 99.

18. Mantz, p. 309.

19. Tom L. Mills moved from Wellington in 1907 to edit the *Feilding Star,* in which he established a Saturday literary supplement. Mills reviewed *In a German Pension* in his supplement of 6 October 1912, saying of KM 'Katherine Mansfield—who, by the way, wrote some things for the STAR supplement, some five years ago, before leaving for London'. The New Zealand National Library file of the *Star* lacks the relevant volumes; the file of the *Star* in the Feilding Public Library lacks almost all the supplements, which being half news-sheet size were apparently not bound in. I think these early KM 'things' are gone for ever. I have hunted everywhere.

20. KM to Vera. Turnbull MS.

21. Personal communication from two of KM's contemporaries.

22. KM to Sylvia Payne, March 1908. Turnbull MS.

23. KM to Vera, January 1908. Turnbull MS.

24. KM to Sylvia Payne. Same letter as note 22. Turnbull MS.

25. KM to Harold Beauchamp, July 1922. *Letters,* 1928, vol. ii, p. 232, where Rubi Seddon appears only as 'R'. Her full name is on the typescript copy of the letter deposited by Beauchamp in the Turnbull Library. Harold Beauchamp's grandson, the late Andrew Bell (Canada) received all of KM's letters to her father as a bequest. He informed me that, without his knowledge, they found their way to an American collector. These letters—of critical importance—remain unavailable.

26. Personal communication from Mrs Maude Morris of Auckland (who was one of the women on the committee at the time).

27. KM to Sylvia Payne. Same letter as note 22. Turnbull MS.

28. See 'An Ideal Family' (first collected in *The Garden Party*), where the tennis parties are set in the recognizable 'corner house' in Fitzherbert Terrace (thinly disguised as 'fashionable Harcourt Avenue').

29. KM to Vera, undated, but on internal evidence early 1908. Turnbull MS.

30. Charlotte (Chaddie) Beauchamp to Sylvia Payne, 14 October 1907 (KM's birthday). Text printed in Alpers, p. 89.

31. *Journal,* 1954, pp. 14–15. Murry omitted the words after 'unintellectual head' and gave no indication that he had altered the text of the notebook.

32. *Journal,* 1954, p. 22. The notebook to which this and the previous note refers (Turnbull MS. accession no. 97273) was begun by KM 14 July 1906 in London, carried to New Zealand, completed during 1907, and brought back to London in 1908.

33. KM appears on the Wellington Technical School register as 'Beauchamp, K. Registration number 903'. Her name was entered in May for Commercial Subjects. The names of two future managing directors are on the same page. For an account of my discovery of this enrolment see: Ian A. Gordon, 'Warmth and Hydrangeas; Katherine Mansfield's Wellington Years,' *New Zealand Listener,* 8 May 1976, pp. 22–3.

34. KM to Vera, undated but clearly after KM's enrolment at the Technical school. Vera was in Sydney from late in 1907 till some time into 1908, visiting family friends. KM wrote to her regularly and Vera (the late Mrs Macintosh Bell of Ottawa) retained the letters, which are now in the Turnbull Library.

35. 'I spend a large part of [these days] tapping out my new *long* story or *short* novel on my little Corona' (KM to Harold Beauchamp 28/7/1922). After KM's death, her Corona Portable was used for many years by LM, who then presented it to the Turnbull Library.

36. KM was a fanatical keeper of accounts, even as a schoolgirl. Her 1906 notebook records such items as 'tarts 6d; buns 6d' and the pattern continued throughout her life. Turnbull MS. accession no. 97287 is a complete weekly household account book covering 1914–16 recording such items as 'safety pins for Jack 9d' and sums 'lent to Jack'. Several of her diaries have quite sophisticated balance sheets in the final pages. The basic cost of the Urewera trip was met by Harold Beauchamp, but KM kept meticulous accounts of her own out-of-pocket-expenses—see Appendix.

37. I was told this recently by KM's sister Jeanne (Mrs Renshaw).

38. KM to Vera, undated. Late 1907/early 1908. Turnbull MS. KM thought it an 'excellent scheme'.

39. Harold Beauchamp, *Reminiscences and Recollections,* privately printed, New Plymouth, New Zealand, 1937.

40. Her allowance was £2 per week in 1908, raised to £3 per week in 1916. In 1919 Beauchamp settled £200 per annum on Vera, Jeanne and Chaddie and £300 a year on KM. KM's allowance was paid monthly through the Bank of New Zealand, London. There are records of cash gifts at Christmas and other payments. Source: KM's accounts, Beauchamp's Instructions to the Bank of New Zealand, London (Turnbull MSS.).

41. A partial text of 'The Scholarship' was printed in the *Scrapbook,* 1939, pp. 93–100. The only full text of this story appears in *Undiscovered Country,* 1974, pp. 253–8.

42. *Journal,* 1954, p. 157.

43. Mantz (and Murry), 1933, p. 333.

44. Cf. *Poems by Katherine Mansfield,* London, 1923, Introductory Note, p. xiii—'he [the editor of the *New Age*] wanted her to write nothing but satirical prose'.

# The Ghost of Katherine Mansfield

## LINDA HARDY

In 1903, Kathleen Beauchamp spent seven weeks on the *Niwaru,* a 'small cargo ship' sailing out of New Zealand, via the Pacific Ocean and Cape Horn, for England. According to Claire Tomalin, the Beauchamp family devoted its first month in England to 'cultural touring', and Stratford in Warwickshire was 'one of their first objectives'.[1] There cannot have been anything singular about the Beauchamps' selection of this 'objective'; as the site of Shakespeare's birthplace, Stratford belonged to the normal itinerary of 'the cultural tourist', an itinerary long since inscribed in the geography, as in the cultural history, of England. Thomas Carlyle had already foretold in 1840 the pre-eminence of Shakespeare, not merely as 'an ornament to our English Household', but throughout a racial and linguistic empire from whose uttermost bound the Beauchamp family would later return:

> England, before long, this Island of ours, will hold but a small fraction of the English: in America, in New Holland, east and west to the very Antipodes, there will be a Saxondom covering great spaces of the Globe . . . Here, I say, is an English King, whom no time or chance, Parliament or combination of Parliaments, can dethrone! This King Shakespeare, does he not shine, in crowned sovereignty, over us all, as the noblest, gentlest, yet strongest of rallying-signs; *in*destructible . . . From Paramatta, from New York, wheresoever, under what sort of Parish-Constable soever, English men and women are, they will say to one another: 'Yes, this Shakespeare is ours; we produced him, we speak and think by him; we are of one blood and kind with him.'[2]

One hesitates to ascribe such sentiments to the fourteen-year-old Kathleen Beauchamp, whose journey to Stratford may merely have obeyed the logic of a colonial itinerary 'chosen' by no-one in particular, though prompted by interests whose very obviousness, Barthes reminds us, is a sign of their ideological over-determination, their capture in the semiotic systems of 'myth'.[3]

An anecdote, then, about Kathleen Beauchamp, which, though it occurs in her biography, belongs rather, or more intelligibly, to the history of 'English', whether one takes that as a Political or as a literary nomination. The conjunction of Beauchamp (family) and Shakespeare (via Stratford) is com-

From *Landfall: A New Zealand Quarterly,* 43:4 (December 1989), 416–32.

monplace enough; yet Kathleen Beauchamp will mutate into Katherine Mansfield, will acquire, in 1988, a 'birthplace' of her own,[4] and will perhaps assume a position, in relation to the literature of New Zealand, not unlike Shakespeare's for 'English' in general: a position of priority and pre-eminence. *If* it is possible to tell such a story, it is because the conception of 'national' literatures in English is articulated through two primary tropes: the figure of the rupture, and the scheme of repetition.

Thus, Carlyle's 'Saxondom covering great spaces of the Globe', exempted thanks to Shakespeare's transcendent genius from time, chance and political insurrection, suffers a thoroughly historical termination; in its place arise the autonomous nations, ex-colonies, whose 'new' literatures are founded in a break with that global 'English' culture now withdrawing behind its proper, and merely British, borders. The formation of *national* culture then proceeds in the elaboration of an origin, a genealogy, and a canon—a repetition *in another place* of the mutual articulation of literary and national identity already *in place* in Stratford, for England. Such a project is underway in our universities, where the inclusion in curricula of New Zealand, Australian, Pacific and American literatures unsettles the meaning of 'English', a term now irrevocably split between its dual significations of national and linguistic identities.

One way of registering the dubiousness of this nationalist project in culture is to focus on the impossibility of the substitution (the repetition with a difference) that I proposed earlier. Katherine Mansfield both has not, and *cannot,* function as a sign of priority and pre-eminence in the 'national' literature of New Zealand; not only do 'we' lack a Shakespeare, but in lacking such a figure, 'we' lack the transcendent origin in which to found 'our' identity.

Let us pursue, a little further, the resonance of that date 1903. For to the year of the Beauchamps' trip to Stratford belongs a short story called 'The Birthplace', where, had they been readers of Henry James, the Beauchamps might have found themselves satirically incorporated in a 'crowd of gaping, awe-struck persons', which in a 'full, swift and steady stream, passed through the smoothly-working mill and went, in its variety of degrees duly impressed and edified, on its artless way.'[5] The manufacturing connotations carried in the last metaphor here ('smoothly-working mill'), are played off against, and mark a vulgar declension from, the pretensions of 'The Birthplace' to be a 'shrine . . . the most sacred known to the steps of men, the early home of the supreme poet, the Mecca of the English-speaking race' (p. 286). Yet for James, mill and shrine are in the end identical with each other, the vulgarity of a quasi-religious cult of 'the supreme poet' at one with the vulgarity of a commerce in 'his' relics.

It is impossible not to read the story as being 'about' Shakespeare's birthplace at Stratford, although at no point is the poet, or the place, granted the unambiguous identity of a proper name:

the Birthplace Trust appears ... as the 'body', the indwelling poet as the 'Spirit', the process of exhibition is known as the 'Show', and the 'Show' includes the telling of certain 'Facts'. . .[6]

The withholding of the names that most readers will instantly supply (Shakespeare, Stratford) neatly parallels the 'spirit's' failure to manifest itself in the shrine, despite the poignant longing of its priest, or caretaker, Morris Gedge, for it to do so: 'He *had* to take it as the place where the spirit would most walk and where he would therefore be most to be met, with possibilities of recognition and reciprocity' (p. 302). In this latter phrase, James allows Gedge, his tragi-comic protagonist, a desire sufficiently hesitant, scrupulous, and courteous ('possibilities of recognition and reciprocity') to be felt as exempt from the vulgarity of the tourist crowd. All the same, Gedge must resign himself to the futility of even such tentative hopes, his very scruples bringing him to the point where, 'in the conflict of theories, the sole certainty surviving for the critic threatened to be that He had not—unlike other successful men—*not* been born' (p. 302). In this instance, the material consequences of the death of the author necessitate a bloodier death, the violent extinction of Gedge's 'critical sense':

'It's dead,' he went on; 'I killed it just now ... If you'll go out and see, there must be blood. Which indeed,' he added, 'on an altar of sacrifice, is all right. But the place is forever spattered.' (pp. 330–1)

Thus, Gedge averts the loss of his position with the 'Body', and of the salary he draws; indeed, as Marjorie Garber glosses it,

[t]he rest of Gedge's career is instructive for academics, for ... once reminded of his jeopardy, Gedge turns completely around, and, freed of the burden of an indwelling author, himself becomes one, gaining such fame as a raconteur that the Body doubles his stipend. (Garber, p. 10)

More generally (and as allegory, 'The Birthplace' makes itself available for 'general' applications of this kind), it might be said that whenever 'possibilities of recognition and reciprocity' fail, the cult of the author is re-installed all the more desperately, in order to mask 'His' displacement by the raconteurs who make it their business to authorise 'His' presence and 'His' identity.

Henry James was, of course, himself a migrant to England from Carlyle's global 'Saxondom', if not from Paramatta then from New York. His corrosive satire on the cult of Shakespeare can be understood at least in part as a hybrid or Anglo-American rewriting of Carlyle's paean to the 'English King'. Indeed, it is the arrival of a cultivated young American couple at The Birthplace which precipitates the Englishman Gedge's violent struggle with his awakening 'critical sense', though James also reminds us that the most eager and populous audience for Gedge's inspired fabrications is likewise American.

My use of the term 'hybrid' in this context is intended to invoke the work of Homi Bhabha on 'the problem of the ambivalence of cultural authority'.[7] In a series of intricate essays, Bhabha has argued against the assumption that the cultural politics of 'colonial discourse' can be read more or less straightforwardly as a drama of domination and resistance, from which will emerge, ideally, a *diversity* of national cultures in place of the Euro-and Anglocentrism of Empire.[8] Bhabha points out that any appeal to the 'diversity' of cultures logically presupposes 'the unity or totality' of each culture in itself; he argues, rather that the instability, or indeterminacy, of the 'discursive conditions of enunciation . . . ensure[s] that the meanings and symbols of culture have no primordial unity or fixity; that even the same signs can be appropriated, translated, rehistoricized, and read anew' ('The Commitment to Theory', p. 21). More specifically, he proposes that we understand the 'effect of colonial power' as having been:

> the production of hybridization rather than the hegemonic command of colonialist authority or the silent repression of native traditions . . . Hybridity is a *problematic* of colonial representation and individuation that reverses the effects of the colonialist disavowal, so that other 'denied' knowledges enter upon the dominant discourse and estrange the basis of its authority . . . ('Signs taken for Wonders', pp. 97, 98).

One kind of 'hybridization' is 'the figure of mimicry'; in an early essay, Bhabha discusses the production of colonial subjects (or 'mimic men', as in the title of a novel by V.S. Naipaul) as effects of 'a flawed colonial mimesis, in which to be Anglicized, is *emphatically* not to be English' ('Of Mimicry and Men', p. 128). One could elaborate from this a reading of Katherine Mansfield as a white colonial, as *'a subject of a difference that is almost the same, but not quite',* and in terms of 'the desire to emerge as "authentic" through mimicry—through a process of writing and repetition' ('Of Mimicry and Men', pp. 128, 129).

Another possibility would be to read James's Morris Gedge, as a 'mimic man', whose extravagant if belated espousal of the cult of 'the supreme poet . . . of the English-speaking race' is suspended uncertainly between 'mimicry and mockery' ('Of Mimicry and Men', p. 127), at once destabilising the meaning of that discourse and estranging 'the basis of its authority'.

But in this essay I want to turn to the possibility that 'the inscription and articulation of culture's hybridity' ('The Commitment to Theory', p. 22) might be traced through the ghostly recurrence of 'Katherine Mansfield' in New Zealand writing—where she figures, *not* as a point of origin, nor as the founding term of a national culture, but as a phantasmic and sometimes troubling sign of displacement. If Bhabha is right to insist that 'the image—as point of identification—marks the site of an ambivalence ('Remembering

Fanon', p. xvii), then it is the image of Katherine Mansfield, wherever 'she' is reinscribed, that displays this slippage of identity, this uncovering of ambivalence within the structures of identification. To adapt Bhabha's more general claim, 'her'

> ... representation is always spatially split—it makes *present* something that is *absent*—and temporally deferred—it is always elsewhere, a repetition. ('Remembering Fanon', p. xvii)

I shall begin with three poems, each of which seems to take up the possibility of an identification with Katherine Mansfield. The opportunity for identification is two-fold: through a visit to or occupation of the house of the dead writer; and in a somatic repetition of the writer's tubercular symptoms in the body of the (female) poet. All the poems carry in their titles the name of Mansfield's villa near Menton in the south of France: 'At Isolla (sic) Bella with Fleur', by Marilyn Duckworth; 'Villa Isola Bella', by Fleur Adcock; and 'A Visit to Isola Bella', by Anne French.[9] The coincidence of titles is scarcely uncanny: since the Katherine Mansfield Fellowship was endowed to provide New Zealand writers with a temporary address at Mansfield's mediterranean villa, the Chemin Fleuri has become a virtually compulsory stop-over for anyone following a serious career in writing in New Zealand (not to mention their friends and relations). But the well-established institutional priority of Isola Bella over Tinakori Road (the Wellington birthplace) has the effect of displacing the national shrine to Katherine Mansfield from New Zealand to France. The place where the ghost of Katherine Mansfield might 'most walk', where one might hope for 'possibilities of recognition and reciprocity', is, from the point of view of a nationalist discourse, problematically *elsewhere.*

Of the three, Duckworth's poem is least resistant to the temptations of identification: it concludes in an awakening from nightmare that is supposed to recall the bloody eruptions of Mansfield's consumptive lungs:

> I don't want dreaming to stop
> So will endure
> The nightmares niggling and crude
> And wake, mouth bubbling with idiot fear
> Like Katherine's dark blood.

Here, as elsewhere, Katherine Mansfield is exhaustively signified by one synecdochical detail: her disease, which seems monotonously to elicit from writers either a masochistic identification or a response compounded of fascination and recoil. At the beginning of the poem, however, Katherine Mansfield is identified merely as the former occupant of the room now shared by the poet and her sister. This room is indeed populated by ghosts ('furies' and 'familiar horrors') but they have no literary specificity, and they pass *between* the sisters in a movement of contagion and bodily invasion; the *mise en scène* belongs unmistakably to the genre of female gothic. The poem is mostly about the difference between the sisters' daytime nostalgia for a shared childhood, and the nocturnal return of 'old nightmares'. 'Katherine's Room' is haunted, then, only by the familial memories that invest it; empty, until the sisters' presence to each other transforms it into a dreamsite ('Tents and air raid shelters/In the forties'). The detail about 'Katherine's dark blood' seems incidental, an afterthought—at any rate, not essential to the poem's staging of its ambivalent reminiscences.

Adcock's poem is more determined to foreground the literary associations of the villa, as it is more wittily conscious of its own literariness. The epigraph cites Mansfield's claim, in a letter to Murry, that 'You will find Isola Bella in pokerwork on my heart'—itself a possibly joky allusion to Bloody Queen Mary's deathbed lament for Calais. But from this point the poem proceeds through a series of disavowals, undoing precisely the identification that Duckworth tries to secure in the closing lines of her poem: 'Your villa, Katherine, but not your room/and not much of your garden. . .'. Here the possibility of posthumous contagion, whereby the poet 'catches' tuberculosis from the dead writer ('the ghost of your hot flat-iron burns my lung') is elaborated as part of a half-humorous, half-affectionate address to 'Katherine'. The trope of prosopopeia, whereby the dead are rhetorically summoned back to life, positions Mansfield as the silent auditor to Adcock's mock-heroic and incomplete similitudes:

>               . . . You
> smoked shameless Turkish all through your TB.
> I drag at Silk Cut filters, duty-free,
> then gargle sensibly with Oraldene
> and spit pink froth. Not blood: it doesn't mean,
> like your spat scarlet, that I'll soon be dead—
> merely that pharmacists are fond of red.
> I'm hardly sick at all.

This denial is at once complicated by a confession that the poet *is* nevertheless afflicted by 'a nameless fever, atavistic fears', but Adcock insists that her 'disease' originates elsewhere:

> Disease is portable: my bare half-week
> down here's hatched no maladie exotique;
>
>      . . . . . .
>
> Whatever haunts my bloodstream didn't start
> below your villa . . .

If a tubercular condition is a conventional synonym for poetic energy and inspiration, as in the juxtaposition of 'ragged lungs and work you burned to do', then it is a condition the two writers share without thereby being placed in any relation of influence or succession. Mansfield's 'harsh breathing' has at most 'left a trace/held in the air'; the ghost is dismissed with a 'Goodnight' and the poet turns away, in a final gesture of negation, 'to open what was not in fact your door/and find my narrow mattress on the floor'.

The non-identity of 'Katherine's' and Adcock's Isola Bella is paralleled in the 'portability' of (poetic) fever: whatever its source, it can't be traced back to Mansfield. Not-quite origin, not-quite destination, Mansfield figures here as a companionable shade, wholly incapable of exerting any transcendental pressure on the writer who addresses her.

The third of these poems, Anne French's 'A visit to Isola Bella', narrates a pilgrimage which fails to get beyond the 'locked gate' of the 'empty' villa. There the poet 'poses' for the camera, doubling as Mansfield in a gesture inspired more by *ennui* than by piety: 'Nothing to do but take/photographs'. The addressee of the first stanza is, in any case, not Mansfield, but a later occupant of the villa, most likely one of those literary 'fellows' and certainly a far stronger presence for the visitor than is Mansfield. Like Adcock, French is sceptical of what we might call the birthplace-effect: the experience of the writer's shrine as a place which harbours 'a *presence* ... diffused, uncontested and undisturbed' (James, p. 335). For although she feels herself to be 'haunted', it is by 'another address', and throughout the poem the sites and sights of Mansfield's French town evoke more powerfully memories of the very place Mansfield left behind:

> The terraced hillside
> the ochre-pink shuttered villas
> the cypresses
> speak of Wellington
> the palms
> the olive groves
> the sea
> all speak of Wellington.

This might be one way of completing the circuit of identification—if the *vieille ville* is at once France and New Zealand, then Mansfield is already at home, amongst us. But this sense of the uncanny familiarity of the place is precisely what a revenant Mansfield would be denied:

> She wouldn't recognize
> the big main road around the bay ...
> Nor the tourists—people like me
> who drop in for the day and fly on
> in the evening to England.

The dissolution of geographical distance and difference fails to abridge the gap of time, and once again Mansfield is suspended in that space of displacement, where identity and identifications are undone.

I have used Bhabha's term, 'hybridization', to name this cultural space where 'Katherine Mansfield' is at once present and absent, repeated and deferred: unlike that mythic Stratford where the encounter of Bard and pilgrim is supposed to secure the identity, across time, of English men and women 'wheresoever [they] are', the shrine at Menton discloses the non-coincidence of one place, time, writer, and another. Nowhere in these poems can we discern the inscription of cultural identity figured as a continuity between the contemporary poet and the dead precursor.

There are other names we might bestow upon this condition—hybrid names such as 'post-modern', or even (in some of its senses) 'post-colonial'.[10] But in this essay, since I am following some traces of the ghost of Katherine Mansfield, the term closest to hand is Janet Frame's 'manifold'. In *Living in the Maniototo*[11] this word recurs frequently, never quite fixed in a definition, but typically to be found in the vicinity of relations which may be schematically represented as those between original and replica, fiction and reality, author and character. The dictionary tells us that in its adjectival form 'manifold' is a 'literary' term meaning 'having various forms, applications, component parts, etc.; performing several functions at once' and adds that the 'original sense' of the suffix '-fold' is 'folded in so many layers etc' (Concise Oxford Dictionary). In Frame's novel, then, the 'manifold' may be construed as an enfolding and involution of such differences and distinctions. Original and replica, fiction and reality, author and character, enter into what Simon During terms a 'dance of identity' (p. 373) where nothing remains the 'same' as it was, least of all the reader's confidence in her own ability to sustain such distinctions. The narrator of *Living in the Maniototo,* variously named as Violet Pansy Proudlock (ventriloquist), Alice Thumb (gossip), Mavis Furness Barwell Halleton (the wife who has 'buried two husbands'), among a plethora of possible identities, is engaged, nominally, in writing a novel about her 'visit to Menton where Margaret Rose Hurndell used to live . . . (Margaret Rose Hurndell is our famous writer)' (p. 49). That novel is displaced, however, by the novel we have in our hands, whose writing 'takes place' in the author's home in Stratford (New Zealand): where 'the streets [are] named after Shakespearean characters' (p. 213). The author also inhabits a 'house of replicas' in Berkeley, California; among its 'likenesses, . . . replicas, prints of paintings, prints of prints, genuine originals and genuine imitation originals, imitation sculptures and twin original sculptures' (p. 17) is 'a wooden mask of Shakespeare . . . toothless, eyeless, with long nose, burn marks on the forehead and two nailed holes in the skull, one on each side' (p. 15). Although a series of 'dead poets' occur in the novel as the 'absent identity givers' (During, p. 373) for a series of places (Baltimore, 'Blenheim', the eponymous Maniototo), Shakespeare can supply only this 'grotesque' likeness or replica of himself, supplemented by the strangely incongruous naming of 'a small noisy town' in New Zealand—a naming which may or may not invest the town with something like the 'power' carried in 'the Maori names . . . [which] were welded to the place by the first unifying act of poetry and not stuck on like a grocery label' (p. 96).

'Poetry' is the power that confers authenticity on 'names', and arrests the drift of language into mere replication or outright mendacity. Nevertheless the reader of *Living in the Maniototo* is reminded that whenever words are allowed to resonate through the full range of their signification, to 'unfold' themselves, they too enact a drifting away from authentic, original, univocal meaning. The distinction between 'guest' and 'host' for example (the author as 'host' to her characters, her 'guests'), is threatened, if not overturned, by etymology, as by the structures of the novel:

> I still marvel . . . at the richness of meaning within the words 'guest' and 'host', with a guest as originally a host, a stranger, hostis, an enemy, a host as a guest, an army, a multitude of men, women, angels; planets, stars; a guest as a parasite sheltered by the host, the host a sacrifice and ultimately a blessed food. (p. 133)

'Zita', the Hungarian-New Zealander living in California, occasions a similar deconstruction of the phrase 'dwelling-place':

> That was Zita, put into doubt by the English language, speaking the word 'dwelling-place': as one who had learned English . . . and who as once an officially Displaced Person could feel the full meaning of the word and its history, knowing or sensing the derivation—the old Teutonic gedwolen, gone astray, the Old Sanskrit dhwr, dhur, to mislead, deceive, stun, stupefy, to hinder, delay, tarry—and abide, remain. (pp. 217–8)

For Frame, language is just such a 'doubtful' dwelling-place, where one may deceive and be deceived, may delay, tarry or remain; but in making 'settlements' through language, we should be able to see 'the prints, trails, frozen shadows of all who have been there before . . .' (p. 164). Margaret Rose Hurndell, a virtual but nonetheless approximate double for Katherine Mansfield (the dates, as well as the name, are wrong), is the one who, for a New Zealander, is pre-eminent among those 'who have been there before' ('our famous writer', in the striking singularity of that phrase). Near the end of the novel, the narrator dreams 'of all the houses I have lived in' (p. 221)—among them, the room at Menton where Hurndell once dwelt and where she, Alice Thumb or whoever, has briefly tarried. The dream substitutes for the still-deferred novel, the one about Hurndell and the Watercress family,—these latter are 'experts' on Hurndell, a fictional 'family' of critics whose encroachments on the author are comically registered in their decision collectively to migrate to Menton, to live 'near where Margaret Rose Hurndell once lived' (p. 117). This note of irreverence and pastiche recurs within the dream/memory, where the door to the Memorial Room is opened with the Margaret Rose Hurndell Key ('which I had borrowed'). But the room itself is mostly evocative of desolation and neglect, a sanctuary for spirits and the dead. The experience offered by the shrine is an ambiguous one: a chill descends, and with it, 'the kind of peace that one feels walking among the dead and listening, as the dead may, at a great distance from the world and its movement and noise' (p. 227). There is a spirit to be encountered here, but it lacks the singularity of that boastful and proprietorial phrase, 'our famous writer'. The spirit here is not the ghost of Margaret Rose, but of death itself.

Perhaps it is not coincidental that, in *Living in the Maniototo,* Mansfield/Hurndell shares with Shakespeare the privilege, among all the named and unnamed 'dead poets' of the novel, of being singled out as most troublingly liable to replication, reinscription—not as texts, but as individuated *people.* 'I want a Shakespeare like the real Shakespeare', writes someone, yearningly (p. 115). Each disappears, nonetheless, into the anonymous 'prints, trails, frozen shadows of all who have been there before', ceding their priority to the ceaseless erosion and production of language in 'the house of replicas'.

I have been reading these texts, variously, as instances of a breakdown, refusal or critique of the consolidation of identity and identification. The figure of identification is the founding trope of a discourse of literary nationalism ('our Shakespeare', 'our Katherine'). The cultural identity of a people is dependent on their collective possession of a unique cultural heritage, and the most potent means of representing this heritage is by personalising it in the singular figure of a pre-eminent and originating writer, whose posthumous presence *in* the culture secures that inheritance, guaranteeing spatial and temporal continuity. That 'Shakespeare' has functioned in this way for 'English' culture is the burden of much of the work being done in cultural theory in England today.[12] The inscription of Mansfield by contemporary New Zealand writers might suggest a desire to recover her as an analogous figure of origin and continuity—but what we find instead are split or divided representations: the signs, I have argued, of cultural hybridity, rather than cultural identity.

There are two fairly obvious supplementary arguments that can be made here, each more specific than the increasingly commonplace invocation of 'the postmodern condition', though not necessarily incompatible with it. The first is that Mansfield has always been associated, in New Zealand, with an orientation toward Europe, and away from that indigenous, Maori culture to which Frame is not alone in assigning a unique priority and authenticity. I shall return, briefly, to this.

The second is that Mansfield is a woman. Neither in law, nor in cultural representation, have women been able to assume the power to name, to confer identity and guarantee lineage, or continuity:

the patronymic . . . keeps the transcendental ego of the dynasty identical in the
eye of the law. By virtue of the father's name the son refers to the father. The ir-

reducible importance of the name and the law makes it quite clear that the question is . . . one of . . . the production and consolidation of reference and meaning.[13]

In this respect, 'the defining predication of a woman, whose very name is changeable' (Spivak, p. 171) is non-self-identity: 'woman' is already in the place of a displacement, of citation and (mis)quotation, of the exchange and circulation of signs in 'the house of the replicas'. So, of course, is 'man', as Morris Gedge discovers, but in the cultural fiction of the patronymic, 'his' displacement can be dissimulated as authoritative origin and centre.

The lapsing of identity through the line of the woman is presumably compounded when the writer is also a woman, when identity is supposed to pass from woman to woman. One might then speculate that it would be possible to uncover a different relation to Mansfield (or rather, to this woman 'whose very name is changeable') in a text written by a man—in, for example, Ian Wedde's novel, *Symmes Hole*.[14]

*Symmes Hole* presents itself as standing in an illegitimate or bastard relation to official culture. It is prefaced by a spurious 'introduction'—or, at least, by an introduction bearing a spurious signature—which proclaims the novel to belong to

> another history—something with the quality of the invisible, the unofficial, the disquieting, the subversive—[which] must not become official or successful: must remain a 'failure' as Herman Melville used the term of *Moby Dick* . . . (*SH*, p. 8)

'Failure' in this positive sense is at once associated with bad smells, noise, the consumption and excretion of disgusting food (the socially unregulated body); with the infections of rumour (socially unsanctioned speech); and with the cunning elusion of recognition (scopic identification and control). Nor does the novel disappoint us; 'Dr. Keehua Roa' of the University of West Hawai'i will sustain whatever assumptions we care to make about his privileged access to the mind of the author.

*Symmes Hole* is indeed a prodigal novel, a 'failure' in terms of an aesthetic of order, decorum, and clarity; productive of linguistic and bodily excess. Its two protagonists are indefatigable, obsessive story-tellers: Heberley, the nineteenth-century seaman-whaler, stumbles on through his stories despite his uncertainty and lack of eloquence; his alter ego, the nameless twentieth-century 'researcher', pursues a 'quest' through a multiplicity of digressions and devious excursions, in space, time, myth, literature. In this telling, 'women' figure as the 'real', as the closure of that gap between discourse, with its deferrals and substitutions, and bodily and metaphysical plenitude. For Heberley, this means finding a home, founding a family; things are more difficult for the narrator, since the women he knows, or fantasises, for all their tendency to merge into each other, fail to coalesce into a singular, mythic, salvific entity. Instead they become, frequently enough, obstacles—not to the completion of his quest, but to its elaboration and deferral. Twice in the novel a woman intervenes, attempting to put a stop to the proliferation of words in which meaning is endlessly complicated and which seems to bypass the simple experiential truths of real life. On each occasion, the 'researcher' resists being cut off, objects to the 'simplification' (pp. 113–115, 293). Any reader (any reader who likes the novel), whatever their gender, has to be on the side of the 'researcher', since what would be cut off, after all, is the novel we are reading, so that it is difficult to share the 'researchers's' own nostalgia for that final peace, or oblivion, to be found in a desperate, desirous, or filial embrace of the female body.[15]

This alignment of the male quest with an almost monstrous verbosity, with a rhetorical copiousness barely under control, and with (in the 'researcher') bodily symptoms of hysteria, might paradoxically be read as the feminising of that quest, its displacement from the masculine heroic mode of epic to the dilatory feminine mode of romance. The attributes of the 'researcher', and of the novel he inhabits, are reminiscent of those traditionally, and censoriously, ascribed to 'women', and associated with 'female' genres:

> Virgil's poem [the *Aeneid*] . . . seems almost to be commenting, in what we would now call self-reflexive fashion, on the differing tendencies and gender associations of both epic and romance: the resolutely teleological drive of epic in its repeated injunctions to 'break off delay' *(rumpe moras)* and the Odyssean or romance delaying tactics which make it the long poem it is and which disrupt or postpone the end promised from the beginning . . . [I]t is the female figures—Dido, Allecto, Amata, Juno (and their agents)—who are the chief perpetrators of delay and even of obstructionism in relation to the master or imperial project of the completion of the text.[16]

Where the perpetrator of delay is 'masculine', and the 'patrons of ultimate closure' (Parker, ibid) are 'feminine', we seem to have a reversal and re-articulation of orthodox cultural fictions. If so, we should have no difficulty identifying the 'researcher's' lameness, which he shares with another (and crucial) alter ego, Melville's Tommo from *Typee,* as a textually over-determined castration.

To argue thus is to produce difficulties for my initial speculation, that in *Symmes Hole* we might find a distinctively *masculine* inscription of Katherine Mansfield. Wedde claims, for his own text, a position on the side of the *feminine*—or, more plausibly, appropriates a position in literary discourse traditionally ascribed to 'women', in order to capture the privileged place within culture of marginality and subversion. The body of his text swells as it hungrily consumes or incorporates the 'material' it is recycling, as if in mimicry of the 'fat lady' classically associated with the ungovernable multiplication of rhetorical 'matter', the proliferation of corrupted and improper writings.

(Parker, pp. 17 ff). This leaves the female writer somewhat starved for nutriment, wasting away.

Which is indeed the peculiar affliction of 'Kathleen Beauchamp', as she appears to the 'researcher' in a hallucination:

> ... Herman's mouth and face encountered a non-Marquesan angularity, depleted sparser squiff of hair, hips with rims like bone china, a parched odour of civilization and impatience ... bunt of loins against him without langour or luxury ... shroud white belly ... gaunt ribs and white, white breasts with little puckered colourless nipples ... delicate clavicles ... one long neck-tendon standing out with the head turned sideways ... ironic angry passion of the wasted profile ... damp, dark fringe of hair ... charnel breath ... (Wedde, p. 72).

The 'researcher' has momentarily become 'Herman', assuming the name and identity of his hero, Herman Melville ('the first Pacific novelist'), an identity claimed through the 'researcher's' appropriation of 'Fayaway', the lush and literally appetising fantasy woman of *Typee*. When Fayaway dissolves into Kathleen, the sexual disappointment is palpable: 'the Marquesan Fayaway fantasy was okay, but this other. . .'.

In epic, the delaying tactic of the woman is typically a seduction of the hero: 'Kathleen', with her 'sadistic mouth' and 'charnel breath', more or less writes herself out of this novel, leaving Herman Melville, veteran of voyages more daring and more significant than a family cruise on the *Niwaru,* to occupy the place of pre-eminence and priority in the literature of 'the Pacific'. As 'Kathleen' herself admits,

> It's just I ... I see better out of the corners of my eyes ... some *little* thing ... And I'm no good close up, I ... there has to be a gap, quite a big one. When it's too close I ... I mean it's just, code it groon and blee, it's ... fear and panic ... I shouldn't, it was a mistake to come back ... from over there, it was ... lovely. It was ... *newborn* ... (Wedde, p. 45).

For Wedde, (re)constructing a 'tradition' centered on the Pacific Ocean, rather than in the passage back and forth between Europe and New Zealand, Mansfield is a peripheral figure, still in contention, perhaps, but only so far as observations of 'little', and local, things may still resonate. The only line Wedde 'borrows' from Mansfield is an image of the Cook Strait ferry, from her story 'Prelude': 'a little steamer all hung with bright beads'. This is repeatedly cited, but always with a distantiating irony, as when it first occurs in conjunction with the Moa Point sewerage outfall (Wedde, p. 18). It is as though Mansfield, impressionist and miniaturist, 'European' and female, has nothing that is not incongruous to say of a Pacific inundated with 'shit'.

It may be because Mansfield has for so long figured the ambivalence of *white* colonial identity, that neither Wedde nor Frame can be altogether sure of her utility in the more difficult negotiation *within* the Pacific, among ex-colonial and colonised peoples, where the capitalist powers of the Pacific Rim (America, Japan) occupy a horizon once filled by the imperial nations of Europe. Whether it will ever be possible for Mansfield to 'come back', and in what ghostly incarnation, I cannot say.

The tombstone placed by Middleton Murry at the site of Mansfield's grave at Avon, in France, is inscribed with some lines of poetry:

> BUT I TELL YOU MY LORD FOOL
> OUT OF THIS NETTLE DANGER
> WE PLUCK THIS FLOWER
> SAFETY

Unattributed, these lines may be invested with the eloquence of anonymity: a sentiment, originating nowhere, spoken by no-one, they may be absorbed silently into the reflections of the pilgrim. Or they may be read as an utterance belonging to the woman whose grave they cover, opening the possibility of a posthumous dialogue or exchange between the bystander and the dead writer. Or we might recall them as a quotation, doubly displaced from their origin via their citation in Mansfield's journal—a favourite quotation, a motto, words she had made her own. Her own—and yet not her own: Shakespeare's. The tombstone of Katherine Mansfield condenses, in this epitaph, the ambiguities of authorial identity, and there the pilgrim, or passer-by, may be haunted by the presence of a series of ghost-writers: Murry, Mansfield, Shakespeare . . . or no-one 'in particular'.

*Postscript:* This essay would now have to take account of Witi Ihimaera's 'Maori response' to Mansfield's stories (*Dear Miss Mansfield,* Viking, 1989); unfortunately a copy of Ihimaera's collection reached me after the essay had left my hands.

*Linda Hardy, September 1989*

## Notes

1. Claire Tomalin, *Katherine Mansfield: A Secret Life* (New York: Knopf, 1987), pp. 18–19.

2. Thomas Carlyle, *On Heroes, Hero-Worship, and The Heroic in History,* in *Complete Works,* Vol. 1 (Boston: Estes and Lauriat, 1884), pp. 340–1.

3. Roland Barthes, *Mythologies* (London: Cape, 1972), *passim.*

4. Restored and opened to the public by The Katherine Mansfield Birthplace Society in Mansfield's centennial year.

5. Henry James, *Selected Tales* (London: Everyman, 1982), pp. 287, 306. Further references in text.

6. I borrow this convenient summary from Marjorie Garber, *Shakespeare's Ghost Writers: Literature as Uncanny Causality* (New York: Methuen, 1987), p. 9. Further references in text. I

am indebted to Garber's book for alerting me to James' story, and for providing a suggestive discussion of it.

7. Homi Bhabha, 'The Commitment to Theory,' *New Formations,* No. 5 (Summer 1988), p. 19.

8. In addition to the essay on 'The Commitment to Theory', I am using: 'Of Mimicry and Man: The Ambivalence of Colonial Discourse', *October,* No. 28 (1984), pp. 125–133; 'Signs taken for Wonders: Questions of Ambivalence and Authority under a tree in Delhi, May 1817,' in *Europe and its others,* vol. 1, ed. Francis Barker et al (Colchester: University of Essex, 1985), pp. 89–106; and 'Remembering Fanon', the foreword to Frantz Fanon, *Black Skin, White Masks* (London: Pluto, 1986), pp. vii–xxvi. Further references in text. My intention is not to represent Bhabha's work, but to draw on it, where it provides terms that are useful to my own discussion of questions of cultural 'identity' and 'identification'. I do not (here) address the issue of racial difference, which is intrinsic to Bhabha's analyses of colonial discourse. I use the term 'colonial' in a more restricted sense, to designate a relation within 'English' culture, whereby the metropolitan English are differentiated from *white* New Zealanders (or Americans).

9. The poems are published in, respectively: *Antipodes New Writing,* ed. Louis Johnson (Antipodes Press, 1987), p. 45; Fleur Adcock, *Selected Poems* (Oxford: O.U.P., 1983), p. 118; Anne French, *All Cretans are Liars* (Auckland, A.U.P., 1987), pp. 17–19.

10. Cf. Simon During, 'Postmodernism or Postcolonialism', *Landfall 155,* vol. 39, no. 3 (Sept. 1985), pp. 366–380. Further references in text.

11. Janet Frame, *Living in the Maniototo* (London: The Women's Press, 1981).

12. See especially, Jonathan Dollimore and Alan Sinfield eds., *Political Shakespeare: New Essays in Cultural Materialism* (Manchester; Manchester U.P., 1985); and Malcolm Evans, *Signifying Nothing: Truth's True Contents in Shakespeare's Text* (Brighton: Harvester, 1986).

13. Gayatri Spivak, 'Displacement and the Discourse of Woman', in *Displacement: Derrida and After,* ed. Mark Krupnick (Bloomington: Indiana U.P., 1983), pp. 169–195. Further references in text.

14. Ian Wedde, *Symmes Hole* (Auckland: Penguin, 1986).

15. I am here recycling some remarks I made at a Stout Centre symposium on *Symmes Hole* at Victoria University in 1987. But similar comments have been made by Ian Wedde, more recently, in a reply to Cynthia Brophy's article on 'Ian Wedde and Postmodernism': *Landfall 167,* vol. 42, no. 3 (Sept. 1988), p. 349.

16. Patricia Parker, *Literary Fat Ladies: Rhetoric, Gender, Property* (London: Methuen, 1987), p. 13. Further references in text.

# THE CRAFT OF THE STORY

◆

# "With Deliberate Care": The Mansfield Short Story

## RHODA B. NATHAN

A skilful artist has constructed a tale. He has not fashioned his thoughts to ac-
commodate his incidents, but having deliberately conceived a certain *single effect*
to be wrought, he then invents such incidents, he then combines such events,
and discusses them in such tone as may best serve him in establishing this preconceived effect. If his very first sentence tend not to the outbringing of this effect, then in his very first step has he committed a blunder.

———Edgar Allan Poe[1]

Assessing an artist's contribution to his field is tricky at best. The subject
must be scrutinized in his time, in the universal terms of his craft, for his original work, and in his derivative techniques. He must be measured against
other practitioners of the genre, those past and contemporaneous. His good
work must be separated from his mediocre efforts, his early work from his last.
Periods of productivity must be weighed against arid patches in his creative
landscape. Katherine Mansfield is not exempt from such treatment. Even the
negative critical judgment of colleagues and critics in her day must be coun-
terbalanced against favorable reviews. For example, her friend and fellow
writer Virginia Woolf wrote this about her less than half a year after her death:
"While she possessed the most amazing *senses* of her generation . . . she was as
weak as water when she had to use her mind." The truth or falsity of Woolf's
harsh criticism must be balanced against the indisputable fact that Mansfield's
short stories continue to be anthologized frequently in our own day while
those of her more distinguished rival do not.

In one area, at least, the task of critical evaluation is simplified by the author's scope. Mansfield, unlike most of her colleagues, wrote only short stories.
Although she began one full-length novel, *Juliet,* she abandoned it. Notes in
her *Journal* hint at another novel extending the New Zealand theme and tentatively called *Karori,* but nothing came of it. Her contribution was to the short
story only. She is probably unique in this distinction. There is scarcely a writer
of her time, and few since, who did not go on to write at least one novel.
Whether she lacked the broader powers and vision to construct novels, as
some of her detractors have hinted, is moot. The stories she left are sufficient.
Berating her for failing to write at least one distinguished novel is analogous

From KATHERINE MANSFIELD by Rhoda B. Nathan. Copyright © 1988 by Rhoda B. Nathan.
Reprinted by permission of The Continuum Publishing Company.

to faulting the composer Hugo Wolf, master of the German art song, or lied, for not writing at least one celebrated opera.

The conventionality of Mansfield's fiction—the term is not used in a pejorative sense—is another useful factor in limiting and directing critical evaluation. All the standard elements of the short story are present in most of her fiction in harmonious balance, much as the well-crafted stories of specialists such as J. F. Powers, J. D. Salinger, and John Updike during their *New Yorker* period. When Mansfield was experimental, it was primarily in her composition of a handful of spoken monologues, often constructed as flashbacks that reveal character, plot, theme, and tone. Her best short stories, "Miss Brill," "The Garden Party," "Bliss," and "The Dill Pickle," among others, are narrated conventionally from a subjective point of view. They comprise integrated elements of the short story as it has been defined by theorists such as Poe in the nineteenth century and Frank O'Connor in the twentieth.

The single most palpable quality permeating Mansfield's stories is her perfectionism. The exemplary New Zealand cycle, episode by episode, through character and conflict, develops with single-minded intensity a unified theme of complex family life recollected through a veil of nostalgia for an unrecoverable past. The action varies but the setting is remarkably unified, supporting the controlled tone of longing. In its finished state, "Prelude" offers the clearest evidence of its author's relentless polishing. Compared to "The Aloe," the original version of the story written just a year earlier, the final story shows clear evidence of "much reshaping and rewriting," according to Murry's introductory essay.[2] In short order the reader discovers the truth of Murry's description of the first version as "less perfect," and agrees with him that the belated publication of "The Aloe" many years after Mansfield's death does indeed offer the "more critically minded a unique opportunity for studying Katherine Mansfield's method of work."

It is instantly apparent that the intensity and compression of "Prelude" are achieved through the author's conscientious, almost excruciating, editing. Throughout the text single words have been altered, excised, and shifted from one position in a given phrase to another. The casual reader might not notice these seemingly insignificant changes, but the text in its entirety shines more brightly as well as gaining in precision. For example, in "The Aloe," when Lottie and Isabel are put to bed in the new house, they lie down "back to back, just touching." In "Prelude" Mansfield amends the phrase to "their little behinds just touching." The second description is anatomically more correct, as the children's bodies are curled into a ball, and only their backsides touch in that position. If they were "back to back," they would be envisioned in a ramrod posture, unnatural if not downright impossible. Further, there is something childlike and vulnerable about the second phrase that is well suited to the affectionate tone. In contrast, an amendment away from the infantile is made in one of the most dramatic sequences in "Prelude." When the handyman has decapitated the duck for that evening's dinner, Isabel, watching the headless body waddling along the path, squeals, "It's like a funny little railway engine." The original version in "The Aloe" was "It's like a funny little darling engine." The seemingly trivial substitution of the word "railway" for "darling" is more calculated than would appear. If indeed "these kids are real," as one impressed reader was to observe, their "realness" has to be consciously convincing. Isabel was the eldest and the most likely to frame a simile or analogy drawn from her own experience. The adjective "darling" would be more suitable to the young inexperienced Kezia.

Other judicious editing excised repetitions of descriptions such as the portrait of Mrs. Fairchild that appears twice in the original. The character of Stanley Burnell is softened into a more sympathetic figure in "Prelude." In "The Aloe" he is described as a "ginger whale," but in "Prelude" his ginger whiskers remain but he is drawn in more human terms. By and large, it is a small alteration but a shrewd one. It would be difficult for the reader to imagine the beautiful and fastidious Linda Fairfax agreeing to wed and bed with a "ginger whale."

There are larger slashes in "Prelude" that are instantly apparent. "The Aloe" contains an eleven-page digression that Mansfield removed, probably to incorporate it into a third part of the cycle. In the interest of preserving a unified point of view she did well, because in these pages her narrative shifts suddenly from Kezia, who has been the center of sentience, to her mother. It justifies Linda's detachment from her children through a flashback showing her devotion to her father, her longing to travel, and her resistance to marriage. But the section, which is indeed illuminating, threatens the integrity of the whole and Mansfield wisely excised it. Ultimately Linda's point of view is presented more subtly in "At the Bay," where she and the other adults are the focal figures. One other lengthy episode involving Linda, Beryl, and another sister at afternoon tea, probably designed to show the differences in the three Fairfax sisters—and surely a reflection of the Beauchamp sisters—is scrapped and saved for another story. It is preserved in an unfinished state in the *Scrapbook*.

Character in fiction is either "flat" or "round," which is to say stereotypical or multidimensional. Mansfield's characters are primarily round—that is, faceted and like "real" people. Even her minor characters—Pat the handyman in the New Zealand stories, Cyril, the wastrel grandson in "The Daughters of the Late Colonel," and the "literary gentleman" in "The Life of Ma Parker"— have distinguishing qualities that individualize them. For example, when Hennie, the small boy in "The Young Girl," buries his face in his cup of chocolate, his childish delight is captured in his emerging nose, on which hangs a blob of cream. His wholehearted immersion in the treat and his subsequent scarlet-faced humiliation frame him as an endearing child and as an effective counterpart to his sullen sister.

Mansfield can sink a character through a single word and still avoid creating a "type." The irritating genteel nurse in "The Daughters of the Late

Colonel" has a laugh "like a spoon tinkling against a medicine glass." In "Marriage à la Mode" Moira Morrison's arty triviality is encapsulated in her painstaking analysis of the appearance of her legs under water, which she concludes are "the palest mushroom colour" to everyone's edification. A Russian cigarette case pulled from the pocket of the unnamed former lover in "The Dill Pickle" tells the story of his selfishness. It is a mute reminder of a broken promise and its owner's callousness. His onetime companion is reminded of their dreams of traveling to Russia together and of his fulfilling their shared plans without her. His guilelessness in offering her the Russian cigarettes in their native case and his hearty recounting of his adventures make his unthinking cruelty memorable.

As well plotted and carefully constructed as Mansfield's stories are, they cannot be confined to any single tradition. The two recognized historical "schools" are the psychological tradition laid down by Poe and the socially observant tradition associated with Maupassant. There are other categories as well: the plotted and the plotless story, the stories of initiation, symbolist stories, and so on. The categories are both endless and overlapping, but Mansfield, like other writers, cannot be confined to any single formula, whether it be the rules set down in Poe's "The Philosophy of Composition," Chekhov's social realism, James's psychological realism, Maurice Maeterlinck's symbolism, or Joyce's stream-of-consciousness technique. Her short stories do not fit into any single framework, any more than does the entire body of Cheever's or Updike's short fiction. As she wrote, she continued to experiment. "Her First Ball" and "The Garden Party" are stories of initiation. They are also fully plotted psychological studies. They have some traces of social realism. "Je ne parle pas français" is a rare attempt at plotlessness. The story "Psychology" is not psychological but a fragment designed to produce a "single effect" with "deliberate care" in obedience to the Poe formula.

Mansfield's youthful devotion to Wilde's brittle comedy surely is responsible for the languid witty dialogue in "Marriage à la Mode" and "Bliss." "A Cup of Tea" is the perfect magazine story. It has all the elements required for a popular journal, including a surprise ending. Its slick commercial "feel" does not negate the perfection of its construction. "Poison" and "Taking the Veil" are effective demonstrations of the symbolist credo that states of mind are most effectively conveyed through concrete images. "The Child Who Was Tired," Mansfield's most feeling and conscious tribute to Chekhov's social realism, is actually far removed from Chekhov's profound but abstract social concern. Chekhov's "Sleepy" expresses his outrage against societal abuse; it is a protest against oppression and close to political socialism. Mansfield's version is more personal and limited. Her sad story focuses on the child herself as a helpless object of personal cruelty, not social injustice. Her symbolical ending of the child's dream gives the story a twist towards the allegorical. Chekhov's has none of that fanciful quality. His story is close to being a documentary of social inequity, its central character serving as an instructive example of victimization.

The following stories reveal still other debts to traditional sources even as they bear the stamp of her originality. "The Canary," a first-person oral monologue to an unseen audience, is reminiscent of Poe's unidentified monologists whose narrations explain their current emotional state in terms of their past history. The speaker in "The Canary" begins: "You see that big nail to the right of the front door? I can scarcely look at it now and yet I could not bear to take it out." The story is secondary to the tone and symbolism. The speaker is highly agitated. Her loneliness is implicit in her attachment to the dead bird, itself a symbol of her yearning for beauty in a pinched sterile life. The nail that held the suspended cage remains on the wall as a symbol of her loss and pain. It is a nail driven through her heart.

In "The Garden Party" also, literal objects have a wider symbolic reverberation than their limited objective selves. When Laura Sheridan leaves the party on her mission to the bereaved family of the dead man, "the kisses, voices, tinkling spoons, laughter, the smell of crushed grass [are] somehow inside her." As the great lawn recedes in the distance behind her, a newer unfamiliar reality is symbolized by the narrow dark lane leading to the cramped hovel in her line of vision. "Women in shawls and men's tweed caps" supplant the trailing skirts and frock coats of the afternoon's festivities. Shadows replace sunlight, silence follows the murmur of tea-party chatter. Only the large garden-party hat, still propped on Laura's bowed head, remains constant, worn in the dusk as a badge of penance as it has been worn in daylight as a symbol of her corruption.

Socially observant narrative that makes its point through irony in the Maupassant tradition may be discerned in plotted stories like "Sixpence." Mrs. Bendall, a timid woman, is bullied by Mrs. Spears, an overbearing visitor, into goading her husband to whip their beloved small son. The child's infraction is minor, and the family is loving and forgiving. Under subtle criticism of her "superior" neighbor, Mrs. Bendall is made to feel incompetent and lax in the performance of her "moral" duty, introducing a new and ugly atmosphere into her peaceful home. Her tired husband, angry at being assaulted by his overwrought wife to do *his* duty as a man, whips the child, and is crushed by the child's forbearance in his pain and humiliation. The worm has been found in the apple. The child forgives his parents but their happiness has vanished.

The irony of the serpent's evil in this Eden is implicit in the throwaway remark about Mrs. Spears's own "exemplary" sons. They have indeed attained perfection in deportment, but it is noted that they prefer to play outside their home, in the toolshed, behind the kennel, even in the trash bin. Her callers marvel that "you would never know there was a child in the house." Mrs. Bendall then recalls that "in the front hall of her neighbor's well-run home, under a picture of fat, cherry old monks fishing by the riverside, there was a thick dark horsewhip."

The contrast between Mrs. Spears's "soft sugary voice" and the repeated brutal whippings that have shaped her children's decorum is an irony lost on

Mrs. Bendall but not on the reader. Her visitor's hypocrisy in the execution of her maternal obligation is yet another unnoted irony. Does Mrs. Spears administer the whippings? Of course not. It would be unseemly for a mother, the symbol of nurture. Who does it then? Why, their father, of course—the respected symbol of authority. Ironically, just as Mrs. Bendell, under the influence of her persuasive friend, is working herself up to persuading her husband to inflict corporal punishment on his beloved child, he "staggers up the hot concrete steps. . . . hot, dusty, tired out," and spoiling for a fight. He needs no convincing. "He felt like a man in a dark net. And now he wanted to beat Dicky. Yes, damn it, he wanted to beat something." The story ends on yet another ironic note. The beaten child, holding up his face in forgiveness, wipes out the father's rage and accepts the sixpence offered him in penance by his father, who is now beating himself for his unprecedented act of brutality.

This is a story crammed with irony. Whereas little Dicky Bendall makes his small mischief in the open, Mrs. Spears's model sons do theirs secretly, away from the bullwhip. In the arena of conflict the tables are turned and turned again. The timid mother is ironically stripped of authority in her own home and is forced into violating her principles. The "superior" guest is exposed as inferior in human terms. All the plotting of the two women to force the man to an act abhorrent to his nature proves to be unnecessary. He has come home in a brutalized condition and was ready to assault someone. "Sixpence" is withal a touching story in its understanding of frailty and the ironies of interpersonal maneuvering for power. The symbols of the omnipresent whip, the sugary voice, and the sixpence coin are effective emblems of control and subordination. It is worth noting that Mansfield must have taken Chekhov's observation about "props" in the theater seriously and adapted them to her own use of symbols. His remark that the audience may be sure that the gun hanging on the wall in the first act is bound to go off in the third is applicable to Mansfield's use of emblems, from the first mention of the tight headband on Mr. Bendall's head to the angry pucker left by his hat when he beats his child at the end.

Mansfield culled her characters from all levels of society, from the privileged station of the Sheridans to the shabby rooms of Ma Parker, from New Zealand to the Continent, from the beefy Germans of the Bavarian Alps to the fleshless spinsters of post-Victorian England. Her themes are manifold. Like all serious writers she tried to tell the truth about her own life, the life about her, and the imagined life. In short, her contribution to the genre of the short story cannot be neatly categorized. She ranged far and she roamed freely, but certain conclusions may be drawn as a guide to the basic constants in her fiction.

Her technique is invariably efflorescent—from the bud to the flower, so to speak. She begins with a single incident or clue, such as the landlady's intrusion into Miss Ada Moss's room in "Pictures" or the unblemished weather on the day of the Sheridans' garden party. We take it on faith that the tension in the story will derive from that single bit of information. She rarely disappoints us. She builds on the fragment layer by layer, establishing the mood—almost always an atmosphere of psychological tension—until the small incident, which Henry James used to call the "germ," unfolds into crisis, climax, and resolution.

A prevailing mood of tension is a constant in Mansfield's work. Unlike her literary model Chekhov, who did little by way of manipulation after he laid down the bare facts of his characters' troubles, she adds, alters, and controls. Miss Brill's illusory self-image is shattered when she is forced to confront herself in a glass held up by her detractors. Laura Sheridan's innocence is destroyed step by step in a calculated series of ugly events that oblige her to confront the truth about her insulated life and the tragedy of others. The unsuspecting lover in "Poison" is forced by an insignificant incident—his mistress's casual inquiry about the mail—to face her inconstancy. Unrelieved tension is the governing mood of the allegorical "A Suburban Fairy Tale," generated by irremediably obtuse parents and their imaginative child.

In stories such as "Prelude," "Her First Ball," "The Doll's House," and "Bliss," tension is created through a contrived alternation between fulfillment and deprivation, satisfaction and yearning, self-indulgence and guilt. Their total sustained effect is one of delicate balance between opposing forces that prevail to the end. Witness the unanswerable question Bertha asks at the end of "Bliss" and Laura's unfinished question at the end of "The Garden Party." They keep their climate of mystery to the very end because their underlying tension is unresolved.

Finally, Mansfield's stories are usually "good reads." Their meaning is accessible even to the general reader who does not wish to trouble his head about the hidden significance in her fables. Their point of view is almost uniformly subjective, and their dialogue is witty, often sparkling. Her narration is economical and colorful, rarely discursive. Her most successful stories are those that originate in her own childhood, her love affairs and marriages, and the characters she encountered in her travels. Her least successful stories are static monologues such as "A Married Man's Story" and "The Lady's Maid." Taking Brander Matthews's definition of the true short story as "complete and self-contained" and marked by a "single effect," we may conclude that Mansfield's finest stories have the requisite "totality" of the prescription.[3] If she failed to rise to James's mandarin detachment, or Chekhov's selfless compassion, or Joyce's psychological intensity, she left at least two dozen works of brilliance and polish and a smaller number of perfect stories.

## Notes

1. Poe's statement of his theory of the short story appeared in *Graham's Magazine,* May 1842, in a review of Hawthorne's collection of short stories titled *Twice-Told Tales,* and was

later revised to appear as "Tale-Writing" in *Godey's Lady's Book,* November 1847. The epigraph is taken from the 1842 version.

2. Although "The Aloe" was written in 1916, it was not published in her lifetime. Murry published it posthumously in 1930, explaining that it could not be included in *The Short Stories of Katherine Mansfield* because "it repeats, in a less perfect form, the material of 'Prelude.'"

3. Brander Matthews, "The Philosophy of the Short Story," *Short Story Theories,* ed. Charles E. May (Athens: Ohio University Press, 1976).

# From Notebook Draft to Published Story: "Late Spring"/"This Flower"

## GILLIAN BODDY

When Virginia Woolf reviewed the first edition of *The Journal of Katherine Mansfield* in the New York *Herald Tribune* she wrote:

> It is not the quality of her writing or the degree of her fame that interest us in her diary, but the spectacle of a mind. . . . We feel that we are watching a mind which is alone with itself, a mind which has so little thought of an audience that it will make use of a shorthand of its own . . . or, as the mind in its loneliness starts to do, divide into two and talk to itself. Katherine Mansfield about Katherine Mansfield.[1]

Lytton Strachey's reaction to the *Journal* was that it was, "quite shocking and incomprehensible. I see Murry lets out that it was written for publication—which no doubt explains a good deal. But why that foul-mouthed, virulent, brazen-faced broomstick of a creature should have got herself up as a pad of rose-scented cotton wool is beyond me."[2]

Before discussing some of the story drafts that are contained in the notebooks and loose-leaf papers of Katherine Mansfield, it is useful to look at the relationship between these and this published journal which was collated from this material.

After working through her many diaries, notebooks, and exercise books, Murry compiled *The Journal of Katherine Mansfield* in 1927. In 1939 he culled more material from the same sources to produce *The Scrapbook of Katherine Mansfield,* now out of print for some time. In 1954 he published an enlarged "Definitive Edition" of the *Journal.* This did not, however, include all the material from the *Scrapbook,* nor was it 'definitive' in the usual sense of including all available or relevant material.

Many who had been close to Mansfield (including D. H. Lawrence) regarded Murry's publication of these private papers and letters, as well as unfinished stories which she had not intended for public scrutiny, as posthumous exploitation, and unjustifiable betrayal. Murry's stated intention, however,

This essay was commissioned especially for this volume. Permission to quote from the manuscripts of Katherine Mansfield granted by the Alexander Turnbull Library.

was to demonstrate and establish what he described to Sydney Waterlow as "the uniqueness of her genius. Her infallible vision is something apart in this age of spoof. I don't think there's much chance of her being really recognised for what she is."[3]

He had collected her private papers assiduously. Two weeks after Mansfield's death her sister Chaddie wrote to their older sister Vera, explaining that Murry intended to publish her unpublished stories, papers, and poems as soon as possible: "He says he has a most unique & fascinating collection which will make a tremendous stir. . . . Constable will take anything he can give them of K's they all think she is a genius & no modern woman like her."[4] She herself could also be seen to have provided some justification for his decision. In 1922, at the Chateau Belle Vue in Sierre, Switzerland, she had written him a letter, to be handed to him only after her death: "All my manuscripts I leave entirely to you to do what you like with. Go through them one day, dear love, and destroy all you do not use. Please destroy all letters you do not use. Please destroy all letters you do not wish to keep & all papers. You know my love of tidiness. Have a clean sweep Bogey, and leave all fair—will you?"[5] In a will, written and witnessed a little later, she was more explicit: "I should like him to publish as little as possible and to tear up and burn as much as possible. He will understand that I desire to leave as few traces of my camping grounds as possible."[6]

Far from tearing up or burning as she herself had done so often, Murry constructed a literary jigsaw. The ironic result is that we know much in intimate detail about the private life of a writer who assumed some 20 different names during her lifetime, who considered herself "a secretive creature to my last bones,"[7] and had even advised Murry "dont lower your mask until you have another mask prepared beneath."[8]

Virginia Woolf privately admitted that she was dismayed at reading the private fears of the friend she had considered so "inscrutable," the writer whose work had been "the only writing I have ever been jealous of."[9] Publicly, no doubt thinking of her own diaries, so frank and caustic in their discussion of others, Virginia Woolf commented: "There is no literary gossip, no vanity; no jealousy."[10] Had she been able to read the notebooks and letters in her entirety, she might well have felt otherwise. In his edition of the *Letters,* for example, Murry omitted several unflattering references both to Virginia and her sister Vanessa.

Murry himself took pains to point out the *Journal* and the *Scrapbook* were not two carefully kept volumes as such, but had been compiled by him from a number of sources: diaries, notebooks, story outlines, drafts for letters, jottings and fragments of all kinds. So while Mansfield may have described herself for her former editor Orage as "a selective camera," this was probably an even truer description of Murry, his editorial selections being determined, of course, by his own attitude. For though he invented nothing and ordered and dated the material as well as he could, he too was an artist in his way and one with a particular image to project. As a result he found it necessary to give greater form and/or coherence to many passages (particularly the untidier ones) through paragraphing, through the occasional alteration of tense, and through tidying up the punctuation. Mansfield frequently omitted the apostrophe in her notebooks, used the ampersand often but inconsistently, and it is impossible at times to distinguish whether a punctuation is a full stop, comma, or dash. In general what Murry attempted to do was to give shape and sense to what was often an uninterrupted flow of words. Inevitably these alterations to the original created changes of emphasis and a loss of spontaneity.

Murry also omitted passages which he felt might reveal too much of the rebellious, restless side of her nature, while those who had known her were protected by the omission of their names. Sometimes he indicated such omissions by initials, a common convention, but of others there is no indication. So where a passage from the Wellington section of Murry's edition has: "I have been tediously foolish many times, but that is past," the manuscript originally read: "I have been tediously foolish many times, especially with Oscar Fox and Siegfried Eichelbaum but that is past."[11] (The former was a handsome young cricketer, the latter one of the group of young men who regularly attended the same balls and parties as the Beauchamp girls. Described as "our local poet" for a debate at Victoria University College in April 1907, Eichelbaum later translated an article about her from a German paper and kept a dance programme initialed by the young Katherine Beauchamp on his office wall for many years.)

From Mansfield's long passage on "Suffering" written at the Isola Bella in Menton in 1920, Murry omitted such bitter comments as: "the knowledge that Jack wished me dead . . . the horrible vulgar letters of this woman . . . and his *cruel* insulting letter about 'no physical attraction' (!!) 'I think she is in love with me' and so on—were they necessary? He now claims his right not to suffer on my account any more."[12]

On reading these notebooks one can only guess at the pain Murry must nevertheless have experienced when he first read them after her death; the frank disclosure of her experiences, thoughts, and feelings—many of them so well concealed during the ten years of their relationship. In a letter to the South African writer Sarah Gertrude Millin, he himself suggested that he might abandon the projected publications because of his own reactions of despair and depression. In some ways it is surprising that he did not omit more of the material: the descriptions of her feelings for Francis Carco while making love to Murry, for instance, or her frank comments about Murry's lack of consideration and understanding.

While it is possible from an emotional point of view to understand some of his editorial decisions, what is much less tenable is Murry's frequent failure to acknowledge omissions, apart from occasional notes that lines have been omitted because of illegibility. In other words, readers have generally assumed for some sixty years that they are reading the complete text of an entry for a particular day, when in fact much may have been left out that would alter the passage.

Therefore, although the 1954 edition described itself as "Definitive," it was still highly selective, and to work out a systematic rationale for its omissions, other than the kinds already discussed, presents considerable difficulties.

Many of the numerous pages omitted were from early notebooks written during adolescence, so Murry may well have judged these to be of merely marginal interest. To many, however, they would be of substantial value in considering the development of her writing, thematically and stylistically, and particularly as further revelation of an enigmatic and complex personality. This entry, for instance:

> August 15th
> She unpacked her box and then went into the sitting room. She was in a curious vague mood, wandering about the room, opening the piano, striking a chord and shutting it again, taking up the books from the table and putting them back, staring out of the window at the heavy grey rain and the poor draggled line of houses, then staring at her own reflection in the glass over the mantelpiece. She leant both her elbows on the mantelpiece, and spoke to the face. "Well" she said, "are you feeling better—less insufferably bored, less hideously foolish. And in a week's time you will be married to him."[13]

The passage continues with the heroine questioning her intention to marry and the "exquisite respectability" she is forced to endure. While this certainly cannot be described as great literature, its handling of the theme of the woman's role, the characteristic habit of the central character talking to her mirror-face, and the stylistic feature of a series of present participles, all look forward to her mature work. The passage also has similarities to others in the published *Journal* and to the autobiographical fiction "Juliet."

The many notebooks and loose pages that provided the basis for the *Journal* and *Scrapbook* contain numerous drafts of stories: some are unfinished, some apparently abandoned after a few pages, some begin with mere jottings that are then followed by a fuller account. Some she returns to several times but never completes. Mrs. Sheridan of the *The Garden Party* is the subject of several such false starts.

Some of these notebook drafts and notes have been published, for example "Juliet" in the Turnbull Library Record. Others were tidied up, typed, and published during her lifetime or shortly after her death.

Any student of Mansfield's writing would find it fascinating to compare these notebook drafts with the final published stories. Very often the alterations are minimal, the elimination of an adjective or adverb, a tighter grammatical construction, alterations to punctuation such as the elimination of exclamation marks. It is as if the story was already predetermined, even heard, in her head before being written on the page, and so requires little alteration. Often it is only in the last paragraphs that the alterations, emendations, and crossings out become more numerous. It seems at such times as if this writer who so detested "plotty"[14] stories was searching to find thematic resolutions without too overt a conclusion. She endeavored instead to leave the story sufficiently open-ended for the reader's imagination to complete, believing "that the characters have a life of their own . . . that they 'go on' long after the book is finished."[15]

At other times, the handwriting reveals much about the creative process. *Je ne parle pas francais,* for example, sprawls across the pages, the large letters looping the words together. Even with the printed text alongside the manuscript defies the reader's comprehension. It seems an urgent race against time, the writer's pen driven by the picture of that inner world she and her characters inhabit, an inner world that was clearly often more real than the external reality surrounding her.

Mansfield believed that writing was a process of selection, that "there must always be a sacrifice." "Prelude," published by Virginia and Leonard Woolf in 1920, evolved from "The Aloe," probably begun in Francis Carco's Paris apartment in 1914 and continued in 1916 in Bandol, in the south of France, after her brother's death. Vincent O'Sullivan's parallel edition of the two provides a fascinating comparison and a real insight into the writer's craft. The printed text of "Prelude" is almost thirty pages shorter than "The Aloe."

The episodes Mansfield omits include a longer section with the Nathan children; a section set in the store on the journey to Karori, which is rather similar to the description in "The Women at the Store"; a lengthy description of Mrs. Fairfield and Linda; and Linda's reminiscences of her father and her meeting with Stanley Burnell. Part of this is reworked in "At the Bay," and there is also a tongue-in-cheek description of a social given by the Liberal Ladies Political League that provides an entertaining comparison with "Her First Ball." Also dropped in a lengthy account of Mrs. Fairfield, Beryl, Linda, and their sister Doady Trout (married to Jonathan of "At The Bay"), much of which reveals her frustration with married life, and the tensions between Beryl and Linda. Beryl's interior life is also far more clearly revealed though a hairbrushing scene shared with Nan Fry, which is clearly based on incidents in Mansfield's relationship with Ida Baker. Finally, whereas "Prelude" ends with Kezia stealing into Beryl's room with her dirty little calico cat, to play with Beryl's make-up, caught on that margin between childhood and womanhood, the unfinished original continues with a crossed-out section about Stanley. The effect of these excisions is to sharpen the focus on Linda and Kezia, and the central relationships of the story.

Similarly, the draft manuscript of "The Doll's House" includes an amusing passage describing the drunken Mr. Kelvey.

> Mr Kelvie [*sic*] was the scandal of the neighbourhood. He drove a fish cart, when he was out of prison or out of hospital. For he was such a hopeless drunkard that the wonder is that he could sit in the cart at all—he never did for long. Horses have scent of the Devil's plan . . . & there he lay angry & swearing until the police could get to remove him.

Such omissions ensure that the focus remains on the Kelvey children, and Kezia. The crossing out of Wellington, in the opening sentence to replace it with the less specific, anonymous "town"—"When dear old Mrs Hay returned to town"[16]—indicates the writer's awareness of the dangers and limitations of autobiographical fiction. The effect is to change the localized setting to one of greater universality. The story's colonial location, with its raw clay banks and the paddocks, remains an integral element, but the plight of the Kelveys cannot be simply dismissed as a problem peculiar to Wellington, just as the significance of the lamp cannot be limited by time or place.

An even more significant alteration of just one word occurs in "The Fly," written in Paris in 1922 shortly before Mansfield's death. Desperately ill, weak, worn out by massive doses of radiation therapy, disillusioned by the war and by her own relationships, Mansfield composed a tale that is surely the final indictment of so much that she despised. Perhaps it is she who is the fly, too exhausted to struggle any longer, finally crushed by an implacable, omnipotent fate. Perhaps the fly is Europe, destroyed by the juggernaut of war; perhaps it is her final denunciation of those men who, she believed, had so often failed to meet her needs, to understand or communicate their feelings. If so the Boss is the last in a long line of "pa-men," which evolved from early characters such as Andreas Binzer in "A Birthday" to Stanley Burnell in "Prelude" and "At the Bay." This feeling is increased when one sees that in the manuscript of "The Fly" among her papers in the Newberry Library, she had originally called that dominant, inarticulate, but manipulative central figure "the Manager." This has been carefully crossed out throughout, and "the Boss" neatly superimposed. The Manager becomes the Boss: as with the shake of a child's kaleidoscope the whole story shifts, the shades of meaning are now subtly different. The tone has changed, the reader's mental picture of this man "who could not remember" alters slightly but significantly as it clicks into place. He now assumes the coarser boss-like characteristics of Mr. Wilberforce of the unfinished earlier "Juliet."

> Mr Wilberforce, a tall grey bearded man, with prominent blue eyes, large ungainly hands and inclining to stoutness. He was a general merchant, director of several companies, chairman of several societies, thoroughly commonplace and commercial.[17]

Far more dramatic and thought-provoking, however, are the differences between "Late Spring" and the posthumously published story "This Flower," included by Murry in *Something Childish and Other Stories.*

A *Journal* entry indicates that "Late Spring" was begun in January 1920 at Ospedaletti. This was during a particularly difficult period just after Murry returned to London following a frustratingly unsuccessful Christmas visit. The Casetta Deerholm at Ospedaletti, which had seemed idyllic a few months before, had become unbearable; the sea below was no longer beautiful in the sunlight, and the dark waves now echoed her own blackness and despair. There was a postal strike and letters from England were displayed. Estranged from Ida Baker, her only companion, unhappy, ill, and isolated, she felt these were the worst days of her life.

On 11 January she wrote "The Man Without a Temperament," an extraordinarily polished piece of writing under any circumstances and, it seems, a bitter denunciation of Murry's inability to meet her needs. Like "Late Spring" and "This Flower," it contains a doctor's diagnosis of a woman's state of health, and the resulting implications for her life's central relationship.

On that day Mansfield commented, "I thought of everything in my life, and it all came back so vividly—all is connected with this feeling that J. and I are no longer as we were. I love him but he rejects my *living* love."[18] The next day after posting the story to Murry, who was in fact flattered by it, she noted bleakly, "When will this cup pass from me? Oh, misery! I cannot sleep. I lie *retracing* my steps—going over all the old life before. . . . the baby of Garnet's love."[19]

The manuscript for "This Flower" is in the Alexander Turnbull Library, Wellington. It is written in a small exercise book which was begun on 17 December 1919, apparently the day after Murry's arrival at the Casetta, although his note disputes this. The passage on the preceding page is a further comment on the story's origin.

> "Any children?" he asked, taking out his stethoscope as I struggled with my nightgown.
> No, no children.
> But what would he have said if I told him that until a few days ago I had had a little child, aged five and 3/4—of—indeterminate sex. For some days it was a boy. For two years now it had very often been a little girl . . ."[20]

(This refers to the preceding passage in which she blames Murry for killing their love, which she describes as a "love child.")

The page on which "This Flower" begins is headed "Hotspur. Henry IV. Act II Scene III." The published version has some minor alterations from this manuscript, particularly in punctuation.

The Newberry Library manuscript in Chicago entitled "Late Spring" is the shorter and presumably earlier version; the pages are torn from another small exercise book. A *Journal* note of 5 January 1920 indicates that she was reading *Henry IV* and continues, "Started my story 'Late Spring'. A cold bitter day. Worked on Tchehov all day and then at my story till 11 pm."[21] Not surprisingly, the manuscript begins with Hotspur's lines from *Henry IV*, which were later inscribed on her gravestone, and retained in "This Flower": "But I tell you my lord fool, out of this nettle danger, we pluck this flower, safety."

If she was drawing on her own experiences as an autobiographical basis, for this story, too, there are at least two possible past events that could have been central to her thinking during this period in which she was so bleakly "thinking of the past always."

The first of these is described by Ida Baker in *The Memories of LM* and supported by Pierre Sichel in his biography of Modigliani. While at Bishop's Flat in 1910, Mansfield became involved with "a young man, hardly more than a boy . . . and very handsome. He brought her lovely presents . . . a tiny painted Russian village . . . At Christmas he brought a beautiful, tiny decorated tree."[22] (This incident is one of the pivotal memories in "A Dill Pickle," published in the *New Age* in 1917 and revised for inclusion with "The Man Without a Temperament" in *Bliss*.)

Soon after moving to Clovelly Mansions early in 1911, Mansfield apparently realized she was pregnant, and wrote repeatedly to the young man, now known to be Francis Heinemann, but without receiving a reply. In April 1911, when LM's father asked her to visit, she felt confident that Mansfield was positive about her expected child. Having opened a bank account to help with the baby, she sailed for Rhodesia and returned in September to find "no baby and a closed bank account. We never discussed the matter, obviously it had all been horrible. I am sure that Beatrice Hastings had been in some way responsible."[23] While others such as Antony Alpers doubt the veracity of this event, it could be that such events in the late spring of 1911 were part of her memories early in 1920. (It has also been suggested that Mansfield may have become pregnant by J. M. Kennedy of the *New Age,* with whom she was briefly involved.)

An earlier period would have provided similar memories. Pregnant by Garnet Trowell, and just married to George Bowden, she had been taken to Bad Worishofen by her mother early in 1909. When, where, and by whom her pregnancy had been diagnosed is not clear, but she had been certain of it by late April, and on this occasion, too, she knew she had been deserted by her lover. In June she miscarried.

Understandably, the stories that subsequently evolved from her German experience denounced the double standard that allowed men to enjoy sexual pleasures while the women suffered the consequences. "Late Spring"/"This Flower" is an attempt at a more sophisticated treatment of the theme.

Placed in the context of January 1920, the writing of "Late Spring"/"This Flower" is particularly interesting. It was clearly a time when—alone, depressed, and disillusioned with love—Mansfield was haunted by the past, a past she had often wished to dismiss simply as "experience" but which she acknowledged, contained "waste—destruction too."[24]

Cherry Hankin has suggested that "the story . . . renamed *This Flower* by Murry" reflects Mansfield's "desperate sense that her illness was destroying her relationship with Murry. The protagonist is a young woman who, similarly ill, enters into a pact with a sleazy doctor to conceal from her husband the truth about her fatal disease. The husband is only too anxious to be deceived."[25]

A comparison of the two versions suggests a rather more complex situation and raises some interesting questions about Mansfield's intentions in the story and her ability to manipulate perspective, thus affecting the reader's response. It also provokes discussion about Mansfield's view of women and their place in society.

Before looking closely at the ideas and the ways they are conveyed in "Late Spring"/"This Flower," it is interesting to see how the two versions differ, although the central subject, presumably the concealed diagnosis of an unmarried woman's pregnancy, is common to both. In "Late Spring" the story is constructed so that it is the doctor who wins our sympathy to some extent; he is the victim of the young couple who collude against him. It is he who feels the woman's voice is "untroubled"; the senses that he is being manipulated by this couple and wonders, "Why the hell had they knocked him up?" It is he who feels mocked by the barrel organ; it makes him feel like "a sick cat," and it is he who escapes almost in a panic. In "This Flower" complete paragraphs remain unchanged, and yet the perspective is very different. It is the woman who has our compassion; she is now clearly the victim, and the men are now united in an unspoken age-old male conspiracy. Although she seems somehow removed, we empathize with her; she sees the doctor giving her "a strange leering look." As she asks him to help her conceal the truth from her lover, we agree that he is an "odious little toad." When the barrel organ begins to play outside, its sound mocks her—reminiscent of an early poem written late in 1908 during Mansfield's love affair with Garnet, when she described its sound as "the drunken, bestial hiccoughing voice of London."[26]

Such a comparison raises a range of questions, many having to do with the story's narratology and perspective. Why, particularly in that situation, did she even consider manipulating the reader's responses in such a very different way in "Late Spring."

Certainly Mansfield stated on several occasions that the writer was androgynous, that she herself was a writer first and a woman second, and early in her life she had several times declared herself to be "child woman more than half man." Some early published work appeared under male noms de plume such as Julian Mark, and she also signed herself Karl Mansfield on at least one occasion. When we consider her use of a variety of narrative forms, direct and indirect, in constructing her stories and characters, her skill in providing multi-personal viewpoints and the constant shifts of perspective, "Late Spring" is perhaps not so surprising. Nor was this the only time she clearly endeavored to align the reader's sympathy with the male rather than the female.

Did she contemplate briefly making him one of those male characters, like the young lover in "Poison" or William in "Marriage à la mode" who are manipulated by women? Always in her writing she felt free to employ different voices, to construct stories and characters that provide a varied perspective. In Switzerland in 1921 she wrote of the relationship between lovers, "We are neither male nor female. We are a compound of both. I choose the male who will develop and expand the male in me; he chooses me to expand the female in him."[27] Perhaps something of this is reflected in such writing.

Certainly the constructs of gender, male and female, were not for her fixed terms. Although she clearly saw women as entrapped psychologically, biologically, and economically, and often presents them as such, she was not a polemicist and at times may seem inconsistent in her view.

In the margin of "Late Spring" Mansfield has written "Too much description!" but the changes in "This Flower" are far more than simple excisions for the sake of conciseness and stylistic improvement.

"This Flower" begins with an additional two paragraphs, which give greater depth and credence to the central female character. The setting of her room is described in a brief accumulation of detail that heightens the contrast with the doctor, a "strange little figure" with a "shady Bloomsbury address."

The physical description of Roy included near the end of "Late Spring" is removed, but two important sections are added. In the first, his lover, watching the doctor he has obtained "squeezing and kneading his freshly washed hands," remembers Roy saying, "My darling ... we'd better have an absolutely unknown man just in case it's—well, what we don't either of us want it to be . . . Doctors *do talk.*" His characterization is further developed in a later change. Whereas "Late Spring" ends with Roy pulling Marina down into a deep chair, "This Flower" ends very differently. Roy leans against her shoulder "as though exhausted. 'If you knew how frightened I've been,' he murmured. 'I thought we were in for it this time. I really did. And it would have been so—fatal—so fatal.'" In this way he indicts himself with his own words, joining those characters like Andreas Binzer in "A Birthday," who "suffers" his wife's labor, and Stanley Burnell, who expects his sugar spooned into his tea and his slippers put out. While blaming women for their insensitivities, he is oblivious of their needs and feelings.

In "Late Spring" the doctor is puzzled by Roy's suggestion of champagne ("was this a joke") and "stammers" his reply "with immense effort," while his subsequent reply is only just "brought out." These phrases are deleted from "This Flower," and consequently it does not occur to the reader that the doctor experiences any misgivings or embarrassment. He has indeed been shown through her eyes to be an "odious toad" who gives her "a strange, quick leering look," his fingers "shaking" as he removes his stethoscope. He answers her "huskily," "Don't you worry my dear . . . I'll see you through." No longer does he snatch his hat and leave in panic, but simply shakes her hand and leaves.

A comparison of the draft manuscript with the published story provides an interesting example of the ways in which a single situation can be developed, the different voices and perspectives. Finally, however, it is the published story to which the reader returns. Through a number of judicious changes Mansfield eliminates any sympathy she may originally have intended for the doctor. It is the woman, now without a name and consequently more universal, who has become the victim. The two men exploit her in different ways, yet they are linked in an unspoken male conspiracy.

For Mansfield, didactic writing was fatal to art; she could not tell anyone "bang out,"[28] and her rule was not to "grind an axe" but "to single out . . . bring into the light."[29] In "This Flower," therefore, she presents a situation of social injustice, one in which, ironically, a young woman is driven into an alliance with a man she despises in order to deceive her lover. Intuitively the reader perceives that to do otherwise would have been impossible.

## Notes

(ATL denotes the Alexander Turnbull Library, Wellington)

1. Virginia Woolf, "A Terribly Sensitive Mind." Review of *The Journal of Katherine Mansfield*. New York *Herald Tribune*, 18 September 1927. Reprinted in *Virginia Woolf, Women and Writing*, ed. Michele Barrett. (New York: Harcourt Brace Jovanovich, 1980.)

2. Michael Holroyd, *Lytton Strachey* (London: Penguin Books, 1968), vol. 2, 358.

3. J. M. Murry to Sydney Waterlow, 11 July 1921, MS Paper 1157/4 (ATL).

4. Charlotte (Chaddie) Pickthall (Beauchamp) to Vera Mackintosh Bell (Beauchamp), January 1923, Bell Collection MS Papers 3985/3 (ATL).

5. To J. M. Murry, 7 August 1922, MS Papers 4000/40 (ATL).

6. Katherine Mansfield's will, 14 August 1922, Public Record Office, London.

7. To L.M., 21 March 1922. *The Letters of Katherine Mansfield*, vol. 2, ed. J. M. Murry (London: Constable Books, 1928).

8. To J. M. Murry, late July 1919, MS Papers 4000/10 (ATL).

9. *The Diary of Virginia Woolf*, vol. 2, ed. Anne Olivier Bell assisted by Andrew McNeillie (London: Harcourt Brace Jovanovich, Ltd. 1978), 227.

10. Virginia Woolf, "A Terribly Sensitive Mind," in *Virginia Woolf, Women and Writing*, 186.

11. Notebook 39 (qMS 1243) June 1907 (ATL) *Journal*, 15.

12. MS Papers 4006/8 (ATL).

13. Notebook 39 (qMS 1243) 15 August 1907 (ATL).

14. To Dorothy Brett, 12 November 1921, *The Letters of Katherine Mansfield*.

15. A Review of *Old People and the Things that Pass*, in *Novels and Novelists*, ed. J. M. Murry: 1930), 125.

16. Notebook 41 (qMS 1277) (ATL).

17. Notebook I (qMS 1242) (ATL).

18. *Journal of Katherine Mansfield, 1904–1922*, ed. J. M. Murry (London: Constable Books, 1928).

19. Notebook 22 (qMS 1265) (ATL).

20. Notebook 26 (qMS 1264).

21. *Journal*, 191.

22. *Katherine Mansfield: The Memories of LM*, Ida Baker (London: 1985), 62.

23. *Katherine Mansfield: The Memories of LM*, 62.

24. To J. M. Murry, 31 October 1920, *Katherine Mansfield's Letters to John Middleton Murry 1913–1920,* ed. J. M. Murry (New York: Knopf, 1951).

25. *Something Childish and Other Stories,* Centenary Edition introduced by C. A. Hankin (1988), 20–21.

26. "The Winter Fire," Newberry Library.

27. *Journal,* 259 (manuscript Newberry).

28. To J. M. Murry, 16 November 1919, *Katherine Mansfield's Letters to John Middleton Murry 1913–1922,* ed. J. M. Murry.

29. *Journal,* November 1921.

# Katherine Mansfield

## S. P. B. MAIS

By the death of Katherine Mansfield England loses one of the most sensitive of all her modern writers. She was a pioneer in the art of telling a short story about nothing and creating an unforgettable atmosphere. Many people to-day, C. E. Montague leading them, are demanding a return to the short story of plot and action. With this Miss Mansfield had no part nor lot. She stuck to her own interpretation of life. Her last volume, *The Garden Party,* was typical. She had her husband's trick of "painting-in."

This sort of thing: "Behind them an old sheep-dog, his soaking paws covered with sand, ran along with his nose to the ground, but carelessly, as if thinking of something else. And then in the rocky gateway the shepherd himself appeared. He was a lean, upright old man, in a frieze coat that was covered with a web of tiny drops, velvet trousers tied under the knee, and a wideawake with a folded blue handkerchief round the brim. One hand was crammed into his belt, the other grasped a beautifully smooth yellow stick. And as he walked, taking his time, he kept up a very soft, light whistling, an airy, faraway fluting that sounded mournful and tender." Now this shepherd has nothing to do with the plot. He occurs in a short story where, you would think, there was not much room for digression. Most of us do not describe the principal characters in our novels with such meticulous care as this. We are too busy hacking away at what to us are the essentials to bother about the externals.

Middleton Murry and Katherine Mansfield by very careful microscopic analysis of the externals drive by implication far deeper into the essentials than we ever get. They seem to paint for the sake of painting, for the beauty of the scene, and the combined effect suddenly shakes you. You have seen something far behind.

One feels as if Miss Mansfield were being wheeled round a confined space. Every trifle assumes a portentous significance. When Beryl pushed the sugar over to Stanley instead of helping him, we are made to feel that we are on the crater of an active volcano. Soon Stanley goes. "Oh, the relief, the difference it made to have the man out of the house." Healthy people thrive on friction. Not so the Beryls of Miss Mansfield's quiet, ordered brain. The only thing of moment that happens during that lazy day at the bay is late at night when Mrs Kember's husband cajoles Beryl to come out with him as far as the

Reprinted from S. P. B. Mais, *Some Modern Authors* (London: Grant Richards Ltd., 1923), 108–113.

fuchsia bush. No sooner had she got there than she wrenched herself free. "Then why in God's name did you come?" asks the man. The story closes on that note.

There are still people who cavil at stories which do not contain two murders, a divorce, three incredible long arms of coincidence, and a journey from China to Peru. They should take a strong dose of Tchehov. They like every picture to tell a story. Miss Mansfield prefers every story to be a picture. The ordinary man's brain is so addled that he does not willingly pay homage to something new even when it is good. It takes him half a lifetime to see Rubens and Rembrandt. It isn't likely that he will appreciate Manet, Monet, Piccasso, or Gauguin.

"At the Bay" is as nearly perfect a description of a day by the sea as I have ever read. There is colour, there is quiet movement, there are real people. The curtain goes up at dawn and goes down in the dead of night. There is no climax, no fifth act: it is, like Tchehov, a slice of life. It implies everything: it says very little. It is, if you like, a Pharaoh's dream. Miss Mansfield does not insult us by acting as Joseph in the interpretation thereof. It takes even a little time to discover that Stanley's wife is not Beryl, but Linda. We ought to have known that from the fact that he did not say good-bye to her, as a punishment.

There is absolute reality in those children playing, in Lottie's difficulty with stiles and her hopeful, "I'm getting better . . . aren't I?" No, no; she isn't consumptive—how you magazine-story readers do jump at things!—better at climbing things. The nearest to rebellion is Jonathan, "like an insect that has flown into a room of its own accord," in his city office wanting to get out— nearest that is, after Beryl, who wanted a lover so much that she invited that "cold little devil" from the disgusted Harry Kember.

Better than "At the Bay" is "The Garden Party."

Laura is like her creator—she stops everywhere to wonder at the beauty of things, the friendliness of the workmen putting up the marquee, the "darling little spots" of sun on the inkpot, the lovely lilies. Suddenly we are surprised, horrified. Something has happened. A man has been killed outside the front gate.

"Not in the garden?" interrupted Laura's mother. "Oh, what a fright you gave me!" she said with relief when she heard the truth. There is all Miss Mansfield in those two sentences, contempt for the whole craziness of life. After the party is over Laura is sent down to the man's cottage with a basket— crumbs of comfort. She sees happiness and beauty in the dead man's face. The inexplicable marvel of life hits her straight in the face. You would scarcely select a meagre plot like this for a story meant to live, would you? And yet—it is impossible to get this vision of Laura out of one's head.

There are readers who prefer "The Daughters of the Late Colonel," worrying whether to give his top-hat to the porter, worrying about the nurse who "was simply fearful about butter!"—Nurse Andrews and her "Lady Tukes" who "had such a dainty little contrayvance for the buttah . . . quite a gayme";

Nurse Andrews, with her laugh "like a spoon tinkling against a medicine-glass" (how apt and excellent a simile), and "I hope it's not very bittah marmalayde"; worrying about the funeral arrangements, "A good one that will last," as if they were buying a nightgown; worrying whether Cyril ought to have the Colonel's watch—Cyril who, on his last visit, had to tell his deaf grandfather how fond of meringues his own father was. Poor, dear, laughable, inconsequent, pathetic old spinsters! Little mercy do you get from your surgical creator. Miss Mansfield is not afraid of her scalpel. She loves the operating theatre. She laughs immoderately at the curious viscera she disembowels. It is all rather horrid, this ruthless dissection, but oh, how it is clever! What art!

Then there is Mr Dove, escaping from the flower-snipping dragon of a mother to propose to Anne, taken to see her pigeons—"the male, bowing and bowing, and away she runs . . . and that's their whole life," laughing away his proposal "it's your check t-tie . . . we'd be like Mr and Mrs Dove," miserable at his misery. "Don't pity me, little Anne." The doves "coo" as he goes. He looks back. "Come back, Mr Dove," said Anne. A masterpiece of understatement.

And "The Young Girl," in her blue dress, her blue eyes, her gold curls, standing on the steps of the Casino, petulant and bored, not allowed to accompany her mother inside, taken off to tea by friends, sulking and rude all the time, taking four cakes after refusing any, aching to get away by herself, left where she was found, her dark coat open, her soft young body in the blue dress like a flower emerging from its dark bud.

I know no picture of a spoilt darling so complete as this—and all compressed into ten pages.

Then there is Ma Parker, in service when she was sixteen, married to a baker, seven of her thirteen buried, "If it wasn't the 'ospital it was the infirmary, you might say," a long history of ulcers, consumption, spine trouble, "emigrimation," "going wrong" . . . and then little Lennie, her grandchild, "taking him to the cemetery, even, never gave him a colour; shake up in the bus never improved his appetite." Even Lennie died, and Ma Parker tries to escape to cry. "There was nowhere." The whole history of generations of charwomen is summed up in her appalling cry: "What have I done? What have I done?"

"Marriage à la Mode" is less tragic. William returning to the exquisite freshness of his wife, for weekends; William, sentimental and hungry for her, tired of work, condemned to meet her only among a riotous mob of poets: Dennis with his jejune, heavy "A Lady in Love with a Pine-Apple," "A Lady with a Box of Sardines," "A Lady reading a Letter"; Bill Hunt with his infuriating: "Well, William, and how's London?" Bill and Dennis, both with enormous appetites, rude, flamboyant, all over the place. "I hardly seem to have seen you," says Isabel, as she sees him off again. He writes to her: "My darling, precious Isabel . . ."—a love letter. She reads it aloud to her congregation: they were almost hysterical. She has eventually the grace to see her vileness. "God forbid, my darling, that I should be a drag on your happiness. . . ." She determines to write. They call to her to go out to bathe. She goes.

There is "Miss Brill" and her fur, sitting by the bandstand watching the lovers, the beautifully dressed boy and girl: "The hero and heroine, of course, just arrived from his father's yacht." Her heart warmed towards them. The girl giggled: "It's her fu-fur which is so funny. It's exactly like a fried whiting." Miss Brill goes home to cry: she even forgets to buy her Sunday treat—a slice of honey-cake at the baker's. Yes; the art is there all right, but Miss Mansfield must have been ill when she wrote "Miss Brill." It is not healthy to dwell on the Miss Brills so lovingly as she does. There is the same low devitalised note in "The Singing Lesson." Miss Meadows, with that letter tearing at her heart—"I feel more and more strongly that our marriage would be a mistake"—keeping on, keeping on, called away from the appalling task to receive this telegram: "Pay no attention to letter must have been mad bought hatstand to-day.—Pasil"; returning to tell her class to sing less dolefully: "It ought to sound warm, joyful, eager." Oh, these spinster schoolmistresses and their passionate aches! How we sigh for the full-blooded lusts of Somerset Maugham's heroes.

There was the reunion of Janey and her elderly husband after her long voyage, when she tells him of the stranger who died "of heart" in her arms the night before. "Spoilt their evening! Spoilt their being alone together! They would never be alone together again." Surely this is where Miss Mansfield topples over on the farther side. This is the hectic flush. She is seeing things awry. She is better when she is merely describing. "Bank Holiday" is better by far, more full of life, colour and action than any of the myriad pictures of it. She returns to her pathos in the picture of old M'Reave, the forgotten father surrounded by his ideal family. "What had all this to do with him—this house and Charlotte, the girls and Harold . . . they were strangers to him. Life had passed him by. Charlotte was not his wife. His wife! . . ." His thoughts go back (all Miss Mansfield's characters think back, never forward—a sure sign of their lack of health) to a time when a little pale face was lifted to his and a voice breathed—"Good-bye, my treasure." She was his wife, that little pale girl— and all the rest of his life had been a dream.

Miss Mansfield had power all right; she dreamt dreams, but they were hot-house dreams. She was a tender, sensitive plant, exotic, meant for the hothouse. To let her loose in England seemed cruel. We are so much more fond of the windy heath plants; we prefer the down orchis to the frail lily, the wild rose to the garden one.

# Allusion, Image, and Associative Pattern: The Answers in Mansfield's "Bliss"

## Judith S. Neaman

"Bliss," Katherine Mansfield's most ambiguous story of initiation, poses many problems, some of which have plagued critics for years.[1] What is Bertha's "bliss"? What does Pearl Fulton represent and to what does her name allude? Why a pear tree instead of an apple? Was Bertha really cold? Is she hysterical? Would *would* "happen now"? Why, at the end of such a crisis of disillusionment, is the pear tree "as lovely as ever"?[2] Yet, Mansfield has answered these questions in the story by interweaving allusions to two sources—the Bible and Shakespeare's *Twelfth Night*—whose major role in "Bliss" has been largely ignored. These allusions not only answer the crucial questions but they also illuminate the meaning of the tale, while simultaneously charting the anatomy of its creation.

Perhaps because critics have seen all too clearly the obvious tree of knowledge blooming in Bertha's garden,[3] none seems to have detected the first overt clue to the thematic importance of the Bible. It appears as a familiar echo in the words, "for the first time in her life, she desired her husband" (p. 349). In Genesis 3.16,[4] among the punishments God metes out to the disobedient Eve is: "thy desire *shall* be to thy husband and he shall rule over thee." In visiting this affliction on Bertha at the very moment that she first experiences marital lust, Mansfield appears to indicate an easy familiarity with the long tradition of biblical commentary. According to both Augustinian and Talmudic interpretation, lust entered the world as a result of the Fall. "Bliss" pursues the theme by chapter and verse.

In the same chapter of Genesis, directly before and after Eve is first sentenced to a life of connubial desire, there are numerous phrases so similar in image and content to those Mansfield uses in "Bliss" that the story seems to be almost a gloss upon the Bible. The evidence that the words of Genesis were deeply embedded in her mind appears in a diary entry of February 1916 in which she remarks that, since she came to Bandol where she wrote "Bliss" in 1918, she has "read the Bible for hours on end." She wrote here of wanting to know "if Lot followed close on Noah or something like that. But I feel so bitterly that they ought to be part of my breathing."[5] Furthermore, during the

Reprinted from *Twentieth Century Literature* no. 2 (September 1986):242–254.

same brief period of feverish work in which she produced "Bliss," Mansfield wrote the story "Psychology," in which a character playfully remarks, "And God said; 'Let there be cake. And there was cake. And God saw that it was Good.'"

In both stories, words or phrases from Genesis appear in brief but they set up reverberations which guide the reader's responses to all subsequent events. In "Bliss," Mansfield's more indirect use of the words of Genesis is overbalanced by a closer attention to the intent and material of it. In fact, the parallels between the biblical work and Mansfield's story are so close that the words of Genesis may inform the reader not only of what Bertha's life was before the day of her maturation but also of what her future will be. In this way, Genesis answers Bertha's last question: "What is going to happen now?" If, like a modern Eve,[6] Bertha has lived in a fool's paradise which is destroyed by knowledge, then she and Harry are destined to repeat, in a modern form, the fate of their first models. This is so much the case that God himself answers Bertha's question about her future. What "will happen now" is that Bertha will desire only her husband and he will dominate her life. "In sorrow [she] will bring forth children" while Harry, who has tasted another form of the forbidden fruit of knowledge, will now eat "the herb of the field" in sorrow . . . all the days of [his] life" (Gen. 3.17). Bertha's future children will be begotten in sorrow and bitterness born of the knowledge she has gained. She will know that Harry sees her as Adam saw Eve after the Fall—as the "mother of all living" (Gen. 3.20), which, in Mansfield's punning paraphrase, is Bertha A' Young.

Because Mansfield's metamorphosis of this chapter of Genesis remains so close to its source, readers will not be surprised to find still further relations between the words and events of "Bliss" and those of Genesis 3. The garden in which this young pair learns the consequences of sin is populated not only by a wondrous tree about which all knowledge revolves but also by animals. Following her own associative thought patterns, Mansfield has linked the denizens of the first garden and the Youngs' garden with the behavior of Adam and Eve and also with Darwinian evolutionary theory. The Norman Knights are also compared to first forebears by their name but they are now the forebears of English society. Mansfield compares them to monkeys, for "Face" Knight, so perfectly matched with her mate, "Mug," is wearing a funny little coat with monkeys all over it and looks "like a very significant monkey."[7]

Here the reader must wonder if Mansfield is using her Bible to deliver a post-Darwinian stab at English society. The rest of Face's outfit echoes Adam's and Eve's first attempt at clothing, which they made in Genesis 3 to hide their shame at their newly discovered nakedness. As God created for Adam and his helpmeet "coats of skins" (3.21) to help them "hide their shame," so Face wears a yellow silk dress that looks like "scraped banana skins" and she is later described as "crouched before the fire in her banana skins" (p. 343). No sooner has Bertha noticed the simian clothing and physiognomy of her guest than

Mr. Norman Knight remarks on parenthood and paradise, "This is a sad, sad fall! . . . When the perambulator comes into the hall—. . . ." The final link of this particular chain which seems to stretch through Mansfield's mind from Bible to "Bliss" is forged when Norman Knight remarks in parting, "You know our shame" (p. 343).

Gradually, it becomes apparent that the innocent Bertha and her hairy mate, an emotional primate if there ever was one, have opened their house and garden to beasts from a number of literary fields. Eddie Warren, his last name removing all doubt of his nature and habitat, is a stuttering rabbit. Terrified by his taxi ride, dressed in white socks and an enchanting white scarf to match, Eddie speaks in conversational tones and patterns that often echo those of Alice in Wonderland's white rabbit.

Pearl has been called a moon to Bertha's sun[8] and a parallel to the pear tree, which has also been identified with Bertha and Harry.[9] However, Mansfield's descriptions of pearl emphasize not only Pearl's lunar qualities (she is dressed "all in silver with a silver fillet binding her head" and her fingers, "like moonbeams, are so slender that a pale light seemed to come from them") but also focus the reader's attention on her "cool arm," "heavy eyelids," and "[mysterious] half smile."[10] Pearl is such an adept at enigma that everyone who encounters her assigns her another identity. Her conversation merely amplifies the mystery, for it is barely audible; she whispers and intimates. Bertha is not even certain what Pearl murmured about the pear tree or if she had guessed that Pearl said, "just that" (p. 347) when she looked out at the tree in the garden. Yet, it is Pearl who asks if there is a garden, Pearl whose "cool arm could fan—fan—start blazing—blazing the fire of bliss that Bertha did not know what to do with" (p. 344).

Enigmatic, dressed in scaly silver, full of whispers and murmurs, Pearl is infinitely tempting. Her lidded eyes conceal her passion for Harry. But she is secretive, intimating, cool-skinned and cool-souled, in other words, "the subtlest beast of the field" (Gen. 3.3). Thus, Bertha cannot see the truth until she glimpses the kiss. With that kiss, Bertha's innocence falls and her blissful illusions are destroyed. Only then does Bertha begin to see her mysterious friend in a new light. No longer the distant and enchanting moon of Bertha's hopes, Pearl now appears to her hostess to resemble the seductive gray cat who had provoked a shiver of sexual revulsion in Bertha earlier in the evening. One critic believes that Bertha's new vision of Pearl is evoked by a horror of the bestiality she perceives in her former love, since she considers that Pearl's purity has been sullied by the heterosexual behavior Bertha abhors.[11] But, if we see Pearl as a serpent, the common Talmudic and patristic interpretation of the serpent's role in tempting Eve seems far more appropriate a view.

According to this traditional understanding of the Bible, it was the serpent's seduction of Eve that first induced her to lust for Adam. Pearl's seduction of Bertha awakens Bertha's lust for her own husband. In fact, Bertha's image of Pearl followed by Eddie, as the seductive gray cat followed the black cat, is so distorted a view of Eddie that it makes little sense if Pearl is not seen as the serpent. Mansfield has, after all, painted Eddie as effeminate at least and homosexual at most, hence hardly a likely candidate for seduction by a woman. Clearly the "grey cat, dragging its belly . . . [as it] crept across the lawn, and a black one, its shadow trail[ing] after" (p. 341), reminds Bertha, and is intended to remind readers of "Bliss," of the serpent of Genesis which God punished by decreeing that it should crawl on its belly.

In every possible way, Pearl fulfills the role of the serpent in the garden. She is one of those beautiful women with "something strange about them" (p. 341) with whom Bertha is always falling in love. Like the rest of these temptresses, she is strangely secretive while seeming to be *so* open and Bertha is certain that they "share" something. Until Bertha gains the carnal knowledge which will be revealed to her, she is incapable of understanding that what they share is a lust for Harry. By the time Bertha realizes that the "bliss" with which she has burned is sexual desire and then sees that desire mocked (all within moments), she has tasted the fruit of the tree and found it a bitter dessert to the banquet of sight and taste she has laid for herself and her guests. That the discoveries which cause her so much pain should take place at a dinner party celebrated in a house with a flowering fruit tree is no coincidence.

Critics who have noted the importance of the imagery of food and eating in this tale[12] have ignored standard biblical associations among lust, fruit, and knowledge so clearly introduced in Mansfield's references to the food and eating which led to the Fall and lead to this fall. Bertha's first important act in the story is associated with these elements. The reader can see this link in her conflict between the enjoyment of temptation and her fear of succumbing to it. First she luxuriates in the beauty of the fruits she has bought for the party. Then, as she begins to fear the intensity she tries to repress it, crying, "No, no. I'm getting hysterical" (p. 339). As the tale and Bertha's growth simultaneously progress, the images of fruit and eating become less abstract and aesthetic and more active and hostile, for their connection with sex, flesh, and desire is clarified. Pearl rolls a tangerine between her luminous fingers. Harry loves the "white flesh" of lobster and "pistachio ices—green and cold like the eyelids of Egyptian dancers" (p. 345). The most emotionally evocative dish is made of eggs, reminding us of the embryonic Youngs and their new infant. In the forms of the new cook's omelettes and the "admirable soufflé," eggs become the crucial bonds in the marriage, inspiring Harry's praise which makes Bertha almost weep "with childlike pleasure" (p. 345).

After Bertha sees Harry and Pearl embracing, the nature of the imagery shifts from its focus on the food to be eaten to a new emphasis on the act of eating it. With this shift, the cannibalism which has been vaguely implied now becomes glaring.[13] When Harry kisses Pearl "with his lips curled back in a hideous grin" (p. 349), the reader, like Bertha, sees him devouring this delectable woman whose serenity he had earlier attributed to a "good stomach."

Hence, fruit becomes the visible apple of temptation (at one point in the story it is a tangerine turning in Pearl's fingers), and eating becomes the act of lust born of knowledge.

If fruits and flesh and the devouring of these represent desire and consummation as well as knowledge, then instruments and the music *not* played on them represent human bodies and sexual frustration and/or repression. Marilyn Zorn quotes Mansfield's letter of May 24, 1918, to Ottoline Morrell in which Mansfield cries, "What might be so divine is out of tune—or the instruments are all silent and nobody is going to play again."[14] For her purposes, Mansfield's succeeding words are irrelevant, for ours, they are central. "There *is* no concert for us. Isn't there? Is it all over? Is our desire and longing and eagerness, quite all that's left? Shall we sit here forever in this immense wretched hall—waiting for the lights to go up—which will never go up."[15] That is precisely what Bertha does at the end, of course, and it is Harry who "shut[s] up shop" or turns out the lights (p. 350). The musical refrains, though they occur only three times in the story, are central and the association between the fruits, the passion, and the music becomes increasingly specific. Music is "the food of love." Like the eating of the fruit, the playing of music, in this tale at least, is forbidden.

At the very outset of the tale, Bertha longs to dance, bowl a hoop, or "simply laugh at nothing" (p. 337) in the streets to express her bliss. "Oh, is there no way you can express it without being 'drunk and disorderly'? How idiotic civilization is! Why be given a body if you have to keep it shut up in a case like a rare rare fiddle?" (p. 337). Bertha's protest against the social requirement that she quash her ebullience becomes a louder aria when Nanny removes the baby from her embrace: "How absurd it was. Why have a baby if it has to be kept—not in a case like a rare string fiddle—but in another woman's arms?" (p. 339).

Finally, the fiddle—shaped like a pear and analogue, like the pear, to a woman's body—grows into a piano. Now fully aware and successfully trying to repress her thoughts and fears about that moment at which she will share the bed with a husband she suddenly desires, Bertha runs to the piano. "What a pity someone does not play! (p. 348). Indeed, Bertha's body has not been played, nor has she played. But now the fruit of carnal knowledge is about to be transmuted into the music of desire and the passion arising from both is about to suffer "a dying fall,"[16] a hidden pun on both the original fall from grace and the musical form of a "dying fall."

Associating the tree of knowledge with the food of love, Mansfield has subtly alluded to Shakespeare's *Twelfth Night,* a play she knew almost by heart, which celebrates the Feast of Twelfth Night or Epiphany. This reference creates a musical tie which binds all the images and references of "Bliss." Like the primary biblical allusion, this secondary Shakespearean allusion from the opening lines of the play not only recapitulates the theme of the Fall but, in so doing, explains in part why Bertha's beloved tree is a pear tree. The lines alone explain the musical references in "Bliss" and show the relations between love, food, and the shattering of Bertha's innocence:

> If music be the food of love, play on;
> Give me excess of it that surfeiting,
> The appetite may sicken and so die.—
> That strain again!—it had a dying fall!
> <div align="right">(<i>Twelfth Night</i> I.1.4)</div>

To observe Mansfield's whole train of thought, the reader must consider the entire play. *Twelfth Night* is a play of pairing and couples, of confused and confusing sexuality, of female love which leads to male-female unions. The pear tree of "Bliss" may be Mansfield's conscious or unconscious pun on pair, as Magalaner suggests, for the story is itself full of pairs and even possibly alter egos.[17] More important, Mansfield was interested throughout her life in "shadow selves," as she called them in a letter to Murry of 1920.[18] But the connections among the pairing and the pear tree and the structure and imagery of *Twelfth Night* run deeper still.

Large portions of the play take place in a garden which belongs to Olivia; there, to oblige Orsino, Viola courts Olivia. Viola is dressed as a man and Olivia does, indeed, conceive a passion for her, only to discover that she is not eligible. It is only after meeting Viola's twin, Sebastian, whom Viola had feared was dead, that Olivia transfers her affection to him and gives him a pearl as a love token. Viola, one cannot help noting, is closely related to the viol or fiddle to which Bertha compares her caged body, and Bertha is, at first, Pearl's wooer, sadly winning her for Harry. Thus, the theme of sexual confusion, of pairing of opposites, of "shadow selves" which Mansfield had cherished so long and embodied in her story "Sun and Moon," is everywhere in "Bliss." Bertha and Harry, Bertha and Pearl (Bertha's gift to Harry), the black and gray cats, Pearl and Eddie, and the spiritual twins, Mug and Face, recapitulate this favorite theme, one which Magalaner has noted.[19] In *Twelfth Night,* as in "Bliss," heterosexual love is the goal toward which the play strives and pairing is, after all, just another name for copulation, suggesting the lust which the fruit of the tree evoked.

But Mansfield's personal and aesthetic interests might have been far more effective than her reading in directing her choice of associations which formed "Bliss." Since girlhood, Mansfield had been both a cellist and a passionate lover of gardens and pear trees. Magalaner notes that, a year before she wrote "Bliss," Mansfield mentioned, in a letter to Ottoline Morrell, the importance of writing about a flower garden with people in it:

> walking in the garden—several pairs of people—their conversation—their slow pacing—their glances as they pass one another.
>
> . . . . . . . . . . . . . . . . . . . . . . . . . . . . . . . . . . . . . . . . . . . . . . . . . . . . . . . . . . . .
>
> A kind of, musically speaking, conversation set to flowers.[20]

In Murry's volume the letter immediately succeeding the letter to Ottoline Morrell was a note to Virginia Woolf about the sketch "Kew Gardens":

> Yes, your Flower Bed is very good. There's a still, quivering changing light over it all and a sense of those couples dissolving in the bright air which fascinates me—[21]

Of all the plants and trees in a garden, a pear tree was one of the most important to Mansfield and, at the time of the writing of "Bliss," she must have been thinking of it. Convinced that she was dying after the major hemorrhage which preceded the writing of this story by a few days, she thought constantly of her beloved brother, Chummie, who had recently been killed in the war. How often the two of them had sat on the bench beneath the pear tree in Tinakori Road in New Zealand and exchanged confidences. The new home which she and Murry first rented in England had a garden with a pear tree.

If these two types of sources, the biographical and the literary, consistently clarify Mansfield's use of images and symbols in the story, it would be illogical to ignore their potential influence upon the meaning of the story. Might they not also, central as they seem to be to Mansfield's consciousness at the time she wrote "Bliss," shed light on the relationship between Bertha and Pearl, for example? Upon this love, some critics of the story have dwelled far too emphatically. Mansfield's friend Virginia Woolf, for example, hated "Bliss," which she considered a shallow, maudlin tale of lesbianism. Later critics, like Nebeker,[22] have argued that Bertha's real goal is Pearl and that the sorrow she experiences is a result of Pearl's rejection of her for Harry. But nothing in the story suggests this. In fact, Bertha considers a bedtime discussion with Harry about what she and Pearl share. She imagines that this conversation will promote the spiritual understanding that will culminate in their first passionate physical union. In both *Twelfth Night* and "Bliss," youthful and innocent love is homosexual, as if both authors were chronicling the normal English schoolgirl stage of maturation. Heterosexual love is the source of the excitement, the growth, the real passion. Bertha's "crushes" on women are nothing new in her life, but her desire for her husband is both new and startling to her. Ultimately, Bertha's disillusionment over the impossibility of fulfilling her terrifying but exciting new desire matures her, for, through this loss of hope, she learns the sorrow of knowledge. Finally, it is Harry's "cool" voice which sets the seal on Bertha's fear and suffering.

Critics have cited Bertha's frigidity as the most incontrovertible proof of her lesbianism. After all, Bertha seems to have admitted to frigidity when she reflected that "it had worried her dreadfully at first to find that she was so cold" (p. 348). Despite the fact that readers conventionally accept a narrator's statements about him or herself, Bertha's self-evaluation, in this instance, cannot be taken at face value, no matter how afraid she is of her first real sexual encounter. Too much of her behavior argues against frigidity.[23] She experiences bliss, she resents the restrictions of a society that demands she "cage" her body, she enjoys her child's flesh and resents the woman who withdraws it from her, she aches to communicate her bliss to Harry though it is hopeless to do so. Bertha is highly sensual, glorying in the colors of fruit, in smells and sights, in feelings she can hardly contain. Surely these are not the responses of a frigid woman. The source of her conviction that she is frigid lies elsewhere—at the site of her "discovery" that she is so cold. It is the same source from which she learns that her desire to dance and sing, to hold her child are symptoms of "hysteria" (pp. 337, 338). That source is the society she identifies as the one which will call her "drunk and disorderly" (p. 338) if she gives vent to her passions; it is the "idiotic civilization" which demands that she imprison her feelings and her body. Harry and she have "discussed" her problem and he has explained that he is "different" (p. 348).

That Bertha's testimony about her own proclivities is not necessarily reliable is attested to by the sardonic tone, the desperate contradiction of her "Really, really—she had everything. . . ."[24] She is missing something—something that throws a pall over her marriage, and surely part of what she is missing is the understanding husband who would not hasten her off the phone, truncate her expression of feeling. Is the rest the passion she lacks or is it, as Mansfield's portrayal of Harry's callousness suggests, the passion he tells her she lacks? Throughout the story, Bertha acts the good wife and mother, observing the conventions of social respectability which pinion her whims and moods. The purveyors of these conventions appear in the forms of Nanny and Harry, yet she still emerges as a passionate woman. When she finally experiences the marital lust so "improper" in a good English matron, Bertha learns that the fruit of desire is death, for there is always a snake in the garden and the music of passion always suffers a "dying fall."

In marrying these sources to produce so carefully unified a story, Mansfield has disclosed the cast of her mind. Critics who have often pointed out how autobiographical the tale is, have neglected one major aspect of Mansfield's autobiography to which both her letters as well as her journals draw attention. Mansfield was devoted to Shakespeare and the Bible and was especially absorbed in Genesis at the time she wrote "Bliss." She spoke of her desire to know the Bible as well as she knew Shakespeare, whose words she recited constantly. In a letter to Murry, dated March 4, 1918, written only a week after completing "Bliss,"[25] Mansfield remarked to Murry: "My Shakespeare is full of notes for my children to light on." Magalaner noted a letter to Murry written just days before the completion of "Bliss" in which Mansfield speaks of her love for Murry in terms of food and eating.[26] She concludes, "'Hang there like fruit, my soul, till the tree die!' The tree *would* die."[27]

*Twelfth Night* is much on her mind. She notes often at this time that she is thinking of death (because of her own severe hemorrhage and Chummie's death), and these morbid thoughts intermingle with visions of gardens and food. She is filled with what she calls either "a rage of bliss" or bliss she longs to "share unexplained." Coincidentally perhaps, both the story and the title of "Sun and Moon" are conceived at this same time. The intellectual and emotional recipe for "Bliss" is revealed in these threads of thought recorded in Mansfield's journals and letters. How she regarded the conclusion of the story is not. Yet, the mystery of the concluding lines is solved by finishing the speech from *Twelfth Night* which both opens the play and sets the musical key of the story.

The work ends on an elegiac note: innocence dies quickly, but those who see their paradise fade survive. They live out long lives in a twilight sorrow, illuminated only by a memory of an irretrievable bliss.

> O, spirit of love, how quick and fresh art thou!
> That, notwithstanding thy capacity
> Receiveth as the sea, naught enters there,
> Of what validity or pitch soe'er,
> But falls into abatement and low price
> Even in a minute!
>
> (*Twelfth Night* I.1.9–15)

*Twelfth Night* tells us what has happened; Genesis tells us that what happened once will happen—again and again. The pear tree remains "as lovely as ever and as still" because, like the tree of knowledge, it remains firmly rooted in perfect Eden. Only Bertha is expelled. The lasting beauty and seductiveness of the tree sound an ironic note of contrast with the imperfection of the love they provoke and disclose. In the mythic world in which the pear tree, now forever out of Bertha's reach, blooms eternally without blemish, Eddie Warren's last words about the eternal quality of the lines: "Why must it always be tomato soup?" bear the wisdom of the Shakespearean clowns; they are set against an archetypal quest for knowledge which will always end in the "too dreadfully eternal" (p. 350) discovery that sweet fruit turns bitter when bliss fades. Accompanied by the unplayed music of *Twelfth Night* Bertha Young relives the epiphany of Genesis in a London garden.

### Notes

1. Saralyn R. Daly (*Katherine Mansfield* [New York, Twayne, 1965], pp. 81–83) refers to Bertha's "bliss" as the passion she and Pearl share for Harry, and agrees with Sylvia Berkman (*Katherine Mansfield, A Critical Study* [New Haven: Yale Univ. Press, 1951]) that Bertha is hysterical. Daly believes that what Bertha first "interprets . . . as 'bliss,'" but shortly calls "hysteria," has arisen because she knows her husband is having an affair . . ." (p. 83). She believes that Bertha is uncomfortable "before animal sexuality" (p. 83) and that Bertha "physically rejects Harry" (p. 86) as the cool pear-tree analogue, Pearl, does not. The pear tree remains lovely, according to Berkman, because it reveals the "immutability of natural beauty in the face of human disaster" (p. 107), whereas Daly (p. 87) points out that "such beauty offers no promise. . . ." She

asserts that Bertha knows what will inevitably happen. Pointing out how Mansfield uses auto-biography to reconcile parts of the self in her writing, Marvin Magalaner ("Traces of Her 'Self' in Katherine Mansfield's 'Bliss,'" *Modern Fiction Studies,* 24 [1978], 420) sees the characters as parts of the whole, so that the lead character is the moon, Pearl, and the tree is Bertha-Pearl. The woman becomes a compound of opposites, the "virginal matron and harlot" amalgamated in "Bertha-Pearl" (p. 420). In his longer study, *The Fiction of Katherine Mansfield* (Carbondale: Southern Illinois Univ. Press, 1971), p. 85, Magalaner again equates Pearl with the moon and Harry with the tree, maintaining that Bertha wants to stave off old age, hence she sees the pear tree as always in full bloom though it is "blasted in advance by Marvell's chill observations on time and eternity." Helen F. Nebeker ("The Pear Tree: Sexual Implications in Katherine Mans-field's 'Bliss,'" *Modern Fiction Studies,* 24 [1978], 545–51) sees "Bliss" as a tale of Bertha's homo-sexual love for Pearl and her disillusionment at the discovery of Pearl's passion for a man. Only what Nebeker calls the "bisexual pear tree" remains perfect. Marilyn Zorn ("Visionary Flowers: Another Study of Katherine Mansfield's 'Bliss,'" *Studies in Short Fiction* [Spring 1980], 173) calls the story a romantic "cry against corruption" of Shelley's "white radiance of eternity" and speaks of her inability to find someone with whom to share her vision which will remain locked in her forever unrealized passion (p. 147).

2. "Bliss," *The Short Stories of Katherine Mansfield,* ed. J. Middleton Murry (New York: Knopf, 1937), p. 350. All further quotations of the story are from this edition and will hereafter be cited in the text by page number.

3. Magalaner casually refers to Bertha as "a more mature Eve than Laura" and to Harry as a "modern Adam" whose fall causes Bertha's "expulsion from the fantasy garden" in *The Fiction of Katherine Mansfield,* p. 77. Berkman, *Katherine Mansfield, A Critical Study,* p. 252, notes that a "ruined Eden" is one of Mansfield's major symbols in numerous stories, especially "Bliss." Zorn, "Visionary Flowers," p. 146, also utilizes the Eden imagery noted by Magalaner. She speaks of the sun images in this story and of Mansfield's consistent use of images "which link the sun and moon" as "holistic" for Mansfield. "They suggest the earthly paradise, the condition of prelap-sarian innocence."

4. All biblical citations are from the King James Version.

5. *Journal of Katherine Mansfield,* ed. John Middleton Murry (New York: McGraw-Hill, 1964), p. 56. In this same entry, Mansfield writes that her Bible reading has continued "with the same desire" as that with which she has always read Shakespeare.

6. For Edenic imagery and references to innocence, see note 3, especially Zorn, who also mentions the prevalence of these images in the story "Sun and Moon," and Magalaner, *The Fic-tion of Katherine Mansfield.*

7. Face's coat is described on page 343 of "Bliss." Magalaner, *The Fiction of Katherine Mansfield,* pp. 82–84, writes of Mansfield's association of the couple with monkeys who mimic and imitate and are part of the gross animalistic aspect typical of the segment of society Mans-field scorns.

8. Magalaner, *The Fiction of Katherine Mansfield,* p. 78; Zorn, "Visionary Flowers," p. 146.

9. Berkman, *Katherine Mansfield, A Critical Study,* p. 195; Magalaner, "Traces of Her 'Self,'" p. 195.

10. "Bliss" (p. 345) actually refers to Pearl's expression as a "strange half smile."

11. Nebeker, "The Pear Tree," p. 546.

12. This imagery is especially noted by Magalaner, *The Fiction of Katherine Mansfield,* p. 82, and "Traces of Her 'Self,'" pp. 415–17, and by Zorn, "Visionary Flowers," pp. 146–47.

13. Zorn, "Visionary Flowers," p. 147; Magalaner, "Traces of her 'Self,'" p. 417, speaks of Mansfield's preoccupation with "consuming and being consumed."

14. Zorn, "Visionary Flowers," p. 144, is quoting from *Katherine Mansfield's Letters to John Middleton Murry: 1913–1922,* ed. John Middleton Murry (New York: Knopf, 1951), p. 211, hereafter cited as *Letters.*

15. *Letters,* pp. 144–45.

16. This phrase appears in *Twelfth Night* in the first speech about music as "the food of love," I.1.4, as quoted below in the text.

17. Magalaner, "Traces of Her 'Self,'" pp. 419, 422.

18. Magalaner, "Traces of Her 'Self,'" pp. 418, 419, quotes this letter (from *Letters,* p. 566) and cites both other letters and journal entries dealing with the same theme. He elaborates on people as parts of one another or "pairs," p. 421.

19. Magalaner, "Traces of Her 'Self,'" pp. 420, 421, and *The Fiction of Katherine Mansfield,* p. 79.

20. Magalaner, "Traces of Her 'Self,'" p. 421.

21. *The Letters of Katherine Mansfield* (New York: Knopf, 1936), pp. 70–72.

22. Nebeker, "The Pear Tree," pp. 547, 548.

23. Magalaner, *The Fiction of Katherine Mansfield,* p. 75, accepts Bertha's testimony that she is "getting hysterical" and that she is "cold." Yet, Bertha's perception of her own marital bliss is clearly one even she doubts. Why, then, should one accept what is clearly something she was told by either society or Harry (that she is hysterical in joy and cold in bed) as accurate? In fact, the extramarital joys Harry pursues may be justified, as Mansfield suggests in the story, by his belief that he is different. If Harry sees Bertha's behavior as license to pursue other women, she is fully justified and can be "cool," even claiming about Bertha "The woman gave me of the tree and I did eat." This fractured version of Genesis 3 is part of what the story is about.

24. See Magalaner, *The Fiction of Katherine Mansfield,* p. 76, and Zorn, "Visionary Flowers," p. 145, on the irony or delusion apparent in this line from page 342 of "Bliss."

25. *Letters,* p. 127.

26. Magalaner, "Traces of Her 'Self,'" p. 416.

27. Mansfield is quoting and elaborating on the line, "Hang there like a fruit, my soul, Till the tree die," from Cymbeline V. 5.236. Another work about confused identities, this Shakespearean play includes the character of Imogen who has just asked her husband why he rejected her. These admiring words are his reply.

# What Does Bertha Want?: A Re-reading of Katherine Mansfield's 'Bliss'

## PAMELA DUNBAR

'Bliss' (1918) is Katherine Mansfield's most controversial story. Criticism of it was first voiced by the writer's friends and contemporaries. John Middleton Murry found its 'mix' of satire and lyricism unsatisfactory; Virginia Woolf condemned it as the superficial product of an uninteresting mind; and T.S. Eliot, though affecting tolerance, damned it as being '[without] moral and social ramification', as 'handl[ing] perfectly [its] *minimum* material', and as being what he would call 'feminine'. Later critics have found the work incoherent, usually because of its employment of an 'unreliable' narrator, or cruel, on account of the fate that it metes out to the heroine.[1]

It seems to me that these criticisms arise in large part from a failure to perceive the radical nature of the narrative with which they are dealing. For 'Bliss', besides being a fairly conventional tale of a love-triangle, also constitutes a daringly experimental evocation of the nature of female sexuality. It is with this radical and subversive aspect of 'Bliss' that I intend to deal.[2]

'Bliss' opens with the heroine Bertha walking down the street in the grip of a near-hysterical mood of ecstasy. There is no apparent cause nor, it would appear, any ready outlet for her condition:

> Although Bertha Young was thirty she still had moments like this when she wanted to run instead of walk, to take dancing steps on and off the pavement, to bowl a hoop, to throw something up in the air and catch it again, or to stand still and laugh at—nothing—at nothing, simply . . . She hardly dared to look into the cold mirror—but she did look, and it gave her back a woman, radiant, with smiling, trembling lips, with big, dark eyes, and an air of listening, waiting for something . . . divine to happen . . . that she knew must happen . . . infallibly.

When the maid finally lets her into the house Bertha goes straight to the dining-room to arrange some fruit. Her ecstatic mood transforms the result of her labours into an emblem of radiant beauty:

> When she had finished with them and had made two pyramids of these bright round shapes, she stood away from the table to get the effect—and it really was

Reprinted from *Women's Studies Journal*, 4:2 (December 1988):18–31.

most curious. For the dark table seemed to melt into the dusky light and the glass dish and the blue bowl to float in the air. This, of course, in her present mood, was so incredibly beautiful. . . . She began to laugh.

'No, no. I'm getting hysterical.' And she seized her bag and coat and ran upstairs to the nursery.

In the nursery Bertha trains her still undirected ecstasies upon her baby daughter, Little B:

she loved Little B so much—her neck as she bent forward, her exquisite toes as they shone transparent in the firelight—that all her feeling of bliss came back again, and again she didn't know how to express it—what to do with it.

Moving next to the drawing-room our heroine finds her attention caught by the view from the windows:

At the far end, against the wall, there was a tall, slender pear tree in fullest, richest bloom; it stood perfect, as though becalmed against the jade-green sky. Bertha couldn't help feeling, even from this distance, that it had not a single bud or a faded petal. Down below, in the garden beds, the red and yellow tulips, heavy with flowers, seemed to lean upon the dusk. A grey cat, dragging its belly, crept across the lawn, and a black one, its shadow, trailed after. The sight of them, so intent and so quick, gave Bertha a curious shiver.

Bertha's reaction to this scene is a divided one: she is deeply moved by the beauty of the pear tree, and a moment later lays claim to the tree as 'a symbol of her own life'. She also sees it—like herself, perhaps—as 'tall' and 'slender'. And she dresses for dinner in white, green, and jade—colours that mimic the tree's own. (Her explicit denial here of any such connection—'She had thought of this scheme hours before she stood at the drawing-room window'—is of course to be read as a sign of unconscious intent.) On the other hand she withdraws instinctively from the sight of the cats—slinky, and sexually engaged.

Bertha and her husband Harry are hosting a dinner-party that evening. Three of the guests turn out to be members of a smart 'arty' set; the fourth is an enigmatic young woman called Pearl Fulton, described in the story as a 'find' of Bertha's. Their chatter, which is smart and superficial, counterpoints Bertha's 'moments' of flaring intensity.

After dinner Bertha and Miss Fulton go together to gaze out of the windows, as Bertha had earlier done on her own. The scene is now lit by a full moon. Bertha experiences a moment of what she believes to be perfect communion with her friend:

The two women stood side by side looking at the slender, flowering tree. Although it was so still it seemed, like the flame of a candle, to stretch up, to point, to quiver in the bright air, to grow taller and taller as they gazed—almost to touch the rim of the round, silver moon.

Bertha then switches her attention to an imaginary conversation which she plans to hold later with Harry about this moment of intimacy but now her ecstatic pulsations suddenly shift from Miss Fulton to the possibility of a first-time satisfying sexual engagement with Harry himself—for, as the text has by now made plain, Bertha Young is still sexually unawakened. And her little fantasy of engagement with Harry anticipates a coming-together far more dramatic and dangerous than that which has (perhaps) already taken place with Miss Fulton in front of the tree:

> something strange and almost terrifying darted into Bertha's mind. And this something blind and smiling whispered to her: 'Soon these people will go. The house will be quiet—quiet. The lights will be out. And you and he will be alone together in the dark room—the warm bed . . .'
> She jumped up from her chair and ran over to the piano.
> 'What a pity someone does not play!' she cried. 'What a pity somebody does not play.'
> For the first time in her life Bertha Young desired her husband.

The evening ends however with the shattering of Bertha's dual fantasy. Overhearing Harry arrange an assignation with Miss Fulton she realises that she has, in her own terms, been betrayed by both of them: her 'lovely pear tree' is all she has to turn to.

At the beginning of the story Bertha's 'ecstasy' is entirely unfocussed. It is registered by the heroine herself as superfluous (and unaccustomed) energy and exultation, and imaged as fire that 'burned in [her] bosom, sending out a little shower of sparks into every particle, into every finger and toe'. But, though the mood demands expression, its subject is uncertain about how she can express it without offending against 'civilisation':

> Oh, is there no way you can express it without being 'drunk and disorderly'? How idiotic civilisation is! Why be given a body if you have to keep it shut up in a case like a rare, rare fiddle?

And as the detail of the forgotten key—a typically Mansfield touch—suggests, she knows nothing of the origin or nature of these feelings.

From the outset—even before she settles down to arrange her tray of fruit—Bertha's reaction to this 'blissful' mood is complex: she both fears it and endeavours to precipitate an increase in its power. Her attitude is also consonant with the expectation of a trajectory of culmination and subsequent release:

in her bosom there was still that bright glowing place—that shower of little sparks coming from it. It was almost unbearable. She hardly dared to breathe for fear of fanning it higher, and yet she breathed deeply, deeply.

Bertha now sets about arranging the fruit on a glass bowl and a blue dish (or a glass dish and a blue bowl—the adjectives are, I suggest, interchangeable because the precise nature of the vessels is immaterial) so that it forms two pyramidal shapes. These shapes appear to her to float in the air, lustrous and dematerialised—like symbols of some abstract and achetypal beauty.

Bertha interprets this vision as a confirmation of what she herself half-jokingly dismisses as her 'hysterical' condition. It is a parody not only of her extravagance of feeling, but also of the excesses of the contemporary aesthetic movement, with its preoccupation with perceptual intensity and the detachment of the art-object from 'real life'. But within the story it functions positively on the whole—as a 'normal' and 'natural' alternative to the absurdly corrupt and sterile artistic pretensions of Harry's dinner-guests, who concern themselves with plays like *Love in False Teeth* and 'Stomach Trouble', and poems beginning with '*incredibly* beautiful lines like 'Why Must it Always be Tomato Soup?'[3]

Obtaining no release from her 'ecstasy' through this act of artistic devotion, Bertha rushes off to visit her baby daughter in the nursery. But it is supper-time there, and Little B is firmly in the clutches of her nanny. Like the 'poor little girl in front of the rich little girl with the doll', Bertha feels herself excluded. However, she does finally manage to snatch up the baby and feed her—with a spoon—while Nanny is out of the room.

One or two critics have tentatively suggested that the two pyramid-shapes into which Bertha arranged her fruit might be intended to symbolise breasts. But if this episode is considered in relation to the succeeding one, in which Bertha laments the way her child has ended up in another woman's charge—and in which she clasps and feeds her eagerly when she gets the chance—then the implication seems clear: Bertha would have done better to have followed her maternal instinct rather than social convention, and to have nursed and taken care of her child herself. Certainly her 'charge' of ecstasy is only renewed after she has fed Little B and while she is still holding her. It would appear then that it is an unconscious desire to nurture her child which Bertha expresses through the shapes into which she arranges the fruit—and moreover that it is this desire which sends her dashing off to the nursery.

Bertha's devotion to her daughter serves not only to indicate her mothering impulses: it is also a hint—another hint, if we bear in mind the likely significance of the pear-shapes—of her tendency to concern herself with the female principle rather than the male. The tendency is associated with a certain predisposition towards self-preoccupation, which also reveals itself in the name, Little B, of her daughter.

As we have seen, Bertha identifies with the pear tree—even to the extent of dressing herself in its colours. But Pearl Fulton—clothed from head to toe in silver, the colour of the moon—is also dressed with an eye to symbolic significance. In addition she is making an outré gesture which would have appealed to her 'arty' companions.

After dinner, as Pearl and Bertha stand side by side in contemplation of the scene which features their respective symbols, Bertha suddenly comes to envisage the pear tree in the shape of a candle-flame that stretches upwards—this detail is repeated several times—towards the rim of the moon:

> And the two women stood side by side looking at the slender, flowering tree. Although it was so still it seemed, like the flame of a candle, to stretch up, to point, to quiver in the bright air, to grow taller and taller as they gazed—almost to touch the rim of the round, silver moon.

Here the symbolism is clear. The tree, taking on the ardent nature of flame, and striving to reach (and, presumably, to penetrate) the chilly and indifferent moon, both expresses and encodes the sexual attraction which Bertha feels for her friend. (Most critics now accept that the episode centres around lesbian desire.) The sexual positioning of the entities within this little fantasy are governed by the 'normal' biological/cultural sexual polarities: the tree (Bertha) takes on the male role in response to the rounded moon (Pearl Fulton), culturally associated with virginity and with the female principle. (In the next paragraph, however, Bertha appears to revert to the female position: she sees both herself and Pearl Fulton 'caught in that circle of unearthly light', and envisages the two of them being showered with silver flowers.)

As we have seen, our heroine permits herself to believe that she has enjoyed a moment of true intimacy with Miss Fulton. Yet there are clear indications, even within the frame of her fantasy, that this belief is false: the flame representing her ardour only 'almost' touches the moon's rim, and both women are described as 'creatures of another world . . . *wondering what they were to do in this one*' (my italics). And a second later Bertha, whose subconscious musings find frequent access to the narrative, admits to herself that she may well have imagined Miss Fulton's murmur of affirmation.

Finally Bertha comes to fix her emotional intensities upon her husband. However, it should be noted that she comes to do this only by way of a reference to her 'moment' of communion with Pearl Fulton. This she recalls a little later when, believing Harry to dislike Pearl, she rehearses the pleading of her friend's case with him:

> 'Oh, Harry, don't dislike her. You are quite wrong about her. She's wonderful, wonderful. And, besides, how can you feel so differently about someone who means so much to me. I shall try to tell you when we are in bed to-night what has been happening. What she and I have shared.'

As those last words something strange and almost terrifying darted into Bertha's mind. And this something blind and smiling whispered to her: 'Soon these people will go. The house will be quiet—quiet. The lights will be out. And you and he will be alone together in the dark room—the warm bed . . .'

She jumped up from her chair and ran over to the piano.

'What a pity someone does not play!' she cried. 'What a pity somebody does not play.'

For the first time in her life Bertha Young desired her husband.

Bertha's evocation of a strange and terrifying Cupid-figure, even though one that is only partially articulated, suggests her anticipation of a communion with Harry far more mysterious, and more disturbing, than any which may already have taken place with Miss Fulton. And that which was identified at the beginning of the story as 'bliss'—a spiritual condition implying a sense of absolute contentment which is its own end—is finally revealed here to be repressed sexual desire, fervently (if like the Cupid-figure, blindly) seeking its own satisfaction. It will be observed too that this desire exists in close association with fear. (In Bertha's confused psyche the qualifier 'almost' in 'almost terrifying' acts, as in other passages, as an intensifier.) Herein of course lies one reason for its repression. It is only through an inarticulate, and only half-acknowledged, passion for the apparently virginal Miss Fulton that Bertha for the first time becomes able to contemplate a fully-committed sexual relationship with Harry.[4] The gap in the text in the extract quoted above indicates, as do similar gaps in other Mansfield stories, a subconscious connection in the perceiver's mind between the two subjects.

Bertha's shift of focus from Miss Fulton to her husband is dramatic. It also marks the final stage in that sequence of events which corresponds to the unfolding of Bertha's desire. There is a final twist in the plot, however, when Bertha realises a few moments later that her husband and her friend are already lovers; and that she, far from achieving an intimate relationship with each of them—as she had hoped to do—is being excluded by them from their relationship with each other.

The story ends with a brief return to that other 'couple'—Bertha and her pear tree. The topic of the pear tree is broached once more in Miss Fulton's ironical farewell to her hostess: '"Your lovely pear tree!"' (the words were originally Bertha's own) before she departs, the poetaster Eddie slinking along in her wake. With Miss Fulton's words resounding in her ears, Bertha rushes over to the windows again—to find that 'the pear tree was as lovely as ever and as full of flower and as still.'

To register the full significance of this complex conclusion we must turn once more to Bertha's initial vision of her garden. The diagrammatic nature of this vision, coupled with the emphatic and intensely personal way in which Bertha reacts to at least one element of it, indicates that it may serve as a kind of objective correlative for her state of mind.

The lone pear tree seen in 'fullest, richest bloom' is unquestionably the dominant element in the scene. It is also the element with which Bertha herself identifies. Why does she do so? The tree's lovely white flowers—'not a single bud or a faded petal'—may at first appear to suggest a kind of bridal, or nubile, openness. But as self-pollination does not normally take place in the case of the pear, and as Bertha has in her garden only a single tree, a different (and opposed) interpretation—that of sterility—may well be more appropriate.[5]

The other features of this scene—the tulips 'heavy with flowers, [that] seemed to lean upon the dusk', and the cats, to which the departing Pearl Fulton and her pursuer Eddie are compared—appear to represent, respectively, generative fulfilment and a crudely instinctual sexuality. Though both are present in the scene, thereby indicating that each has a certain relevance to the heroine's own psyche, neither compels her attention in the way that the tree does. Bertha does however bestow a fleeting shudder upon the cats—something which, in the complex psychical organisation with which the story deals, no doubt indicates deep seated fascination on her part for them.

In sum, the garden forms an emblem of Bertha's sexual proclivities.[6] However, mediated as it is by Bertha herself, it represents, not these proclivities in themselves, but these proclivities subtly influenced by the heroine's own idealised image of herself. The pear tree, beautiful and inviolate, stands for her own desired self-image; the tulips (presumably) for that aspect of 'sexual' fulfilment which she has in some sense achieved, but largely ignored, in Little B; the cats for an instinctual sexuality which Bertha herself perceives as bestial, and emphatically rejects. One might add that this little emblem of Bertha's garden marks the transition in the text from (or break between) the fruit and child scenes, in which sex is not directly involved, to the two later encounters in which sexual engagement with another—with all its attendant risks and complexities—is at issue.

The episodic narrative which flanks this emblematic scene, and through which Bertha herself moves, does not actually conflict with the image of her which the emblem presents. But it does reveal the full extent of the split in her sexual identity—between that which is approved and acknowledged, and that which is repressed. It also gives some indication of the consequences of this repression.

Unable to engage readily in a fulfilling sexual relationship with her husband, Bertha is overcome by strong feelings of sexual desire. She does not realise, or else refuses to acknowledge, the significance of these feelings. Nevertheless they are imperious, dictating her mood and her responses to those objects and persons she encounters during the evening—and eventually even guiding her towards Harry, their apparent ultimate object.

Mansfield's description of the manner in which the heroine comes to focus attention first on the fruit-arrangement, then on her daughter, then on

Pearl Fulton and finally on Harry himself, does appear to suggest a dedicated and reasonably consistent—if subconscious—attempt on Bertha's part to find an outlet for her feelings.

This is not, however, the case. Any desire on Bertha's part for a renewed sexual engagement with Harry is mingled both with fear and with a sense of potential disillusion: 'Was this what that feeling of bliss had been leading up to? But then, then—' The notion of a climax (in both senses of the word) has been held out to us, yet no climax has been achieved. We are presented in 'Bliss' neither with the conventional happy ending of romance, nor with the sense of illumination which ought to conclude an 'education' story.

The plot of the story, then, fails to resolve itself into a conventional narrative progression. But its subversion of convention and of its attendant expectations indicates no cruelty on the part of the author, nor indeed any incompetence. They are a direct reflection both of the non-goal-directed nature of Bertha's sexuality and the way in which the alien 'climate' within which she is located causes her to repress her own desires. (I will return to this point a little later.) And far from being evidence of Mansfield's 'cruelty', Bertha's turning at the end of the story to the solitary pear tree for consolation is the logical consequence both of the character as it has been constructed, and of the position in which society has placed her.

Bertha's anxieties, and the repressions which they have given rise to, are not envisaged by Mansfield—nor indeed by Bertha herself—as a purely private malaise. They have their being within a social context—that of the arty metropolitan upper middle class. And within the story it is the Youngs' dinner-guests, together with Harry himself, who serve as a microcosm of that context.

Though Mansfield's manner of narration excludes us from these characters' inner lives, their social chatter, threaded through as it is with images of rape, mutilation, and sexual predation, reveals their obsessions. Some of the characters also appear to be fixated upon food—in Mansfield's writings a frequent indicator of an aggressive and overbearing attitude towards sex.[7] As Hanson and Gurr point out in their monograph on Mansfield, Bertha appears to have considerable natural sexual vitality.[8] Her inhibitions are presented as a reaction to the sadistic and crudely salacious attitudes that characterise the social milieu of which she is a part.

Sex, then, has become for Bertha a matter on the one hand of innocence and spirituality in which bodily impulses play no part; on the other an affair of crude lust that denies the 'higher' aspects of the personality.[9] Her emblematic garden reveals with stark clarity this schizophrenic attitude. The attitude is also written into the story's opposing metaphors of stillness (associated with the pear tree) and extravagant motion, with its implications of a fast lifestyle. It is perhaps worth noting that the latter finds its most striking, and parodic, expression in Eddie Warren's nightmare taxi ride:

'I have had such a *dreadful* experience with a taxi-man; he was *most* sinister. I couldn't get him to *stop*. The *more* I knocked and called the *faster* he went. And *in* the moonlight this *bizarre* figure with the *flattened* head *crouching* over the *little* wheel. . . . I saw myself *driving* through Eternity in a *timeless* taxi.'

And indeed, in what becomes a sort of 'in-joke', the story throughout associates taxis with basic, physical sex. Both Harry and Pearl arrive for the evening in taxis (it is implied that they have been together before the dinner begins), and when Bertha observes that her friend lives in taxis, Harry outrageously replies '"She'll run to fat if she does . . . Frightful danger for blonde women."'

The consequences of the schizophrenic attitude towards sex which we have been discussing bear of course most heavily upon women. For instance, Mrs Norman Knight, alone of the dinner guests, finds it necessary to advertise her degraded attitudes through the clothes that she is wearing—in her case, her 'monkey' dress. The only way for a woman in particular to survive within such a culture may be to behave like the enigmatic seductress Pearl—acting publicly as a devotee of the goddess of chastity, carrying on an assignation in secret.

In 'Bliss', then, Mansfield devotes herself to rendering female sexual desire. The satirical sections of the story are directly relevant to its central preoccupation, in that they reveal the 'ground' within which Bertha's sexuality has developed, and been repressed. Mansfield renders Bertha's desire as originating with the heroine and her own needs rather than, as was the case with literature in the Petrarchan romance tradition, with a highly specific attachment on the part of a male lover to an object of desire which both focussed and rendered coherent that desire. In transferring woman from object to subject position, and in focussing upon this subject rather than upon the single, unifying object of male attraction, Mansfield has deconstructed both her subject and that subject's desire.

This desire is rendered, not as goal-directed, but as fluid and tentative. Giving the appearance of randomness, yet conveying a strong sense of inner compulsion, it moves from fruit-arrangement to child, from woman to man. Nominally portraying a consciousness at the mercy of an impoverished social vision, Mansfield has also depicted in her heroine a sexual passion that gains in strength and richness through its association with artistic sensitivity and maternal affection; and one that connects heightened emotion with a wider range of experience than the simple act of sexual gratification. Desire and sexuality come then to relate to the whole field of female experience—in contrast to the single focus and goal-directed pursuit of the (male) courtly lover.

Furthermore, in presenting us with a subject who aims to dissolve the conventional division between the Self and the Other by seeking identification with the Other rather than absorption, or conquest, by it, Mansfield is also interrogating the conventional Self-Other duality.

Attempts had of course been made in the English fiction of the nineteenth century to convey the distinctive nature of woman's sexual desire—usually as part of an attempt to render female aspiration in general. Perhaps the most notable achievement of this endeavour is to be found in the novels of Charlotte Brontë.

But with the advent of the Modernist period and its new faith in the supremacy of inner experience, there was increased interest in conveying the nature of desire itself. A number of early twentieth-century writers devoted themselves to suggesting, and rendering, the nature of distinctively female sexuality. (Relevant here is the Modernist tendency to go against long-established tradition by associating the human consciousness in general not with the male psyche, but with qualities which our culture has traditionally defined as female, or feminine—passivity, fluidity, receptivity, acute sensibility, irrationality.) Molly Bloom's soliloquy at the end of Joyce's *Ulysses* (1922) is the most celebrated of these attempts to foreground woman's desire; Mansfield's 'Bliss', published in 1918, is one of the first, and in some ways the most radical.

Of critical significance in establishing the new climate of opinion associated with the Modernist movement were the early works of Freud. Mansfield herself made no direct reference to him in any of her writings.[10] But A.R. Orage, editor of the *New Age,* a radical magazine which published some of her early stories, was an early Freud enthusiast.[11] He and his lover Beatrice Hastings were for a time close friends of Mansfield. It is inconceivable that Mansfield should not at least have been present at discussions of Freud's earlier works in her avant-garde Bohemian coterie. Her knowledge of German would also have given her access to the original, German-language versions of them—generally published five years or so before the first English translations—had she wished.

In 'Bliss' Bertha's several references to herself as 'hysterical' are clearly popular uses of the word. But her language is treacherously double throughout her story, and these references no doubt serve as a clue to the story's probable subtextual engagement with the subject of hysteria in something approaching its clinical sense—the study of which placed Freud on the path to the development of the science and techniques of psychoanalysis.

Freud's *Studies on Hysteria* was published jointly with Dr Josef Breuer in 1895. It offers a tentative early version of his theory of repression. This is presented in association with the phenomenon of hysteria: 'hysterical symptoms are the expression of [the patients'] most secret and repressed wishes'.[12] In analysing Dora's case, Freud also associated hysteria with 'a disturbance in the sphere of sexuality' and by implication with a tendency towards homosexuality.[13] His *Three Essays on the Theory of Sexuality,* published five years after *Studies on Hysteria,* develops some of these ideas—notably by associating hysteria with sexual repression. It also suggests that the sexuality of women—like that of children—tends to be, in the celebrated Freudian phrase, polymorphous and perverse (i.e., departing from the 'normal').

In 'Bliss' we have a fairly close correspondence with these ideas in Bertha's free-flowing desires and their ready movement across the sexual divide, as well as in the story's emphasis on the power of the repressed impulse. Like some of Freud's later works, 'Bliss' also appears to link hysterical neurosis with arrested development, with narcissism, and with bisexuality. But Mansfield, like Freud, was prepared to identify the neurotic case as a model for the norm: her Bertha is both a sadly maladjusted figure and (by implication) a representative of her times, of her sex, and of humanity in general. It is also worth emphasising, particularly in view of recent feminist criticisms of Freud's role in the Dora case,[14] that in 'Bliss' we have a very early rendering of a 'case' of hysteria in which no analyst (generally as in the Dora case, a man) appears to put his own perhaps inevitably misleading construction on events: the narrative is expounded wholly from the subject's point of view. The author has, in all except the most necessary sense, been banished; and any partisan interpretations must, within the conventions of the fiction, be taken to be Bertha's own.

'Bliss', then, is preoccupied with Katherine Mansfield's vision of the complex, and distinctive, nature of female desire, and the way in which this has been conditioned by the prevailing cultural context. It challenges the sole sway of the notion of sexual polarity and attraction, and it makes clear the differing character of the woman/woman relationship (hesitant, 'mystical', beautiful) from the woman/man connection (mysterious, terrifying, 'sublime'). It is best regarded as offering an ironic subversion of traditional narrative patterns rather than a kind of failed enactment of them. And, though it offers no solutions, it—like *Anna Karenina,* another popular subject of contemporary debate—asserts the problem it engages with in a courageous and radically innovative manner.

## Notes

1. 'I threw down *Bliss* with the exclamation, "She's done for!" Indeed I don't see how much faith in her as a woman or writer can survive that sort of story. I shall have to accept the fact, I'm afraid, that her mind is a very thin soil, laid an inch or two deep upon very barren rock. For *Bliss* is long enough to give her the chance of going deeper. Instead she is content with superficial smartness; and the whole conception is poor, cheap, not the vision, however imperfect, of an interesting mind'. Virginia Woolf, *A Writer's Diary,* London 1959:21. 'In Bliss the moral implication is negligible: the centre of interest is the wife's feeling, first of ecstatic happiness, and then at the moment of revelation. We are given neither comment nor suggestion of any moral issue of good and evil, and within the setting this is quite right. The story is limited to this sudden change of feeling, and the moral and social ramifications are outside of the terms of reference. As the material is limited in this way—and indeed our satisfaction recognises the skill with which the author has handled perfectly the *minimum* material—it is what I believe would be called feminine.' T.S. Eliot, *After Strange Gods,* London 1934:35–36. On the charge of incoherence, see e.g. Walter Allen, *The Short Story in English,* Oxford 1981:169–70, and Claire

Tomalin, *Katherine Mansfield: A Secret Life,* London 1987:170; on that of cruelty, Elaine Showalter, *A Literature of their Own,* London, 1982 (new revised edn):246; and Margaret Drabble, 'The New Woman of the Twenties: Fifty Years On', *Harpers & Queen,* June 1973:106–7, 135.

2. See Elizabeth Abel, 'Narrative Structure[s] and Female Development: The Case of *Mrs Dalloway*' in *The Voyage In: Fictions of Female Development,* ed. Elizabeth Abel, London 1983:163, for the contention that women's narratives typically contain two plots—one 'that is shaped to confirm expectations and a subplot at odds with this accommodation.'

3. See Susan Gubar, 'The Birth of the Artist as Heroine' in *The Representation of Women in Fiction,* ed. Carolyn G. Heilbrun and Margaret R. Higonnet, Baltimore and London 1983, especially pp. 27 and 39, for a discussion of how Mansfield redefines creativity in order to include, and valorise, woman's domestic crafts.

4. A somewhat similar episode occurs towards the end of 'Psychology', another story in the *Bliss* volume, when a brief encounter with an adoring 'elderly virgin' serves to unblock the heroine's formerly diminished passion for her (heterosexual) lover. An alternative, though similar, explanation for Bertha's switch of attention from Pearl Fulton to Harry is offered by Saralyn R. Daly, *Katherine Mansfield,* New York 1965:85–86, who argues that Bertha is subconsciously aware of her husband's relationship with Miss Fulton. So Pearl Fulton's attraction to Harry provokes Bertha's desire for him. This interpretation follows the theory of imitative, or 'mediated' desire (see Rene Girard, *Mensonge romantique et verite romanesque,* Paris 1961; translated as *Deceit, Desire, and the Novel,* Baltimore 1965).

5. See Helen E. Nebeker, 'The Pear Tree: Sexual Implications in Katherine Mansfield's *Bliss*', *Modern Fiction Studies,* XVIII, 1972–73:545–51.

6. There are also resonances in it of the Genesis myth of the Fall—another tale of innocence and sexual knowledge pertaining to a garden. In Mansfield's modernist, and more socialised, version of the story, however, the heroine's sexuality is more circumspect, and her fate is harsher: in her case the hero is in alliance with the Serpent.

7. See e.g. Mary Burgan, 'Childbirth Trauma in Katherine Mansfield's Early Stories', *Modern Fiction Studies,* XXIV, 1978:399, for a discussion of this subject.

8. Clare Hanson and Andrew Gurr, *Katherine Mansfield,* London 1981:62 'Her suppressed but real sexual force is indicated in the fire and sun imagery which dominates the first half of the story'.

9. Mansfield's attitude towards rampant sexuality is evident from her comment on D.H. Lawrence's *The Lost Girl:* 'His hero and heroine are non-human. They are animals on the prowl . . . They submit to the physical response and for the rest go veiled—blind—*faceless—mindless.* This is the doctrine of mindlessness.' *Katherine Mansfield's Letters to John Middleton Murry 1913–1922,* ed. John Middleton Murry, London 1951:620 (letter dated December 1920).

10. Though see for example her short story 'Psychology', in which the hero observes, '"I think it's because this generation is just wise enough to know that it is sick and to realise that its only chance of recovery is by going into its symptoms—making an exhaustive study of them—tracking them down—trying to get at the root of the trouble."'

11. See Antony Alpers, *The Life of Katherine Mansfield,* Oxford 1980:369 'Orage had been fond of saying that Freud was the greatest analyst of the age'.

12. Sigmund Freud, *Case Histories I: 'Dora' and 'Little Hans',* Penguin Freud Library, vol. 8, p. 36.

13. Ibid., p. 54.

14. See e.g. *In Dora's Case,* ed. Charles Bernheimer and Claire Kahane, New York and London 1985.

## *Reference*

Mansfield, Katherine. 1945. *Collected Short Stories.* Constable (reprinted Penguin, 1981).

# Poetry and Performance in Katherine Mansfield's "Bliss"

## GARDNER MCFALL

> Oh, to be a *writer,* a real writer given up to it and to it alone! . . . There are moments when Dickens is possessed by this power of writing: he is carried away. That is bliss.
>
> Katherine Mansfield, 1920
> (*Journal,* 203)

"Bliss" exemplifies Mansfield's mature fiction shaped by her lyric impulse and her mastery of poetic tradition squaring with the circumstances of her life. Here, her concision, mobilization of imagery and rhythm, irony, ambiguity, and submerged lyric voice require that we read the story with the kind of close attention generally reserved for poems. In doing so, we can see in what respect Mansfield's fiction is poetic. We can also see how, under the pressure of Mansfield's illness and exile, it emerges as a site of revisionary performance, compensating for reality.

When Mansfield wrote "Bliss," she was in Bandol, recuperating from a recently diagnosed "spot" on the lung. Aside from Ida Baker, whose arrival in France on 12 February 1918 irritated her, Mansfield had only the 1900 *Oxford Book of English Verse* for companionship.[1] Her steady attention to it resulted, as she told Murry, in its being "full [of] notes" by early March (*Collected Letters,* 2:107). Among the poems there, she fell under the spell of Shelley's "The Question," which she quoted twice in her letters to Murry that month and which she alluded to in her journal. On 18 February she wrote him:

> On my table are wild daffodils . . . They are so lovely that each time I look up I give them to you again. We shall go expeditions in the spring and write down all the *signs* & take a bastick and a small trowel & bring back treasure. Isn't that lovely where Shelley speaks of the "moonlight coloured may" . . .
>
> Its still (I think) very cold & I am in my wadded jacket with the pink 'un round my legs. (*Collected Letters,* 2:78)

---

This essay was commissioned especially for this volume.

On 19 February Mansfield had her first hemorrhage of the lung. Her anxious thoughts turned immediately to Murry, for she was frightened, and to her work, which she feared would be left incomplete:

> . . . of course I'm frightened . . . I don't want to be ill . . . away from Jack . . . I don't want to find this is real consumption . . . and I shan't have my work written. *That's what matters.* How unbearable it would be to die—leave "scraps," . . . [Mansfield's ellipsis] nothing real finished . . . *Jack and my work*—they are all I think of (mixed with curious visionary longings for gardens in full flower).[2]

Her parenthetical words point to Shelley's poem in the *Oxford Book* ("Methought that of these visionary flowers / I made a nosegay" [715]), and suggest the poem's connection to "Bliss," with Bertha's vision of the full, flowering pear tree.[3] Her reference shows how rapidly she had appropriated the poem, how both her experience and Shelley's words were converging even as she worked on "Bliss," started seven days before.[4]

In a letter to Murry of 20 and 21 February, she invoked Shelley's poem again:

> Do you remember, or have I mentioned lately that poem of Shelley's *The Question.* It begins: "I dreamed that, as I wandered by the way / Bare Winter suddenly was changed to Spring" . . . [Mansfield's ellipsis] I have learned it by heart since I am here; it is very exquisite, I think. Shelley and Keats I get more and more *attached* to. Nay, to all poetry. (*Collected Letters,* 2:83)

She quoted these same lines by Shelley in a letter to Ottoline Morrell on 22 February (*Collected Letters,* 2:86). Why "The Question" particularly should have captured Mansfield's imagination is not hard to divine. In the poem, a dreamer gathers an elaborate bouquet of "visionary flowers," only to realize he has no one to give it to. The poem ends:

> I hastened to the spot where I had come,
> That I might there present it—O! to whom?[5]

The dreamer's lush landscape, constituted by language in a detailed listing of flowers, creates a presence in the poem, while the closing question falls on thwarted desire and a recognition of human absence. Mansfield appreciated the poem's movement from longing to deprivation, for it matched her emotional experience with those closest to her, her brother Leslie, whom she had lost in 1915, as well as Murry, whose absence she felt keenly on the heels of his 1916 attraction to Ottoline and the onset of her illness. Her letters record that during this separation, Mansfield dreamed of Murry, only to find him not there upon waking (*Collected Letters,* 2:20). She wrote him: "I have such a longing for you. . . . The absence from you eats at my heart" (*Collected Letters,* 2:81). Although she projected a brave exterior about her illness in her letters to

Murry, her hemorrhage understandably accentuated her need of him and her desires for an immediate, happy future together.

Mansfield sketched a movement from longing to deprivation in "Bliss." Shelley's lines, which she quoted to Murry and Ottoline, are recapitulated in the second sentence, where Mansfield's dreamer, Bertha, is caught up in a "sudden" transformation: "What can you do if you are thirty and, turning the corner of your own street, you are overcome, suddenly by a feeling of bliss— absolute bliss!"[6]

Shelley's sudden seasonal change (from "Bare Winter" to "Spring") echoes in Bertha's emotional swing. Later in the story, Bertha ascribes her feeling to the season: "She felt quite dizzy, quite drunk. It must have been the spring" (308). Living apart from Murry in a sunny, but chilly France, Mansfield's emotional life was virtually "bare winter." There was every reason why she would have dreamed, like Shelley's dreamer and like Bertha in "Bliss," of a sudden spring. In fact, she wrote Murry: "This will all pass & I shall get better, our spring will come—& it will be warm & you will write to me & we shall be together again" (*Collected Letters,* 2:11).

Coupled with Murry's absence was the repressed, yet still troubling matter of Leslie's death, which would have been called up by the passing of his birthday on 21 February, and which she mentioned in a letter to Murry on 26 February (*Collected Letters,* 2:93). Although Mansfield had put the worst of her mourning behind her, her continued longing for him is suggested by the re-emergence in "Bliss" of imagery from a 1915 entry in her *Journal* following his death. There she wrote recollections of herself and Leslie in the Acacia Road garden, noting the "slender" (83) pear tree, and the "round moon [that] shines over the pear tree" (85). In the entry, the "moonlight deepens" (85) as brother and sister say their good-byes: "The shadows on the grass are long and strange; a puff of strange wind whispers in the ivy and the old moon touches them with silver" (85).

The movement of her journal entry from union to farewell corresponds obliquely enough with Shelley's poem and, inevitably, with "Bliss" to show how "The Question" tapped into Mansfield's continued loss and grief. It touched that dreaming part of her that still wished for her brother (in many ways her expectant, but ruined dreams of their shared life parallel Bertha's disillusionment), and figured in the compensatory writing of "Bliss," where Bertha's vision of the flowering pear tree stands removed from human failure and death: "as lovely as ever and as full of flower and as still" (*Stories,* 315). Here was the emotional ground Shelley's poem was laid upon, and in this "soil," to borrow Woolf's figure which she used in criticizing "Bliss,"[7] the story took root.

Mansfield was also reading other poems in the *Oxford Book.* She told Murry: "I *keep* (as you see) wanting to quote poetry today—When I get back I shall be like a sort of little private automatic machine in the home. You wind

me up & a poem will come out—Ive learned so many here while I lie awake—"
(*Collected Letters*, 2:94).

She singled out Marvell's "Upon Appleton House" for quoting in a letter
to Murry of 26 February. The lines appeared in the *Oxford Book* as the last six of
"A Garden: Written after the Civil War":

> Unhappy! Shall we never more
> That sweet militia restore,
> When gardens only had their towers,
> And all the garrisons were flowers;
> When roses only arms might bear
> And men did rosy garlands wear?
> (*Collected Letters*, 2:94;
> *Oxford*, 386–87)

In her letters to Murry at this time, Mansfield often expressed her wish to
regain their garden, which she associated with domestic happiness (*Collected
Letters*, 2:77, 93, 97). It is understandable that Marvell's poem appealed to her
in that it would have not only called up the past New Zealand gardens of her
youth and the 1915 Acacia Road garden she knew with Leslie, but symbolized
a future one she hoped to share with Murry. Suffering a triple exile from the
"garden," she conflated possibly Marvell's poem as well as Shelley's in her 19
February admission to "curious visionary longings of gardens in full flower"
(*Journal*, 129–30).

In any event, her head was full of poetry when she finished "Bliss" on 27
February. On that day, she wrote Murry:

> . . . I am so seized with the wonder of the english tongue—of english poetry—
> and I am so overcome by the idea that you are a poet and that we are going to
> live for poetry—for writing—that my heart has begun dancing away as if it will
> never stop—& I can see our cottage and our garden & you leaning against the
> door & me walking up the path . . . (*Collected Letters*, 2:97)

On 28 February, she mailed him the story:

> Ive just finished this new story *Bliss* and am sending it to you. But though my
> God! I *have* enjoyed writing it I am an absolute rag for the rest of the day . . .
> Oh, tell me what you think about *our* new story . . . Please try and like it and I
> am now free to start another. One extraordinary thing has happened to me since
> I came over here! Once I start them they haunt me, pursue me and plague me
> until they are finished and as good as I can do. (*Collected Letters*, 2:97–98)

In these letters, almost in the manner of Bertha, Mansfield reveals the
bliss-producing role of writing in her life. Her exclamation points, her em-

phasis on "Bliss" as *"our"* story, her sentences such as "one extraordinary thing has happened" and "I am so seized with the wonder of the english tongue" are echoes of the story she had finished. Her request of Murry ("Please try and like it") sounds like Bertha's plea on behalf of Pearl ("Oh, Harry, don't dislike her" [*Stories,* 313]).

Mansfield's composition of the story gave her a new "vision" of her life with Murry, complete with a garden (Marvell's "sweet militia" restored) and a mutual dedication to art, the only third party to their relationship Mansfield could embrace.[8] The story momentarily filled her sense of absence, reawakened and affirmed the 1915 image of union with her brother, and, if we consider her choice of words, supplanted her illness. It is, she tells Murry, her stories that haunt, pursue, and plague her, not the tuberculosis. In other words, a significant mental and emotional alteration was wrought in Mansfield's writing of "Bliss." Language redeemed or compensated for an inadequate world, and this sort of transaction is what concerns us in the story.

On the mimetic level, "Bliss" depicts Bertha Young's ironic realization that she and her husband love the same woman, Pearl Fulton. Structurally, the story builds on a reversal of Bertha's expectation and ends in what is taken for disillusionment. We witness Bertha at a private moment when she is disabused of any pretense of having an ideal life. As she catches sight of her husband kissing Pearl, her status as wife and friend is called into question, and the precipitous ending of the story just beyond this point forces the reader to consider what for Bertha must be a crushing blow.

Yet the language of the story works against this conclusion and, indeed, achieves what the plot denies. While the plot is cast as a straightforward quest narrative ending in disappointment, the language indicates a different, opposite objective. Managing a second mode of discourse, the story achieves a reformulation of bliss as it occurs tropologically throughout the *Oxford Book* in the poems of Shakespeare, Milton, Wordsworth, and Browning, among others. It plays off the traditional figure of bliss, that is lust, found for example in Shakespeare's sonnet 19 ("a bliss in proof, and proved, a very woe" [*Oxford,* 199]), against what Mansfield felt bliss to be, namely writing or language. Through the story's competing and arguably subversive mode of discourse, language (or subjective vision) balances and compensates for human failure.

Mansfield's appropriation and reformulation of the trope is evident from the beginning of the story in the elaborate account of Bertha's feeling of "absolute bliss": ". . . as though you'd swallowed a bright piece of that late afternoon sun and it burned in your bosom, sending out a little shower of sparks into every particle, into every finger and toe" (*Stories,* 305). Her description harkens directly to the first line of an anonymous sixteenth-century lyric in the *Oxford Book:*

> My heart is high above, my body is full
> of bliss. (80)

Bertha's feeling of bliss, which is evoked in language that suggests lust, appears throughout the story as a recurring motif. After her arrival home, she stands in the dusky dining room: "But in her bosom there was still that bright glowing place—that shower of little sparks coming from it" (*Stories,* 305). Later, she holds her baby in the nursery: "And, indeed, she loved little B so much—her neck as she bent forward, her exquisite toes as they shone transparent in the firelight—that all her feeling of bliss came back again" (307). By the time Bertha encounters Pearl, the shower of sparks in her bosom has become a full blaze: "What was there in the touch of that cool arm that could fan—fan—start blazing—blazing the fire of bliss that Bertha did not know what to do with?" (311). Finally, in her momentary dreamlike inspection of the garden with Pearl, she wonders: "How long did they stand there? Both, as it were, caught in that circle of unearthly light, understanding each other perfectly, creatures of another world, and wondering what they were to do in this one with all this blissful treasure that burned in their bosoms and dropped, in silver flowers, from their hair and hands?" (312–13).

If Mansfield's title were not sign enough, certainly her initial description harboring the older trope, and its recurrences throughout the text should tell the reader that Mansfield is up to more than detailing a love triangle from the viewpoint of the betrayed. Playing on "bliss" as it appears in the *Oxford Book,* she deploys it to place vision (indicated by Bertha's pear tree) above or outside human escapades. There are, after all, two things Bertha sees at the end of "Bliss." One is her husband kissing Pearl in the foyer; the other is the flowering pear tree in the garden, whose perfection has been, from the start, a subjective "vision," one of Bertha's own making: "The windows of the drawing-room opened on to a balcony overlooking the garden. At the far end, against the wall, there was a tall, slender pear tree in fullest, richest bloom; it stood perfect, as though becalmed against the jade-green sky. Bertha could not help feeling, even from this distance, that it had not a single bud or a faded petal" (308).

It is this vision that remains intact, though Bertha's interpretation of it as a "symbol of her own life" (308) is cast into doubt. The story appears to say: human relations fail; we scarcely know ourselves and are betrayed, if not by ourselves, by others close to us; however, the final vision of the pear tree, a literary figure and the embodiment of Bertha's longing, endures, and stands removed from the disillusioning events that have transpired. Of course, it is because her longing has been thwarted that it remains perfect as represented in her vision of the tree. There are implications here for the writer's task which, in Mansfield's case as we have seen, involved the subordination of absence and longing to the form of fiction.

Just as Mansfield borrows the figure of bliss from the *Oxford Book,* she also appropriates the blossoming tree, a common enough image. She would have found it in Browning's "Home-thoughts, from Abroad" contained in the anthology:

> Hark, where my blossom'd pear-tree in the hedge
> Leans to the field and scatters on the clover
> Blossoms and dewdrops—at the bent spray's edge—.
> (866)

Mansfield's anxiety about her appropriation of the image is suggested in her choosing to have Bertha's tree remain full flowering throughout the story. She resists employing it as an equation for inconsistent human feeling and action, which she was unable to do in her poem "The Lilac Tree" from 1908; there a lilac tree corresponds with the fruition and loss of love:

> Soon must the tree stand stripped and bare
> And I shall never find her there
> Oh, lilac tree, oh lilac tree
> Shower down thy leaves and cover me.

In "Bliss," nature (insofar as it is part of Bertha's vision) is not subordinated to human crisis, but aloof in all its contrasting perfection. Mansfield has traveled a great distance from her 1908 poem, but the influence of the poets appears as keen if not more so, evidenced by her need to revise the clearly borrowed trope. She reverses Herrick's tact in "To Blossoms," also contained in the *Oxford Book:*

> But you are lovely leaves, where we
>   May read how soon things have
>   Their end, though ne'er so brave:
> And after they have shown their pride
>   Like you awhile, they glide
>     Into the grave. (269)

Mansfield's contrasting use of the figure (she might have had at least one petal fall from the tree to underscore Bertha's revelation about Harry's affair if this were the story's central concern) shows her unsentimental insistence on the enduring power of subjective vision as it results from longing, and, implicitly, the formalization of it represented by the text, or art.

The irony of the story, which critics generally locate in Bertha's revelation at the end,[9] resides rather in Bertha's inability to express herself (or read people and situations properly) juxtaposed with the text's achievement of expression. Bertha is constantly frustrated by her inarticulateness ("Oh, is there no way you can express it" [*Stories,* 305] and revises her attempts at expression ("No, that about the fiddle is not quite what I mean" [305]). She speaks in phrases marked by Mansfield's inverted commas, indicating these phrases are not authentic:

"But while I am making coffee in the drawing-room perhaps she will 'give a sign.'" But what she meant by that she did not know, and what would happen after that she could not imagine. (312)

Mansfield's intention to have Bertha lack authentic expression is revealed in her comment to Murry that Bertha was an "artist manque enough to realise that those words and expressions were not & couldn't be hers—They were, as it were, *quoted* by her, borrowed . . . she'd none of her own" (*Collected Letters,* 2:121).

Yet Bertha appreciates and longs for performance, which is often couched in artistic terms: "Why be given a body if you have to keep it shut up in a case like a rare, rare fiddle?" (*Stories,* 305). Later she wonders: "Why have a baby if it has to be kept—not in a case like a rare, rare fiddle, but in another woman's arms?" (306). Bertha behaves like an eager director, who has set the stage for her acting dinner guests. Her attention to the arrangement of fruit whose color will "bring the carpet up to the table" (306) and her attire that imitates the pear tree hint at her investment in what is about to happen, in what she has earlier thought would be "divine" (305). When the guests finally assemble, they remind her of "a play by Tchekof" (311).

Mansfield once referred to her writing as "regular performance" (*Journal,* 262). That Bertha is duped, that her actors and actresses rewrite the script throws Mansfield's authorial performance into relief. She achieves what is denied Bertha who, upon contemplating being alone with her husband after dinner, jumps up from her chair and runs to the piano:

"What a pity someone does not play!" she cried. "What a pity somebody does not play." (*Stories,* 314)

Her anxieties are subverted into a longing for performance that is not fulfilled. The bundle of inadequacies that constitute Bertha's character and the failings of those around her are contrasted by the text in which they appear. Mansfield's performance suggests, through Bertha's concluding vision, that the figure or the fiction endures, whatever the outcome of human events.

This contradiction in what the plot recounts and language implies is signaled in the way language unravels the plot even as it progresses, and holds two levels of discourse in balance: the mimetic depiction of Bertha's dinner party with its ensuing revelation and the play of tropology centering on bliss and the flowering pear tree. Mansfield's process of fiction conforms to Anne Mellor's definition of romantic irony as a "form or structure that simultaneously creates and de-creates itself."[10] (5). The first sentence of the story illustrates this: "Although Bertha Young was thirty she had moments like this when she wanted to run instead of walk, to take dancing steps on and off the pavement, to bowl a hoop, to throw something up in the air and catch it again, or to stand still and laugh at—nothing—at nothing, simply" (305).

Retraction and contradiction mark the sentence where "simply" cannot be said to apply. Immediately following the first sentence, which aims at a mimetic account, a lyric elaboration of Bertha's "bliss" ensues. These two modes of discourse thread throughout the story and are balanced in the final scene:

> Bertha simply ran over to the long windows. "Oh, what is going to happen now?" she cried. But the pear tree was as lovely as ever and as full of flower and as still.

The question of action is answered with a still-life description, a perfect figure, a remaining vision. In Bertha's cry ("Oh, what is going to happen now?") we hear the echo of Shelley's dreamer ("That I might there present it— O! to whom?"). Although the anguish of thwarted desire is implied by both texts, in Mansfield's story it is checked by the compensating vision itself.

Yet even as we track this compensating function of Bertha's vision in the story, "Bliss" resists closure. The ambiguity achieved by the juxtaposition of Bertha's sight of her husband kissing Pearl, and the vision of the perfect tree further places the story in the tradition of Romantic irony:

> English Romantic irony, broadly put, consists in the studied avoidance on the artist's part of determinate meanings, even at such times as he might wish to encourage his readers to *produce* such meanings for himself; it involves the re-fusal of closure, the incorporation of any potentially available "metacomment" within the primary language of the text, the provision of a linguistic sign which moves towards or verges on a "free" status. . . .

Mansfield's refusal to direct us in how we must read the story (though it *is* a lesson in reading) rivets us to her performance as writer. For Mansfield, the text is analogous to Bertha's subjective vision, and maintains a compensating or balancing function in relation to life. As she tells us in a 1922 journal entry: "There is no feeling to be compared with the joy of having written and fin-ished a story. . . . There it was, *new* and complete" (285). Elsewhere, and ironi-cally, given our knowledge of the strain in their relationship, she insists in a 1921 letter to Ottoline Morrell: "Work is the only thing that never fails."[12]

In "Bliss," we have the fusion of Mansfield's life and reading. We witness an active dialectic whereby texts (in this case, poems from the *Oxford Book*) res-onate with her experience to produce a fiction whose romantic tropology, identified with subjective experience (and poetry), vies with a linear, mimetic account expected of prose. The situation of "Bliss," involving a triangular rela-tionship, reversal of expectation, and deception, was not new in Mansfield's work. She employed this configuration of elements as early as 1908 in a short sketch entitled "The Unexpected Must Happen."[13] What was distinctive about "Bliss" was the incorporation of poetic, noncausal elements to reveal the ambiguity of human relationships, and to suggest the triumph of creative vision over pain and disappointment. "Beauty triumphs over ugliness in Life . . ." she wrote. "And that marvellous triumph is what I long to express" (*Letters*, 2:452–53).

Mansfield's "Bliss," far from the love triangle it recounts, points to lyric bliss discovered in the act of writing. It points to longing, whose perfection involves the production of vision or text. Mansfield's bliss was not the lust of the anonymous sixteenth-century lyric or that of Shakespeare's sonnet. It was not Milton's eternal bliss ("On Time," *Oxford*, 318), or Wordsworth's "bliss of solitude" ("Daffodils," *Oxford*, 605), or Browning's "bliss to die with" ("The Last Ride Together," *Oxford*, 865). Mansfield's was the bliss of language that could balance or compensate for an inadequate world.

## Notes

1. On 6 February 1918, shortly before Mansfield started "Bliss," she wrote Murry: "Four years ago today Goodyear gave me the Oxford Book of English Verse. I discovered that by chance this morning" (*The Collected Letters of Katherine Mansfield,* ed. Vincent O'Sullivan and Margaret Scott [Oxford: Clarendon Press, 1984– ], 2:78; hereafter cited in the text.

2. *Journal of Katherine Mansfield,* ed. John Middleton Murry (London: Constable Books, 1927; New York: Knopf, 1927; Definitive Edition, 1954; London: Hutchinson, 1984), 129–130; hereafter cited in the text.

3. Marilyn Zorn supports this view in her article "Visionary Flowers: Another Study of Mansfield's 'Bliss'" (*Studies in Short Fiction* 17:2 [1980]: 141– 47): "'Bliss's' theme encompasses exactly the visionary joy and cry against corruption which we associate with the Romantics. One of the unacknowledged sources for the story is Shelley's poem 'The Question'" (143).

4. In a letter dated 12 and 13 February 1918, Mansfield wrote Murry: "I lay down under a pine tree & though I spent some time saying 'the wells and springs are poisoned' they were not really. I began to construct my new story. Until I get back to you & we are safe in each other's arms there is only one thing to do & that is *work work work*" (*Collected Letters*, 2:70).

5. See Arthur Quiller Couch, ed. *The Oxford Book of English Verse 1250–1900* (Oxford: Clarendon Press, 1900), 715; hereafter cited in the text.

6. *The Stories of Katherine Mansfield,* ed. Antony Alpers (Oxford: Oxford University Press, 1984), 305; hereafter cited in the text.

7. After reading "Bliss" in the August 1918 issue of the *English Review,* Woolf wrote in her *Diary:* "I threw down Bliss with the exclamation, 'she's done for!' Indeed I don't see how much faith in her as a woman or writer can survive that sort of story. . . . her mind is a very thin soil, laid an inch or two deep upon very barren rock. . . . the whole conception is poor, cheap, not the vision, however imperfect, of an interesting mind. She writes badly too" (*The Diary of Virginia Woolf 1912–1922,* ed. Anne Olivier Bell [New York: Harcourt, 1979] 1:179).

8. That their work became a sign of Mansfield and Murry's love is suggested by an exchange of letters. On 5 February 1918, Murry wrote Mansfield: "I feel that in you & me our love & our work are become the same thing, inextricably knit together" (*Letters*, 111). On 10 and 11 February, she replied: "all I write or ever will write will be the fruit of our love" (*Collected Letters,* 2:66).

9. C.A. Hankin, *Katherine Mansfield and Her Confessional Stories* (New York: St. Martin's Press, 1983), 147.

10. Anne K. Mellor, *English Romantic Irony* (Cambridge: Harvard University Press, 1980), 5.

11. David Simpson, *Irony and Authority in Romantic Poetry* (Totowa: Rowman and Littlefield, 1979), 190.

12. *The Letters of Katherine Mansfield,* ed. John Middleton Murry. 2 vols. (London: Constable, 1929; New York: Knopf, 1929), 2:385; hereafter cited in the text.

13. This sketch is deposited at the Alexander Turnbull Library, Wellington, New Zealand.

# Katherine Mansfield's Images of Art[1]

### KIRSTY COCHRANE

Katherine Mansfield's images of art include living things that have the power to transform something else, or that can themselves be transformed. In "Sun and Moon," flowers are the agent of transformation. Elsewhere, this function is performed by lights or lamps, which may be seen to provide the conditions for awareness of human sympathy and its preciousness. With flowers, however, an elaborate scale of imagistic use can be discerned. First of all, flowers are intrinsic to the stories in their fundamental role of fact and image. Beyond this, they often possess the mediating property of disposing characters toward the experience of art. Ultimately they may be found functioning in ways which both symbolize and enact the condition of art: being fact, metaphor, and emblem.

Already in the nine-year-old Katherine Mansfield's first published story, "Enna Blake," there exists an impulse to reshape in fictional form the primary human experience of gathering plants to bring home and reassemble as objects of beauty or offerings of love in another setting.

> 'I should think it would be very nice to get some moss', Enna said; so off they trudged. The girls spent a very happy day, and got a great many nice ferns and some beautiful moss. And that night Enna thought it was the nicest day she had ever spent in the country.[2]

That child's voice, vision, and impulse, are there with the same purity in stories from Katherine Mansfield's maturity. In these, this fundamental imagery from childhood transforms our view of the adult world; for instance, a child may see the plants and flowers and trees of the outdoor world transfigured in indoor settings, or see the familiar daytime house and garden undergo a mysterious metamorphosis through the effects of night.

The story where this quintessential imagery lies at the very heart of meaning is "Sun and Moon." On 10 February 1918 Katherine Mansfield wrote to John Middleton Murry from Bandol, in the South of France:

> I *dreamed* a short story last night, even down to its name, which was *Sun and Moon*. It was very light. I dreamed it all—about children. I got up at 6.30 and wrote a note or two because I knew it would fade. I'll send it some time this week. It's so

This essay was commissioned especially for this volume.

nice. I didn't dream that I read it. No, I was in it, part of it, and it played round invisible me. But the hero is not more than 5. In my dream I saw a supper-table with the eyes of 5. It was awfully queer—especially a plate of half-melted ice-cream.[3]

It is almost typical of Katherine Mansfield to trivialize the importance of her story like this. Her attitude in this letter provides a cue for Anthony Alpers to remark in his fine edition of Mansfield: "A case of mental reaction to a major work, written down within hours of finishing *Je ne parle pas*" (*Stories,* 561). Is this indeed simply a very insignificant story? I don't think so; quite the contrary. This is how it begins.

> In the afternoon the chairs came, a whole big cart full of little gold ones with their legs in the air. And then the flowers came. When you stared down from the balcony at the people carrying them the flower pots looked like funny awfully nice hats nodding up the path.
> Moon thought they were hats. She said: 'Look. There's a man wearing a palm on his head.' But she never knew the difference between real things and not real ones.
> There was nobody to look after Sun and Moon. Nurse was helping Annie alter Mother's dress which was much-too-long-and-tight-under-the-arms and Mother was running all over the house and telephoning Father to be sure not to forget things. She only had time to say: 'Out of my way, children!' (*Stories,* 300)

From inside they looked like hats, from outside you might see they were trees being brought in.

"Sun and Moon" was written all in one piece very fast on the same day in 1918 that she wrote to John Middleton Murry about her dream of it. It is remarkable, among her stories of childhood because the children in this case are so very young; they are at the threshold of realizing an individual consciousness. At least, Sun is there; Moon has not yet reached it. It achieves the very delicate task of making very young children real without sentimentality. Where sentimentality is found in the story it belongs to adult characters, not to the narrative consciousness. The story uses a vocabulary which is entirely that of the boy, Sun. The two children are so young they are a world in themselves. They scarcely know that they are boy and girl. "There was nobody to look after Sun and Moon." These names are self-concepts. Chummie, Boy, Sonny, Son: the child makes elementary and total sense of his nickname, and names his sister in terms of his perception. The story comes close to the fundamental sources of individual consciousness. As Katherine Mansfield said, "I was in it, part of it, and it played round invisible me." Her role in it seems to have been that of her "hero," Sun. Perhaps she was sensitive to the psychological truth of this transference. Certainly she was not comfortable about exposing the story without the framing of its larger context, her collection *Bliss.*

Sun and Moon are so young that they exist in a universe that has scarcely formulated a notion of individual identity, though it possesses established routines and expectations of behavior: their real names are unknown to us. Their world is upstairs in the nursery. Their experience of larger society is scarcely begun; they have not yet fully comprehended the difference between "real things and not-real ones." From their perspective looking down from the balcony above, the real flowers could be not-real, and again looking up from below into the refrigerator the ice-cream house could be real. When they are dressed for the party they seem decorated, like the table downstairs, for the strange new downstairs world, so that they themselves look not-real to the adults: they look "a picture." "What a picture! Oh the ducks! Oh the lambs! Oh the sweets! Oh the pets!" Not children at all. The known dining-table of their downstairs world has been transformed by flowers and water into an outside garden. The stern behavior of the daytime father is transformed into night-time jolliness. At the end of the story the table, like Mother, is in a disarray never known or countenanced in the daytime world. The little pink house was broken. Sun cannot perceive it was only ice-cream; it was a lovely reality. This is a first experience of disillusionment. There was high-pitched excitement, and joy; there is despair. The newly created world has been destroyed.

> But—oh! oh! what had happened? The ribbons and the roses were all pulled untied. The little red table napkins lay on the floor, all the shining plates were dirty and all the winking glasses. The lovely food that the man had trimmed was all thrown about, and there were bones and bits and fruit peels and shells everywhere. There was even a bottle lying down with stuff coming out of it on to the cloth and nobody stood it up again. And the little pink house with the snow roof and the green windows was broken—broken—half melted away in the centre of the table.

> "Come on, Sun," said Father, pretending not to notice. (*Stories,* 304)

The formulaic symbolism that the story uses to express this first experience of disillusionment works very powerfully, but even more remarkable here is the sustained oblique perspective made up of the elongated or foreshortened view which the children's physical relationship to the adults gives them, together with their innocence. Their sightline is part of their innocent vision. In what sense was the child's original perception of reality not "real"? Perspective in this story is something literal, deriving for instance from the children's line of vision upstairs looking down, so that their "point of view" is something actual, as well as being a matter of emotional attitude. This can cause us to ask: what is real? How can we tell? Is truth after all a matter of perspective?

The images that provide Sun with his insights about reality and the transience of beauty are images of art; the little pink house was a work of art, an emblem of security, placed as the emblematic centerpiece on the dining table decorated also with roses brought in from the outside world, a dining-table that is at the heart of the parameters of his known world. The children themselves, even to the rosettes on Moon's shoes, were presented to the guests as their parents' artificial creations. People become artworks; people destroy their own creations. The sympathetic universe of Sun and Moon is broken. There is no certainty in the world.

Images of change, living images of one thing that becomes another, or that has the capability of allowing one thing to become another, are powerful in Katherine Mansfield's stories. Among these, images of light are innate. Such images may seem to act as agents of alteration, to create the condition of art. Such is the effect of the lighted ship at the end of "The Wind Blows." Vehicle of passage, agent of alteration, it holds the potentiality for other kinds of being. The lighted ship is a powerful image *for* art, and its context is an experience of emotional sympathy.

> 'Look, Bogey. Look over there.'
> A big black steamer with a long loop of smoke streaming, with the port-holes lighted, with lights everywhere, is putting out to sea. The wind does not stop her; she cuts through the waves, making for the open gate between the pointed rocks that leads to. . . . It's the light that makes her look so awfully beautiful and mysterious. . . . *They* are on board leaning over the rail arm in arm.
> '. . . Who are they?'
> '. . . Brother and sister.'
> 'Look, Bogey, there's the town. Doesn't it look small? There's the post-office clock chiming for the last time. There's the esplanade where we walked that windy day. Do you remember? I cried at my music lesson that day—how many years ago! Good-bye, little island, good-bye. . . .'
> Now the dark stretches a wing over the tumbling water. They can't see those two any more. Good-bye, good-bye. Don't forget. . . . But the ship is gone, now.
> The wind—the wind. (*Stories,* 194)

Together, in a combined leap of imagination, brother and sister have left the shore and are on board the lighted steamer, looking out toward themselves and the little town. They experience the desire to travel in sympathy with each other. They want to go away—the "where" remains unresolved; it's the departure, the journey itself that is longed for. What is before them? Life is before them; and then there is a sudden change of consciousness and focus towards another, future, farewell, in which "that windy day" is no longer present; and that change helps the reader to emerge at the greater distance in space and time, which is the author's present, and then ours. The image of the lighted ship moving out of the dark harbor to an unknown destination is charged with emotion. With the brother and sister we have moved in and out of consciousness. This powerful image precipitates a further change in our awareness. Behind the theatricality of the adolescent "good-byes" is hidden the scarcely bearable knowledge of a future already in the process of arriving at its final enactment.

The lighted ship is a symbol of passage, through space, in time, and for the transmission of wisdom. The lamp is a symbol Katherine Mansfield uses quite consistently. In "Prelude" the new house is first seen by the child Kezia in lamplight; as she is lifted down from the buggy in the darkness it seems a living thing.

> The soft white bulk of it lay stretched upon the green garden like a sleeping beast. And now one and now another of the windows leaped into light. Someone was walking through the empty rooms carrying a lamp. From a window downstairs the light of a fire flickered. A strange beautiful excitement seemed to stream from the house in quivering ripples.
>
> "Where are we?" said Lottie, sitting up. Her reefer cap was all on one side and on her cheek there was the print of an anchor button she had pressed against while sleeping. Tenderly the storeman lifted her, set her cap straight, and pulled down her crumpled clothes. She stood blinking on the lowest verandah step watching Kezia who seemed to come flying through the air to her feet.
>
> "Ooh!" cried Kezia, flinging up her arms. The grandmother came out of the dark hall carrying a little lamp. She was smiling.
>
> "You found your way in the dark?" said she.
>
> "Perfectly well." (*Stories*, 228)

This living house is itself a potent image, but within it the lamp is described as "a bright breathing thing," and the grandmother trusts Kezia to carry it. The child now brings the lamplight into the drawing room. For her, it illuminates the corners of a stable world, and identifies the real. The lamp makes the house safe and true. Its light brings into focus and isolates those it illuminates. Two evenings later it does this for Linda as she sits remote from others in the room, and she is made restless and wanders outside (where she sees the moonlit aloe), and realizes the difference between her mother's apparently contented inner life and her own. But the image of the lamp properly belongs to a serene grandmother and a peaceful house. When at the bay the children are playing in the washhouse and Kezia begins to fear the shadowy corners, she is comforted by the thought that "somewhere, far away, grandma was lighting a lamp" (*Stories*, 462). But in "The Voyage," the child's emotional trauma is such that even in the company of her father and grandmother the lantern on the wharf "seemed afraid to unfurl its timid, quivering light in all that blackness; it burned softly, as if for itself" (*Stories*, 470). "As if for itself": the normal and natural function of a lamp is to burn for others. Kezia's grandmother lived for others; the lamp is her symbol. Kezia accepts it. The motto of Katherine Mansfield's first Wellington high school is, by a nice coincidence, "lumen accipe et imperti" ("receive the light and pass it on"). The illumination of Katherine Mansfield's art brings much out of darkness into the light of consciousness. In "The Doll's House," "the lamp was perfect. It seemed to smile at Kezia, to say 'I live here'. The lamp was real" (*Stories*, 500). The doll's house is itself an artifact, a creative image of reality, with its lamp inside it. When, at the end, one rejected little Kelvey says to another, "I seen the little lamp," we may see that the lamp has transformed their reality, as it has ours.

But it is with Katherine Mansfield's flower imagery that we find her most fundamental images of art. Flowers in her stories can create an effect of the same kind as that which surrounds the lighted ship, or the grandmother's lamp, whereby the observer's perception of reality is somehow transformed. More profoundly than that, however, they can be found working as both agent and emblem of alteration.

In "Her First Ball," pink and white azaleas are in tune with Leila's mood, becoming flags streaming and eventually a flying wheel, while Leila herself, standing up for her first dance, floated away like a flower that is tossed into a pool. "The Voyage" takes place in darkness, and moves toward light. When the Picton ferry was docking in the early dawn Fenella thought, "Oh, it had all been so sad lately. Was it going to change?" Later, as she walks up her grandparents' path, we sense the relief of the transition out of darkness into light. Though the morning is still cold there is some promise, and a new sweetness of smell: "Up a little path of round pebbles they went, with drenched sleeping flowers on either side. Grandma's delicate white picotees were so heavy with dew that they were fallen, but their sweet smell was part of the cold morning" (*Stories,* 475). Those daisies are a catalyst. They offer an intimation of change, and a sense of renewed hope. In "At the Bay" the falling flowers of the manuka tree cause Linda to meditate on the meaning of life. "Why, then, flower at all?" (*Stories,* 452)—but these daytime flowers have an intrinsic beauty that makes their existence worthwhile; and feeling this, unexpectedly Linda feels something for her child too. Her brother-in-law Jonathan, relaxed in conversation, offers the garden as a resonant image of undirected energy, and unfulfilled life. "The shortness of life! The shortness of life!" he says. "I've only one night or one day, and there's this vast dangerous garden, waiting out there, undiscovered, unexplored" (*Stories,* 464).

The structural importance of flowers in "Sun and Moon" was obvious; they were the locus for transformations of reality. Flowers are brought inside to make an artificial lake and garden; manufactured fabrics are made to imitate flowers. The story is a study in red and white. There were the flowers that arrived looking like hats, the roses and rose-petals that transformed the dining table into a garden with a lake, the red table napkins that were made into roses, Sun's shirt with red and white daisies on it, and the final devastation of untied ribbons and roses. The little ice-cream house, with its nut door-handle, standing in its artificial garden made of real flowers, is a complete, created world, emblem of Sun's reality, and agent of his disillusionment.

To the five-year-old child Kezia in "Prelude" flowers are part of a world that needs to be made coherent. The new untamed garden is so large and diverse "she did not believe that she would ever not get lost in this garden" (*Stories,* 238). It needs to be brought within her artist's perspective. The richness and profusion of its flowers delighted her; her impulse is to share this delight, to organize this beauty into a pattern, to offer it as a gift. Her grandmother will be the natural recipient. For instance, the child might begin with an empty matchbox. "First she would put a leaf inside with a big violet lying on it, then she would put a very small white picotee, perhaps, on each side of the violet, and then she would sprinkle some lavender on the top, but not to cover their heads."

She often made these surprises for the grandmother, and they were always most successful.

> 'Do you want a match, my granny?'
> 'Why, yes, child, I believe a match is just what I'm looking for.'
> The grandmother slowly opened the box and came upon the picture inside.
> 'Good gracious, child! How you astonished me!' (*Stories,* 239)

They are collaborators; they both value the work of art. Here the child's impulse is already the artist's, to record and find pattern and meaning in the living world. The matchbox may be a house for the family group of flowers, framed thus outside in the garden. The matchbox picture both is in itself, and presents to the beholder, an image of art. In "At the Bay," nasturtium leaves and other plants at the beginning were bathed in beneficent dew; but inside at breakfast time the red and yellow nasturtium flowers are found in an old salad bowl decorating the table, and Mrs. Fairfield has a smile of contentment. Grandmother and child share an appreciation of the natural world and the desire to re-create, in a new patterning, its beautiful forms inside. The jar of seapinks on the dresser in their bedroom at the bay is a living and very transitory work of art, bound by time, as are the living woman and child whose pattern of life it enhances. We are told that the seapinks are *like* "a velvet pincushion" (*Stories,* 455)—they no longer just haphazardly exist in natural beauty, they have been re-made, and have thus become an artifact. That posy is now a miniature work of art, a microcosm for the story, or an emblem that reminds us of the artist's function to make permanent that which is transient, and renew our vision of the world.

Images of transience and transformation, whether of a lighted ship moving on the water, a lamp flickering within a house, or flowers gathered in a posy, provide Katherine Mansfield with images of art. Supremely through these, she succeeds in her artistic intention of recreating the existentialist moment of experienced life.

### Notes

1. Developed from papers given at the Katherine Mansfield Centennial Conferences, Newberry Library Chicago, and Victoria University of Wellington, September–October 1988.

2. *The Stories of Katherine Mansfield,* ed. Antony Alpers (Oxford: Oxford University Press, 1984) 2; hereafter cited in the text as *Stories.*

3. *Letters and Journals of Katherine Mansfield,* ed. C. K. Stead, (Harmondsworth: Penguin Books, 1977), 99.

# THE ARTIST IN CONTEXT
◆

# Spheres of Influence:
## A Critical Perspective

### RHODA B. NATHAN

Katherine Mansfield's reputation has suffered more from her untimely death than did the legacy of other writers whose lives were also claimed at an early age by tuberculosis. Chekhov, for instance, whose stories were so influential to Mansfield, was judged to have fulfilled his promise. D. H. Lawrence and Henry David Thoreau, who died of the same disease, appeared to have completed the work they had undertaken although they died young. In Mansfield's case, however, there was always the sense that her voluminous body of short stories constituted a "prelude" to the larger opus that was never begun. She is even denied the classic justification applied to the untimely death of Stephen Crane, who died at an even earlier age, but whose end was explained as a consequence of romantic excess and willful self-destruction. Perhaps some of the onus for the critical community's judgment must finally rest with her. She alone, of the cited doomed authors, dwelled on her frustration in the volumes of her letters and later, in her *Journal* and *Scrapbook*. As her health failed, she was obsessed about her dwindling time, her precarious health, and her despair at her inability to realize her talent fully. Nowhere in the fourteen volumes of Thoreau's *Journal* can the reader find a single reference to his own health among the entries reflecting on nature, politics, culture, and history. Chekhov's enormous body of prose other than his stories and plays is likewise free from self-reference. Perhaps by refraining from calling attention to projects still in the offing but destined to remain unfulfilled they escaped the reservations always applied to Mansfield's work.

Even so astute a critic as Frank O'Connor, having praised Mansfield's "Prelude" as "remarkable" and a "masterpiece" in his book *The Lonely Voice*, wonders whether she could have "exploited her own breakthrough into magic" as Joyce and Proust succeeded in doing. He speculates that death "came too soon" after some "tantalizing hints" of further development. The question he puts to himself, "Are they really works of art that could have given rise to other works of art and followed the law of their own being?," goes unanswered. Isobel Clarke, an early biographer, attributed Mansfield's relative

From KATHERINE MANSFIELD by Rhoda B. Nathan. Copyright © 1988 by Rhoda B. Nathan. Reprinted by permission of The Continuum Publishing Company.

failure of appreciation to a cultural preference of the reading audience of her day. "The English public does not encourage short stories," she wrote. "It prefers the novel, and for choice, a very long one." Apparently, writers such as Lawrence, A. E. Coppard, and Somerset Maugham, who began with the short story, lived long enough to become novelists of note and were thus exempt from disapprobation or from being regarded as literary lightweights or being stuck at a way station before reaching their ultimate destination as novelists. Mansfield never wrote anything other than the short story, and there are few indications that she intended to move beyond that form, which she mastered at an early age. And although she could very well join Crane in the category of excessive indulgence and self-destructiveness in the romantic nineteenth-century tradition, she is firmly entrenched in literary history as a twentieth-century figure, and is therefore denied the flaming stamp of excess, even though her life bore ample witness of it. Her work must therefore be judged on its merit as it stands, and must be evaluated according to its contribution to the genre of the short story, without the indulgence of a hypothetical literary output of a longer life. Her stories must stand on their own, as do Guy de Maupassant's, and in our own day, the short stories of the *New Yorker* writers, many of whom have exclusively written short stories for decades. The emergence of the gifted short story writer of the twentieth century, craftsmen such as Peter Taylor and William Trevor, has justified the genre as independent of other literary forms. Today the author need no longer defend himself against the charge of miniaturizing or for preparing for something larger, like a novel.

Mansfield's legacy has been a manipulated one, clouded by the expurgation of her *Journal* and letters, principally by her husband J. Middleton Murry, whose motives were probably, at best, directed towards protecting his late wife, and, at worst, towards starting a "cult" of Katherine. Sentimental profiles such as Clarke's and excerpted love letters between Mansfield and Murry, published under such steamy titles as *Passionate Pilgrim* and profusely illustrated, have the impact of Valentine cards and demean her professionalism. Today, after some intervening years and a lessening of public curiosity about the scandalous aspects of her life, it is possible to view her work dispassionately. In addition, in the interest of satisfying those who still require a weightier body of work to measure a writer's achievement, it is possible to evaluate the stories, taken together, as larger than the sum of their parts. The New Zealand stories, for instance, have the weight of an episodic novel, much as Frank O'Connor's linked tales of his Irish Catholic boyhood do, or James Joyce's stories in *Dubliners*. Her startlingly perceptive stories of courtship, love, and marriage can stand as a cycle of personal relationships in the vein of George Moore's sonnet cycle on the subject called *Married Love* or Maupassant's collection of tales of domestic life.

It might be useful to examine Mansfield's short stories alongside the short fiction of Franz Kafka, her exact contemporary and a writer who made his mark in the short story and revealed himself in his *Journal* and letters as she did, and whose conflict with his authoritarian father, closely documented in his *Letters to My Father,* is reminiscent of Katherine's conflict with her "pa-man" father. To complete the analogy, Kafka died of tuberculosis at the age of thirty-one after a long, anguished, fully recorded struggle with the disease. Like Mansfield, he left a lot of unfinished work for his editor to sort out. Also, like Mansfield, he was, both in his life and art, a divided person. To have been a Jew in turn-of-the-century Prague was to experience guilt and pessimism, attitudes that became the center of his moral vision. Mansfield's colonial origins, which she bore with a mixture of nostalgia and chagrin, rendered her, like Kafka, a divided self, never completely at home in Europe, where she did most of her writing, and chafing when she returned to New Zealand. But the bohemian self-exiled Mansfield, the epitome of the "modern" in her personal life, never became a "modernist" in her fiction, whereas Kafka's fiction is a very textbook of modernism.

John Updike, in his foreword to *The Complete Stories* of Franz Kafka, writes that "sixty years after his death, Kafka epitomizes one aspect of modernism: a sensation of anxiety and shame, whose center cannot be located and therefore cannot be placated." Updike notes that Kafka's stories are marked by a great deal of building towards the formulation of plot, with a lot of contortion in the process, but rarely does he complete his fictional journey. Mansfield's stories are exempt from these hallmarks of modernism. As daring as she was in touching upon subjects that were still avoided in her day, her stories are relatively free of the modernist angst that marked Kafka and his European contemporaries. Structurally, her stories, unlike Kafka's, are, with rare exceptions, complete. If the term "well made" could be expropriated from the theater to apply to narrative fiction, Mansfield's stories, like Somerset Maugham's, might be regarded as relentlessly well made. Even her fragments demonstrate discernible movement towards resolution. The division within herself did not direct her, as it did Kafka, towards extended psychological preparation for action that often did not develop. Her backgrounds, both actual and psychological, internal and external, are shrewdly and efficiently laid down in preparation for a dramatic moment of crisis that ends in epiphany as well as resolution. "The Dill Pickle" and "Bliss" are illustrative of her creative process. Although neither ends happily, each concludes with a resolution responsive to the story's central theme. In both stories, the characters are forced by incontrovertible evidence to confront the truths of their lives that are pushing up through thickly planted and cultivated illusions. The stories end without a trace of moral ambivalence and with no psychological issue unresolved.

Perhaps the key to Mansfield's carefully finished stories lies in her essential personal difference from modernists such as Kafka. The most apparent distinction between them is that while he was philosophical and mistrusted the politics and culture of his society, as did his fellow modernists James Joyce and Thomas Mann, she did not. This bohemian daughter of a Victorian colonial family never doubted her personal safety nor her political survival. She could always go home again, and she often did, both literally and nostalgically. Therefore her fiction simply does not concern itself with the anxiety, guilt, and anomie associated with modernism. On another level, the vocational one, she differed from most of the modernists as well. Kafka, for instance, left instructions to have his manuscripts burned after his death. Like many of his fellow modernists, he was ambivalent about his choice of career. Mansfield was not. She was determined to publish as much as she could and struggled to complete as many of her stories as possible in the face of her failing powers. Even as she shuttled from one place to another in search of restoration, she wrote incessantly to her friends about her race to beat the clock. A letter to Lady Ottoline Morell is typical. She wrote it while she was partially bedridden and struggling to complete the ambitious "The Daughters of the Late Colonel": "I couldn't stop. I wrote it all day and on my way back to bed sat on the stairs and began scribbling the bit about the meringues." Her debilitating disease did not exempt her from work. Unlike Kafka, who worked on and off on projects that he never finished, she treated her illness as a goad to her creativity.

To place Mansfield in critical perspective with her contemporaries, her personal and professional relationships with two literary giants of her day should be considered. D. H. Lawrence and Virginia Woolf were significant presences in Mansfield's life—Lawrence personally and Woolf professionally. She met Lawrence in 1913, when she and Murry, like Lawrence and Frieda Weekley, were living together but not yet married. Although Jeffrey Meyers declares that Lawrence was destined to have a "profound emotional impact" on her, he appears to have had no literary influence on her at all. When she and Murry joined with Lawrence in a short-lived publication venture, a magazine called *Signature,* she was harshly critical of Lawrence's writing. Even years later, when she disapproved of something she had read, primarily for looseness of structure or self-reference that bordered on the egotistical, she would condemn it as a "*Signature* style of writing." The little magazine lasted for only three issues, at the end of which Mansfield dissociated herself from the entire venture, expressing disappointment with Lawrence's contribution—a personal essay with fictional overtones, called "The Crown."

If Lawrence's fiction had no influence on her work, Katherine and Murry, as personalities, had a striking impact on Lawrence. He used them and his feelings about them in a number of short stories, and modeled Gudrun Brangwen on Katherine and Gerald Crich on Murry in his novel *Women in Love* in 1920, five years after the ill-fated *Signature* enterprise. The character of Gudrun was not flattering to Katherine, emphasizing the qualities Lawrence found least attractive in her. For her part, Katherine declared the sexually aggressive and destructive Gudrun repellent. However, the two couples remained friends, and wrote for the same literary magazines, *Rhythm, The New Age,* and *Athenaeum,* during their long and occasionally stormy friendship. The bond between them was strong enough for Frieda, by then married to Lawrence, to give Katherine her old wedding ring to wear when she married

Murry, and Katherine never took it off, leaving instructions that she be buried with it. Katherine liked Lawrence for his enthusiasm and his "merry, rich, laughing self," as she confided to her friend Dorothy Brett in a letter, while her reactions to his writing remained uncharitable to the end. In 1920, reflecting on Lawrence's current work of fiction, *The Lost Girl,* she makes it abundantly clear that she could never be influenced by him as an artist: "Lawrence denies his humanity. He denies the powers of his imagination. He denies life—I mean *human* life. His hero and heroine are non-human. They are animals on the prowl. They do not feel: they scarcely speak. . . . They submit to their physical responses and for the rest go veiled, blind—faceless, mindless." Her unforgiving judgment of Lawrence may very well be explained as rancor kindled by his classifying her art as "miniature" through the thinly disguised portrait of Gudrun in *Women in Love.* Their complex relationship endured until Katherine's death. Lawrence, who rarely complained about his own lung ailment and thought the less of Mansfield for her open discussion of her symptoms, which he judged to be exaggerated, outlived her by seven years.

Mansfield's relationship with Virginia Woolf was more professional than personal. Although she wrote to Virginia and visited with the Woolfs frequently, Virginia made it clear that Katherine was not in her social class and kept herself somewhat aloof from the young colonial artist. Although the Woolfs handset, printed, and published "Prelude" in their Hogarth Press, during her lifetime they treated her with the condescension of acknowledged royalty, as the Bloomsburys surely were, to a little New Zealand upstart. After "Bliss" was published, Virginia threw the story aside with a disgusted "She's done for," but after Katherine's death confessed that she was the only writer whose talent had ever threatened her own position. Katherine, for her part, was as critical of Virginia's work as she was enthralled by the elder writer's personal qualities and social position. In her review of Woolf's novel *Night and Day* in *Athenaeum* she offered some tactful remarks about the novel's "deliberateness," but in the privacy of her own *Journal* she slapped her for coldness and bloodlessness. She disliked Woolf's dehumanizing abstractions as much as she deplored Lawrence's excessive animal heat, the very antithesis of Woolf's defects.

The aristocratic Virginia Woolf, the bourgeois Katherine Mansfield, and the working-class D. H. Lawrence could never be considered to have constituted a "movement" or a "school" of writing. They were drawn together by accident, through mutual advantage, by professional circumstances, and the profession they had in common. They shared no stylistic qualities or social points of view. They cooperated when it suited them and engaged in sporadic rivalries. It is highly likely that the three were in fact drawn to each other by their emotional and physical instabilities, each of them being supported and protected by more stable marital partners. All three died painful and premature deaths, leaving these same mates to outlive them for many years as keepers of the flame.

# Katherine Mansfield and the Search for Truth

## DAVID DAICHES

Even in the most realistic fiction there is always some degree of symbolic value attached to the particular incidents selected for presentation. Everything has its representative aspect, however obscurely or implicitly. And this applies not only to the events in a story but to the objects described or referred to as the setting, and to the phrases employed in the dialogue. Indeed, the nature of language is such that any attempt to communicate the nature of a situation involves a suggestion of the type of thing before the specific thing can become clear. But in fiction the suggestion of the type is not merely a means through which the specific is arrived at; it exists in its own right and possesses its own importance. For the literary artist the full quality of an event, or whatever it is that he is describing, resides largely, if not primarily, in its symbolic aspect, the degree to which it is an adequate symbol of the aspect of experience of which the given event is but one example. This is but another way of expressing the old commonplace about the universal and the particular in art; but it is important to look at the matter in this way if we are to understand some of the main problems, both of attitude and of technique, that have faced writers of fiction in the present century.

Modern fiction has been concerned, to a greater degree than fiction in the eighteenth and nineteenth centuries, with two questions. The first is, What symbol will suggest most effectively the required aspect of experience? And the second is, What aspects of experience do you want your symbol to suggest? The second is the problem of selection that we have discussed in the first chapter; the first is the problem of presenting the results of selection. Increase of psychological knowledge and increase a self-consciousness concerning the way the mind works have tended to make writers more and more aware that the first problem is a problem, and one result of that awareness has been the choice of an ever slighter and more subtle kind of symbol. Indeed, the refinement of symbols has been going on continuously in English fiction from the days of Richardson and Fielding, though in the last generation the process has been speeded up tremendously. If we compare the symbols in *Tom Jones* with the symbols in *The Egoist*—remembering that symbols, in the sense in which

Reprinted from David Daiches, *The Novel and the Modern World* (Chicago: University of Chicago Press, c1939), 65–79.

we are using the term, can be incidents, images, conversations, even characters—we can see that though there has been a considerable refinement in symbols between Fielding and Meredith both writers are unsubtle compared, say, with Proust. Fielding's two squires, and Tom himself, are coarse as symbols—which is not a defect in Fielding's art, as it was an art to which the coarse symbol was entirely appropriate—and Sir Willoughby and his imps are not very much subtler. It is perhaps a defect in Meredith's art, as the kind of psychological probing he was attempting requires a more delicate handling of the symbolic aspects than the almost picaresque narrative of Fielding. There is a much more noticeable increase in the refinement of symbols between Meredith and, say, Virginia Woolf than between Fielding and Meredith.

This process had been going on for some considerable time at an accelerating pace when it was speeded up further by the impingement of our second problem—the problem of selection. To become conscious about selection to the extent that writers of the present century have, involves also an increased self-consciousness in the use of symbols. And that means an increase of subtlety in the employment of incident, image, character, etc., as symbols. Modern fiction thus presents us with a new subtlety both in its view of the significant in experience and in its handling of symbols in expressing that significance. We are presented with individual—as distinct from traditional or conventional—views of reality, and such views emerge from the delicacy of the symbolism employed in the story. Writers begin to worry about "truth"—the "truth of the idea," the "essential truth of the situation." Truth, in the definition here implied, emerges from proper selection combined with proper handling of symbols. These were two aspects of literary art about which the Victorians were hardly conscious. The first they took for granted and the second they saw no reason to worry about. The search for truth that Katherine Mansfield pursued all her life, and which culminated in her retirement at Fontainebleau, they would not have understood as a general problem of adjustment to experience, and would have understood even less as a problem of technique in short-story writing. The problem that Katherine Mansfield faced was essentially a problem of her generation, not to be understood by those who came before or, presumably, by those who will come too long after. If she saw it as a problem independent of movements of civilization, that was simply because she was so intensely aware of it both as an artist and as a person.

The Victorian writer was also concerned with truth, but it was a quite different kind of truth. In an age when traditional values determine selection in art—the artist either agreeing or revolting, but in either case accepting the tradition as relevant, as something significantly true or significantly false—truth for the novelist is what he observes, the object of observation having been previously modified, as well as selected, in terms of a preconceived attitude, and the records of the observation being conditioned by the types of emotion, the organization of impulses, reactions, etc., produced by convention, education, public opinion, example, and all kinds of ritualistic practices and magical beliefs that are normal features of any fairly stable civilization. And when a decision had to be made concerning the truth or the falsehood of a work of art, it was made on grounds that can be illustrated, perhaps, by Alexander Macmillan's letter to Thomas Hardy, written after Hardy had sent Macmillan the manuscript of *The Poor Man and the Lady* in 1868:

> I have read through the novel you were so good as to send me with care and with much interest and admiration, but feeling at the same time that it has what seems to me fatal drawbacks to its success, and what, I think, judging the writer from the book itself, you would feel even more strongly—its truthfulness and justice.

Thus in the first paragraph of the letter the question of truth is raised—linked, however, to a much less objective quality, justice. The letter continues:

> Your description of country life among working men is admirable, and, although I can only judge it from the corresponding life of Scotland, which I knew well when young, palpably truthful. Your pictures of character among Londoners, and especially the upper classes, are sharp, clear, incisive and in many respects true, but they are wholly dark—not a ray of light visible to relieve the darkness, and therefore exaggerated and untrue in their result.

True *but* dark, and *therefore* untrue. That is what the argument in the last sentence amounts to. Truth of observation is not "truth"; for the thing observed ought to have been modified before observation by the conceptions about life in general of the observer, and if that has not been done the necessary modifications must be made afterward. If you paint $x$, your view of $x$ must be modified by your consciousness that $y$ and $z$ also exist, and that $y$ and $z$, as well as $x$, have qualities and values of a certain kind. To allow yourself to view $x$ without the modification in your observation that comes from bearing in mind the existence and the qualities of $y$ and $z$ will result in your giving an "untrue" picture of $x$. The fourth paragraph of the letter is equally illuminating:

> I like your tone infinitely better. But it seems to me that your black wash will not be recognised as anything more than ignorant misrepresentation. Of course I don't know what opportunities you have of seeing the class you deal with. . . . But it is inconceivable to me that any considerable number of human beings—God's creatures—should be so bad without going to utter wreck in a week.[1]

This culminating argument is no argument at all, but simply a piece of magical incantation. (It has not infrequently been used by liberals as an excuse for not doing anything about fascism.) The phrase "it is inconceivable to me" deliberately removes the argument from the plane of objective reality, while the parenthetical "God's creatures" suggests that if he believed Hardy he would be going counter to some belief enjoined by his religion and therefore the facts, even if they appear so to observation, cannot be really so. Much more obvious examples could be given—the reception in England of Zola's work would be an outstanding one of this view of truth as some amalgam made up of the facts of observation, a conventional view of what things ought to be, and various magical elements, with the facts of observation not necessarily the dominating component; but we have chosen this letter because it shows us a critic of intelligence faced directly with the problem of truth in fiction in its simplest form and presenting his argument with clarity and moderation.

Truth viewed in terms of the conventions and assumptions of a stable civilization ceased to be regarded as truth when it became obvious that that civilization was losing its stability, when its criteria of value were ceasing to be universal, and when its conventions were coming to be viewed as irrelevant. Consciousness of the arbitrary nature of any such "classical" standard of truth in fiction, together with the growing interest in psychology and the increase in self-awareness that psychological knowledge was bringing, resulted in the complete realization on the part of the more sensitive writers of the false objectivity involved in the traditional approach and technique. The consequent attempt to discount these distorting factors in selection, observation, and method of recording led to dependence on a controlled, but nonetheless personal, delicacy of response to detail. This, as in Katherine Mansfield's case, had implications for technique as well as attitude. There came a shift of emphasis in the whole organization of narrative. Objective truth having been discredited—shown up as anything but objective—that author who was aware of, and sensitive to, contemporary currents of thought was led either to be a scientist, as he fondly thought, using psychology as his science, or else to depend on a personal sense of truth as Katherine Mansfield did. The scientific alternative has proved its barrenness as a substitute for a traditional criterion of value in experience because psychology—the science most favored—is, like all sciences, explanatory but not normative. The psychologically "scientific" writers were thus slipping in some external criterion of value even when they thought they were most scientific and objective. The stream-of-consciousness technique is simply a technique and cannot itself determine the end for which it is to be used. The French naturalists had made the same kind of mistake, believing that fiction could give a scientific account of reality; all they did was to choose different events from those chosen by the romantic writers; and in their case it was a revolt within a tradition, the new selection being the equal and opposite of the old, the old being regarded as wrong rather than irrelevant. (To choose black instead of white is not to abandon the whole tradition which produced the choice of white; for it still involves the recognition that the choice is between black and white—that both black and white are significant choices: to say, however, that color is not important and the thing that matters is texture, or shape, would mean an abandonment of the old tradition.)

The rejection of the use of formulas in observation, therefore, had a twofold result. On the one hand, it encouraged writers to seek an illusive norm in science, with many resulting confusions both in creation and in criticism and, on the other hand, it encouraged dependence on a personal sense of truth—a seeking for greater objectivity by making art more subjective. The paradox involved here is one that confronts us frequently in the history of art. The search for complete objectivity leads to complete subjectivity. Katherine Mansfield finds the "greatest truth of the idea" in the reactions of her own sensibility. Joyce created a microcosm of all human activity out of his own very limited personal experiences in Dublin. The final limit of subjectivity resulting from a search for complete objectivity is reached in Joyce's *Finnegans Wake.* Yet the aim is always to get completely outside one's self. "I can't tell the truth about Aunt Anne unless I am free to enter her life without self-consciousness," writes Katherine Mansfield in her *Journal.* And again: "Calm yourself. Clear yourself. Anything that I write in this mood will be no good; it will be full of *sediment.* . . . One must practise to *forget* oneself." The mind must be a perfectly clear glass through which objective truth can pass undistorted. Then the personal sense of truth will correspond with reality. This doctrine involves the cultivation of a certain type of sensitivity to a point where observation or recollection is sufficient to set in motion a whole set of personal value judgments with their implications. The observer is confident that his reactions represent some kind of ultimate correspondence with what is observed or recollected.

What is this sensitivity that Katherine Mansfield cultivated so deliberately, to the point where it tended to defeat itself? It is simply an ability to see in objects what others, not possessed of this sensitivity, are unable to see; an ability to see as symbols objects which to others are not symbols at all or are symbols of more obvious things. It implies a quality in the observer and does not refer to anything in the thing observed. The potentiality for arousing emotion possessed by an object depends entirely on the mind of the observer of the object, not at all on inherent qualities in the object. If by our way of writing we can persuade others to see as we see, to view as a subtle symbol what they otherwise would regard merely as a stray fact, our literary work is sensitive, as Katherine Mansfield's is sensitive.

Are we to conclude that the search for objective truth is, as far as the artist is concerned, in the nature of things vain? Without going into any of the problems of epistemology, we can say that for the artist at least there is no escape from the two alternatives: reality is judged either by a traditional sense of truth or by a personal sense of truth. Whatever science or philosophy may be, literature is a presentation of facts—real or imagined—which implies at the same time, through the method of presentation or simply by the choice of facts presented, or by both, an interpretation of those facts. This—to put the matter at its crudest—is what distinguishes a story from a mere record of events; what distinguishes a tragedy from an account of unpleasant happenings. (There is, of course, no one definition of tragedy, types of interpretation differ, but interpretation of some kind there must be.) There is always interpretation, and often where there seems to be none the interpretation is most profound and most original. Tchekov and Katherine Mansfield both appeared to many contemporary critics to be presenting merely casual arrangements of detail. That was because they approached those writers' work looking for an interpretation in terms of a tradition and not in terms of a personal sense of value. As a rule it takes the critic longer than the artist to adapt himself to the changed atmosphere of a civilization.

Sensitivity—at least in so far as the term has been applied to writers like Katherine Mansfield—is thus the measure of difference between the personal and the conventional, or traditional, types of interpretation of observed experience. If applied to a writer working wholly within the tradition of a stable civilization, it would refer to the writer's ability to apply the traditional interpretation to realms where it would be thought by the insensitive to be inapplicable or irrelevant. Ability to communicate this sensitivity is, of course, necessary if it is to be the quality of an artist. We have no means of judging unexpressed sensitivity. "Mute inglorious Miltons" are just not Miltons, because it is communicative ability and not attitude that constitutes the differentiating qualities of the artist: if they are mute they are not Miltons. Some critics may be much more sensitive than some writers; they differ in their inability to express the results of that sensitivity in art.

The two main questions concerning European and American literature of recent times are centered on two main points: the type of observation of experience and the way of communicating the results of that observation. Katherine Mansfield's response to experience was such that she was able to extract, and present, the greatest significance from a very limited phase of it. She seems to have been driven almost against her will to the short-story form, and when she tried to write a full-length novel she found herself simply unable to do it. *At the Bay* and *Prelude* are the longest things she did, but they are no more than introductions to a novel. She preferred to approach human activity from the very limited single situation and work "out," setting going overtones and implications by means of her manipulation of symbols, rather than to start from some general view and work "in" by means of illustrative fable. The latter is the method of most great art in the realm of fiction and drama. The artist observes particulars, arrives by induction at some general view concerning aspects of human activity, and embodies this general view in a particular story. The movement is, so far as we can tell in judging from the finished product, from particulars to a universal and then to an illustrative particular. Katherine Mansfield's artistic activity involves no such threefold process: she starts with one particular, and such universal aspects as there are emerge very indirectly, by implication, as a result of her organization of detail. We are not suggesting, of course, that in either case the process is conscious. But it seems clear that Shakespeare, for example, observed men, then came to some general conclusions about certain aspects of human behavior, and finally illustrated these conclusions in his plays. It seems equally clear that with Katherine Mansfield the particular cases of initial observation provided the story. That was why she was so anxious to observe "without self-consciousness," to observe with utter clarity, because there was no subsequent process of comparison and reflection to refine and correct the original observation. In this type of literature it is the actual form of the story which gives symbolic (universal) value to the incidents. There is thus no simple relation between form and content, no story $x$ presented through a medium $y$. The nature of the medium reflects back on, and to a large extent determines, the nature of the content. It is, like lyrical poetry, a type of writing where conception unites instantaneously subject (matter) with style (form). If we asked ourselves what is the story of *The Daughters of the Late Colonel,* for example, we should find it very difficult to express even the idea behind it, the conception underlying it, in any other terms than those employed by the author herself in telling it. It is a commonplace of criticism that what a work of literature says can only be adequately expressed by the work itself. And it is true, in a sense, of all great literature. Yet we can summarize the ideas behind *Hamlet,* give an abstract of the play that will mean something to a reader, even if every man's summary would differ from his neighbor's. But even this can hardly be done with the best and most characteristic of Katherine Mansfield's short stories. Katherine Mansfield expresses a personal sense of truth embodied in a personal vision of an aspect of human behavior. It is literature as vision rather than as fable.

We can perhaps distinguish between two main types of literary activity. There is, first, literature as fable—a story to illustrate a point, to put it most crudely. Anthropologically, the prototype of this kind of activity would be the myth, but it can be developed with infinite degrees of subtlety and sophistication. *Oedipus Rex, Hamlet, Bleak House, Uncle Tom's Cabin, The Way of All Flesh, A Farewell to Arms*—to take quite random examples—are all, in vastly different degrees of subtlety, works of this kind. Most fiction and drama would come into this division. It is for this kind of literature that Aristotle legislated in his *Poetics,* where he rightly said that plot was what mattered most. For fable literature plot is by far the most important element; it is the action that illustrates the thesis—that makes the point. (The situation is, of course, being deliberately simplified for the sake of clarity.) The other type of literature we may call the literature of vision, of which the type is lyric poetry, at least in some of its aspects. The extremes at both ends are the fable proper, such as we find in Aesop, and the visionary lyric, such as we find in Blake. The latter type of literature is much rarer in prose than it is in poetry—for the distinction cuts across the prose-poetry division—and thus we can agree with Mr. Middleton Murry when he says of Katherine Mansfield that "her affinities are rather with the English poets than with the English prose-writers." Katherine Mansfield's desire for truth was not desire for a more adequate fable but for a more intense vision. Her whole life, as well as her work, goes to prove this: for what other purpose was her final retirement to Fontainebleau? The story as fable hardly matters with her. She tells in her *Journal* that she has scores of stories waiting to be written, but they must wait—wait until she can contemplate them with the proper intensity of vision. To this kind of writing the *Poetics* is totally irrelevant. A great deal of unnecessary squabbling about critical principles would have been avoided if critics had recognized the fundamental nature of this distinction between two types of literature.

The literature of vision tends to come into prose as a part of the reaction against what is regarded as an overformulated, and therefore not sufficiently objective, type of fable literature. The personal sense of truth replaces the formulas of a civilization. The next stage is, presumably, a new realization that some sort of formula must be applied to experience before it can be objectively described in fiction at all. The paradox of the search for objectivity leading to greater subjectivity is admitted, and there is a return to the classic ideal again as a way out. There is some hope that the new formula—although it may be wishful thinking to see any signs of it at all—represents not simply a return to arbitrary convention but is some kind of reintegration on a higher level. Perhaps the Hegelian dialectic applies to the progress of literature, and out of thesis and antithesis we get synthesis. This is not to claim that literature gets progressively better, but simply that, once a certain degree of self-consciousness regarding the psychological and other processes involved in determining attitudes and value judgments has been attained, formulas will become more easily recognized for what they are, and thus more foolproof. The true literary artist does not need to be concerned about the nature of the formula in vogue in his day, because he is able to use it simply as a formula for discussing reality and does not confuse it with reality itself. In other words, he is not affected by the formula's being more or less foolproof, because he is not a fool anyway. There are, of course, types of formula which no genuine artist can accept—formulas which instead of interpreting reality contradict it, which instead of enabling the writer to integrate conflicting elements into a pattern force him with a Procrustean hand into a cramped pattern which finds no reflection in his own sensibility. That is one reason why great literary art is impossible in a fascist country.

### Notes

1. Quoted by W. R. Rutland, *Thomas Hardy: A Study of His Writings* (Oxford: Basil Blackwell, 1938), Appen. I, pp. 353–54.

# An Author in Search of a Subject

### FRANK O'CONNOR

Katherine Mansfield is for me something unusual in the history of the short story. She was a woman of brilliance, perhaps of genius; she chose the short story as her own particular form and handled it with considerable skill, and yet for most of the time she wrote stories that I read and forget, read and forget. My experience of stories by real storytellers, even when the stories are not first-rate, is that they leave a deep impression on me. It may not be a total impression; it may not even be an accurate one, but it is usually deep and permanent. I remember it in the way in which I remember poetry. I do not remember Katherine Mansfield's stories in that way. She wrote a little group of stories about her native country, New Zealand, which are recognized as masterpieces and probably are masterpieces, but I find myself forgetting even these and rediscovering them as though they were the work of a new writer.

It may be that for me and people of my own generation her work has been obscured by her legend, as the work of Rupert Brooke has been, and the work is always considerably dimmer than the legend. The story of the dedicated doomed artist, the creature of flame married to a dull unimaginative man persists; persists so strongly, indeed, that one has to keep on reminding oneself that the story is largely the creation of the dull unimaginative man himself. Most of us who were young when the *Journal* was published took an immediate dislike to John Middleton Murry, and I suspect that some of the scornful obituaries that appeared after his death were the work of men who had taken the legend of Katherine Mansfield too seriously. Meanwhile, Murry, a man with an inordinate capacity for punishment, continued to publish letters of hers that seemed to show him in a still worse light.

Obviously there was some truth in the legend since Murry himself believed it, and since the mark left on one's imagination by the *Journal* and letters remains; and yet I get the impression that in the editing of the book he was unfair to himself and far, far too fair to his wife. There must have been another side to her which has not yet emerged from the memoirs of the time. Friends of Murry and hers have told me that they seemed less interested in each other than in the copy they supplied to each other—a likely enough

Reprinted from Frank O'Connor, *The Lonely Voice: A Study of the Short Story* (London: Macmillan Press Ltd., 1963), 128–142.

weakness in two young writers who were both in love with literature, though one wouldn't gather it from what either has written. Francis Carco, after his flirtation with Katherine, portrayed her as a rapacious copyhound, while in "Je ne parle pas français" she caricatured him as a pimp. Childish, spiteful, vulgar if you like, but something that has been carefully edited out of the legend. One might even say that by creating the legend Murry did his wife's reputation more harm than good, for by failing to describe, much less emphasize, the shoddy element in her character, he suppressed the real miracle of her development as an artist.

Therefore, if I emphasize what seems to me the shoddy element it is almost by way of experiment. Most of her work seems to me that of a clever, spoiled, malicious woman. Though I know nothing that would suggest she had any homosexual experiences, the assertiveness, malice, and even destructiveness in her life and work make me wonder whether she hadn't. It would be too much to exaggerate the significance of her occasionally sordid love affairs, of which we probably still have something to learn, but the idea of "experience" by which she justified them is a typical expedient of the woman with a homosexual streak who envies men and attributes their imaginary superiority to the greater freedom with which they are supposed to be able to satisfy their sexual appetite. It is the fallacy of Virginia Woolf's *A Room of One's Own,* and one has only to think of Emily Dickinson or Jane Austen rejoicing in the freedom of a traveling salesman to realize how fallacious it is. The trouble with "experience" in the sense in which Katherine Mansfield sought it is that by being self-conscious it becomes self-defeating. The eye is always looking beyond the "experience" to the use that is to be made of it, and in the process the experience itself has changed its nature, and worldliness no longer means maturity but a sort of permanent adolescence.

> I crouched against him like a wild cat. Quite impersonally, I admired my silver stockings bound beneath the knee with spiked ribbons, my yellow suede shoes fringed with white fur. How vicious I looked! We made love to each other like two wild beasts.

If Katherine Mansfield really did write this after one of her amorous orgies—and in one way or another this was what she was always doing—the "copy" she was collecting was on a par with the "experience" and could only result in a permanent attitude of knowingness concealing a complete emotional immaturity. I sometimes wonder if Middleton Murry really knew what he was writing when he told so charmingly the story of their love affair—*her* suggestion that he should share her flat, *her* use of his surname when she said goodnight that compelled him to call her "Mansfield," *her* "Why don't you make me your mistress?" He was an innocent man: it is he who says somewhere in perfect innocence that Lawrence was as much in love with Frieda's husband as with Frieda herself, but surely it should have occurred to him that from the first moment Katherine Mansfield was adopting the position of the man in their relationship.

There is one quality that is missing in almost everything that Katherine Mansfield wrote—even her New Zealand stories—and that is heart. Where heart should be we usually find sentimentality, the quality that seems to go with a brassy exterior, and nowhere more than with that of an "emancipated" woman. In literature sentimentality always means falsity, for whether or not one can perceive the lie, one is always aware of being in the presence of a lie.

"Je ne parle pas français" is a good example. It is generally accepted as a free description of Katherine Mansfield's first meeting with Francis Carco, and Carco himself admits the resemblance. It describes a sensitive, dreamy girl brought on an illicit honeymoon to Paris by a Mother's Boy who, because he does not wish to hurt Momma, abandons her there to the care of his pimp friend—drawn from Carco—though the pimp friend, finding no use for her, abandons her as well.

A touching little story, and if one could read it "straight," as I am told such stories should be read, one's sympathy would go out to the heroine, every one of whose glances and tears is lovingly observed. But how can one read it straight? The first question I ask myself is how this angelic creature ever became the mistress of anybody, let alone of such a monster of egotism as her lover. Is it that she was completely innocent? But if so, why doesn't she do what any innocent girl with money in her pocket would do on discovering that she has been abandoned in a strange city by a man she had trusted and go home on the next train? Not perhaps back to her parents but at least to some old friend? Has she no home? No friend? None of the essential questions a short story should answer is answered here, and in fact, when I read the story "straight," knowing nothing of the author's life, I merely felt it was completely unconvincing.

Knowing what I do now, I do not find it much more satisfactory. Was Murry, to whom Katherine Mansfield submitted it first, supposed to read it "straight"? "But I hope you'll see (of course you will)," she wrote to him, "that I'm not writing with a sting." Apparently he did not see. Indeed, being a very sensitive man, he may even have wondered at the insensitiveness of a woman who could send such a story for his approval.

But even more than by the element of falsity in these stories I am put off by the feeling that they were all written in exile. I do not mean by this merely that they were written by a New Zealander about Germany, England, and France, three countries any one of which would be sufficient to keep a story-teller occupied for several lifetimes. I mean that there is no real indication of a submerged population, a population which is not by its very nature in need of a coherent voice. To Katherine Mansfield as to Dickens the lower classes are merely people who say "perishall" when they mean "parasol" and "certingty" when they mean "certainty." Reading the stories all through again I experienced the same shock I experienced thirty years ago when I came on "The Life of Ma Parker" and I found myself saying, "Ah, so this is what was missing! So this is what short stories are really about!"

Like much of Katherine Mansfield's work, this story is influenced directly by Chekhov, with whom she always tended to identify herself from the time when she palmed off on Orage a flagrant imitation of Chekhov's famous story about the little baby sitter who is so tired that she smothers the crying baby. "The Life of Ma Parker" is imitated from an equally famous story, "Misery," in which an old cab driver who has lost his son tries to tell his grief to his customers and finally goes down to the stable and tells it to his old nag. Ma Parker, too, having lost her little grandson, is full of her grief, but when she tries to tell her employer about it he merely says, "I hope the funeral was a—success."

And at this point I always stop reading to think, "Now *there* is a mistake that Chekhov wouldn't have made!" and I do not need to go on to the point at which Ma Parker's employer rebukes her for throwing out a teaspoon of cocoa he had left in a tin. Chekhov knew that it is not heartlessness that breaks the heart of the lonely, and it is not Ma Parker's employer who is being coarse but Katherine Mansfield. It is not the only example in her work of a story being spoiled by her assertiveness.

At the same time the story is impressive because Ma Parker is a genuine member of a submerged population, not so much because she is old and poor, which is largely irrelevant, as because, like Chekhov's teachers and priests, she has no one else to speak for her.

It is generally agreed that the principal change in Katherine Mansfield's work occurs after the death of her brother, Chummie, in the First World War. It seems to have been her first contact with real personal grief, and her reaction was violent, even immoderate. "First, my darling, I've got things to do for both of us, and then I will come as quickly as I can," she writes in her *Journal*. What the things were she revealed when she asked herself why she did not commit suicide. "I have a duty to perform to the lovely time when we were both alive. I want to write about it, and he wanted me to. We talked it over in my little top room in London. I said: I will just put on the front page: To my brother, Leslie Heron Beauchamp. Very well: it shall be done."

Of course, it is all girlishly overdramatic in the Katherine Mansfield way, but that is no reflection on its sincerity. After all, it was done, and done splendidly.

She had always been fond of her brother, though to my mind—still speaking in the part of devil's advocate—this is scarcely sufficient to explain the violence of her grief, which sent a normally affectionate husband like Murry home from the South of France, ashamed of himself for thinking of a dead boy as a rival. Once more, I begin to wonder whether the assertive, masculine streak in her had not made her jealous of her brother. There is nothing abnormal about that: it is possible for a woman to love a brother dearly and yet be jealous of the advantages which he seems to possess; and of course, the jealousy cannot survive death, for once the superiority, real or imaginary, is removed, and the beloved brother is merely a name on a tombstone, the struggling will has no obstacles to contend with and the place of jealousy tends to be taken by guilt—by the feeling that one had grudged the brother such little advantages as he possessed, even by the fantasy that one had caused his death. All this is well within the field of ordinary human experience; it is the immoderacy of the reaction in Katherine Mansfield that puzzles me.

I feel sure that something of the sort is necessary to explain the extraordinary change that took place in her character and work—above all in her work, for here the change does not seem to be a normal development of her talent at all but a complete reversal of it. In fact, it is much more like the result of a religious crisis than of an artistic one, and, like the result of a lot of other religious crises, it leaves the critic watchful and unsatisfied. "Did he give up the drink too soon?" is a question we must all have had to ask ourselves from time to time in connection with our friends. For Katherine Mansfield, the woman, the crisis was to end in the dreary charlatanism of Fontainebleau and become the keystone of her legend, but from the point of view of Katherine Mansfield, the writer, that gesture seems immoderate, heroic, and absolutely unnecessary. No one need point out to me that this viewpoint is limited, and that it is not for a critic of literature to say what act of heroism is or is not necessary, but he must do it just the same if he is to be true to his own standards.

It seems to me that Katherine Mansfield's tragedy is, from the inside, the tragedy that Chekhov never tired of observing from the outside—the tragedy of the false personality. That clever, assertive, masculine woman was a mistake from beginning to end, and toward the close of her life she recognized it herself. Writing of herself, characteristically in the third person, she said, "She had led, ever since she can remember, a very typically false life." This is my complaint of John Murry's legend: because he loved Katherine Mansfield he gave no indication of the false personality, and so blotted the true and moving story of the brassy little shopgirl of literature who made herself into a great writer. With that sentence of hers one should compare the passage I have already quoted from Chekhov's letter to Souvorin—"Could you write a story of how this young man squeezes the slave out of himself drop by drop, and how, on waking up one morning, he feels that the blood coursing through his veins is real blood and not the blood of a slave?" That, I fancy, is how Katherine Mansfield would have wished to be described, but Murry could not bear to see how much of the slave there was in the woman he loved.

The conflict between the false personality and the ideal one is very clear in some of the stories, and nowhere more than in the second book in which the two personalities stand side by side in "Je ne parle pas français" and "Prelude." The false personality, determined largely by the will, dominates the former story; an ideal alternative personality—*not* the true one because that never emerged fully—determined by a complete surrender of the will, dominates the latter. As a result of the conflict in her, Katherine Mansfield's reply to the activity imposed on her by her own overdeveloped will is an antithesis—pure contemplation.

For obvious reasons she identified this contemplativeness with that of Chekhov, the least contemplative writer who ever lived, but her misunderstanding of the great artist with whom she identified herself was a necessary part of her development.

> How *perfect* the world is, with its worms and hooks and ova, how incredibly perfect. There is the sky and the sea and the shape of a lily, and there is all this other as well. The balance how perfect! (Salut, Tchehov!) I would not have the one without the other.

One can imagine the embarrassed cough with which Chekhov would have greeted that girlish effusiveness. His contemplativeness, the contemplativeness of a doctor who must resign himself to the death of a patient he has worked himself to death trying to save, was a very different affair from Katherine Mansfield's, and if, as a wise man he resigned himself, it was never because he had not suffered as a fool.

In one story, "The Garden Party," Katherine Mansfield tries to blend the two personalities, and her failure is even more interesting than the success of stories like "Prelude," where one personality is held in abeyance. Apparently, part of her assertiveness came from her resentment of the aimless life of the moneyed young lady in the provincial society of New Zealand, and during the religious crisis, part of her penance has to be the complete, uncritical acceptance of it. In the story the Sheridans' garden party is haunted by the accidental death of a carter who lives at their gate. Young Laura does not want the garden party to take place; she tries to talk her family out of it but is constantly frustrated and diverted, even by her beloved brother Laurie.

> "My word, Laura! You do look stunning," said Laurie. "What an absolutely topping hat!"
> Laura said faintly, "Is it?" and smiled up at Laurie, and didn't tell him after all.

In the evening, at her mother's suggestion, Laura goes to the carter's cottage with a basket of leftovers from the party. It is true she has her doubts—"Would the poor woman really like that?"—but she manages to overcome them with no great difficulty. For one reader at least, the effect that Katherine Mansfield has been trying to achieve is totally destroyed. The moment she moves from her ideal world, "with its worms and hooks and ova," into a real world where the critical faculty wakes, she ruins everything by her own insensitiveness. It is exactly the same mistake that she makes in "The Life of Ma

Parker." Any incidental poetry there may be in bands, marquees, pastries, and hats—and there is plenty—is dissipated in the sheer grossness of those who enjoy them. The Duc de Guermantes, determined not to hear of the death of an old friend in order not to spoil his party, at least knows what is expected of him. Nothing, one feels, can be expected of the Sheridans.

That is why in the best of the New Zealand stories there is no contact with the real world at all. In his excellent life of Katherine Mansfield, Mr. Antony Alpers quotes a brilliant passage by V. S. Pritchett, contrasting the absence of a real country from "At the Bay" with the flavor of old Russia in Chekhov's "The Steppe," but when Mr. Alpers replies that this quality is absent from Katherine Mansfield's story because it is absent from New Zealand he misses Mr. Pritchett's point entirely. The real reply to Mr. Pritchett— which he probably knows better than anybody—is that to introduce a real country into "At the Bay" would be to introduce history, and with history would come judgment, will, and criticism. The real world of these stories is not New Zealand but childhood, and they are written in a complete hypnotic suspension of the critical faculties.

This is clearest in the episode in "Prelude" in which Pat, the Irish gardener, decapitates a duck to amuse the children and the headless body instantly makes a dash for the duck pond. It would be almost impossible for any other writer to describe this scene without horrifying us; clearly it horrified the critical and fastidious Katherine Mansfield since it haunted her through the years, but she permits the little girl, Kezia, only one small shudder.

> "Watch it!" shouted Pat. He put down the body and it began to waddle— with only a long spurt of blood where the head had been; it began to pad away without a sound towards the steep bank that led to the stream. . . . That was the crowning wonder.
>
> "Do you see that? Do you see that?" yelled Pip. He ran among the little girls tugging at their pinafores.
>
> "It's like a little engine. It's like a funny little railway engine," squealed Isabel.
>
> But Kezia suddenly rushed at Pat and flung her arms round his legs and butted her head as hard as she could against his knees.
>
> "Put head back! Put head back!" she screamed.

For me this is one of the most remarkable scenes in modern literature, for though I have often accused myself of morbid fastidiousness, of a pathological dislike of what is obscene and cruel, I can read it almost as though it were the most delightful incident in a delightful day. No naturalist has ever been able to affect me like this, and I suspect that the reason is that Katherine Mansfield is not observing the scene but contemplating it. This is the Garden of Eden before shame or guilt came into the world. It is also precisely what I mean when I say that the crisis in Katherine Mansfield was religious rather than literary.

These extraordinary stories are Katherine Mansfield's masterpieces and in their own way comparable with Proust's breakthrough into the subconscious world. But one must ask oneself why they *are* masterpieces and afterward whether they represent a literary discovery that she might have developed and exploited as Proust developed and exploited his own discovery. They are masterpieces because they are an act of atonement to her brother for whatever wrong she felt she had done him, an attempt at bringing him back to life so that he and she might live forever in the world she had created for them both. They set out to do something that had never been done before and to do it in a manner that had never been used before, a manner that has something in common with that of the fairy tale.

For instance, to have described the world of childhood through the mind of any of the children would have made this the child's own particular world, subject to time and error, and so the only observer is an angelic one for whom the ideas of good and evil, right and wrong, do not exist. Not only does the narrative switch effortlessly from one character to another, but as in a fairy tale speechless things talk like anyone else. Florrie, the cat in "At the Bay," says, "Thank goodness, it's getting late. Thank goodness, the long day is over"; the infant says, "Don't like babies? Don't like *me*?" and the bush says "We are dumb trees, reaching up in the night, imploring we know not what"; while Beryl's imaginary voices, which describe how wonderful she looked one summer at the bay, are not more unreal—or real—than those of Linda Burnell and her husband.

These stories are conscious, deliberate acts of magic, as though a writer were to go into the room where his beloved lay dead and try to repeat the miracle of Lazarus. In this way they can be linked with the work of other writers like Joyce and Proust, who in their different, more worldly ways were also attempting a magical approach to literature by trying to make the printed page not a description of something that had happened but a substitute for what had happened, an episode as it might appear in the eyes of God—an act of pure creation.

Whether Katherine Mansfield could ever have exploited her own breakthrough into magic is another matter; and here, I think, we are getting closer to the discomfort of V. S. Pritchett before "At the Bay" and my own before that whole group of stories because they continue to fade from my mind, no matter how often I reread them.

Are they really works of art that could have given rise to other works of art and followed the law of their own being? Or are they in fact an outward representation of an act of deliberate martyrdom—the self-destruction of Fontainebleau, which was intended to destroy the false personality Katherine Mansfield had built up for herself. If they represent the former, then the old Katherine would have had to come back in however purified a form. She could never have escaped entirely into a magical version of her childhood and would have had to deal with her own sordid love affairs, her dishonesties, her cruelties. There are tantalizing hints of how this might have happened, for in "The Young Girl" and "The Daughters of the Late Colonel" I seem to see a development of her sense of humor without her coarseness.

But death came too soon, and at the end we can only fall back on the legend that her husband created for her and which has placed her forever among "the inheritors of unfulfilled renown."

# Katherine Mansfield

## J. MIDDLETON MURRY

There are very few writers who have been put more fully into the possession of the public than Katherine Mansfield has been. Quite deliberately, as soon as possible after her death, I made it my duty to gather together and to publish her *Journal* and her *Letters*. It seemed to me a matter of cardinal importance that the world should know what manner of woman—or girl (for she wasn't much more when she died)—Katherine Mansfield was. If ever there were a writer whose life and work were one and inseparable, it was she. I can think only of Keats to compare with her in this respect, that her letters are essential to a real understanding of her work. They form a single whole with her stories: one naturally fulfils and completes the other. Indeed, there were moments when it seemed to me that her letters more completely expressed the nature of her genius than even the most remarkable of her stories. There have been moments when I have felt the same about the poetry and the letters of Keats.

When I set myself to publish the *Letters* and *Journal* of Katherine Mansfield, I was acting, not in a personal capacity, as a man eager to erect a memorial to one whom he had loved and lost, but as a conscious literary critic deeply convinced of the peculiar quality of Katherine's genius and determined to establish it before the world. I disregarded completely all the expostulations of those who—a little overweeningly—professed to be more sensitive than I and tried to represent my action as the violation of an intimacy. Perhaps they were sincere; but I had made up my mind that Katherine Mansfield no longer belonged to me, but to the world. Above all, I believed it my duty to pass on what she herself had called her 'legacy of truth', and I believed that the world would find it as precious as I did.

> Honesty is the only thing one seems to prize beyond life, love, death, everything. It alone remaineth. O those that come after me, will you believe it? At the end, *Truth* is the only thing *worth having*; it's more thrilling than love, more joyful and more passionate.

And my confidence was justified, as I felt it would be. Today her *Journal* and her *Letters* are European classics.

Reprinted from J. Middleton Murry, *Katherine Mansfield and Other Literary Studies* (London: Constable Books, 1959), 71–93.

I do not propose, therefore, to indulge in personal recollections of her. They are unnecessary; and if the reader should desire to know more about our ten years' life together, the full story is told in the first volume of my autobiography. For herself, in her habit as she lived, the *Journal* and *Letters* must suffice, together with the simple verdict of one of her most intimate friends: 'Katherine had a greater genius for being *simply a human being* than anyone I have ever known, or read of'.

It is a simple verdict, and a true one. It is implied in the fact that her *Letters* and *Journal* and her short stories are a single whole to an extent that can be paralleled only in the case of Keats. What does that really mean? It means that there was no difference in kind between her casual and her deliberate utterances; it means that her art was not really distinct from her life; it means that she was never what we understand by a professional writer; it means that she was distinguished by the peculiar gift of *spontaneity*.

I do not wish this word spontaneity to be misunderstood. It is not used to imply that Katherine Mansfield wrote as a bird sings, without effort. On the contrary, I hope to show that an effort—of a very arduous and particular kind—was involved in her writing. When I speak of the peculiar spontaneity of Katherine Mansfield's writing, I use the word in a critical sense precisely as I should apply it to Keats. Keats even in his short life passed through many periods of what he called *agonie ennuyeuse*, 'tedious agony', periods of creative sterility and inward despair. One such period intervened immediately before the writing of the great 'Odes', which mark the topmost pinnacle of spontaneous utterance in our poetry since Shakespeare. Spontaneity, in this critical sense, means an absence of any cleavage or separation between the living self and the writing self. The art corresponds to the human experience: every major advance in the art corresponds to a progression of some sort in the human being. When the human being is confused, at a standstill, bewildered in its own living experience, then the voice of the art is silent. Utterance comes only as the result of inward clarification. That, I think, makes clear what I mean: first, by claiming spontaneity as the distinguishing mark of Katherine Mansfield's genius, and second, by insisting so definitely that she was not a professional writer. She was not a person who constructed patterns of objective beauty; she was not a person who 'told stories'; she was essentially a person who responded—through the instrument of a 'more than ordinary organic sensibility'—to her experience of Life.

From the beginning Katherine Mansfield was marked by a curious eagerness for experience. Her youthful passion for the philosophy of Pater (who bade us 'burn with a hard gemlike flame') and Wilde, her early habit of keeping (and destroying) what she afterwards smilingly called those 'huge complaining diaries'—intimate records of her own experiences—of which only tiny fragments survive, her fierce determination not to be swallowed up again, after her English education, in the life of New Zealand; and, of course, earlier than all these, that intense and innocent childish awareness of life—of even the subtleties of adult psychology—which was afterwards to supply the substance of some of her most magical work: these were all symptoms of an intrinsic eagerness for experience which is in the last resort unanalysable. We have, as Walter Bagehot said, simply to accept the fact that the essential to a great artist is 'an experiencing nature'. Katherine Mansfield seems to have been born with one.

As is generally known, Katherine Mansfield went to London to 'finish' her education. There she became passionately enamoured of music and wanted to become a professional musician. Whether she would have realised her genius in that medium, I don't know. I am no judge of music. The fact that I used to think her playing and her singing marvellous means nothing—except that I am sure that had she so desired she could have achieved an extraordinary reputation as a *diseuse.* However—instead of being allowed to stay on as a musician in London, she had to go back to New Zealand. She went, reluctantly and rebelliously.

Her development as a writer dates from her return to England in July 1908. It was by no means a triumphant return. Her family was bitterly opposed to her determination to go back to England; and she carried her way only after a fearful struggle. Her family had, naturally, not the faintest belief in her capacity to succeed as a writer. It was not a *possible* occupation for a New Zealand girl a generation ago; and they were resolved to give their rebellious daughter no more than the absolute minimum of help. And Katherine herself, in 1908, was undecided whether she would be a musician or a writer. Of the ensuing three years of her life—from 20 to 23—little is known: so far as might be, she deliberately destroyed all trace of it. Scarcely any of her journal entries remain—the one which does, and is printed at the beginning of the published *Journal,* bears witness to exhausting suffering, endured in isolation. The outcome of this period was the series of bitter and disillusioned sketches which were afterwards published as her first book—*In a German Pension*—in 1911. In after years it was only with the utmost reluctance that Katherine consented to have these sketches republished. She wanted to disown them completely. The same mood of embittered disillusion with life is expressed—I think more powerfully—in two stories of life in the New Zealand back-blocks which she wrote in the end of 1911. One of these—*The Woman at the Store*—she sent to me as editor of a small and unsuccessful literary review, I was deeply and durably impressed by it. And that is how we met. That I fell in love with her and she with me would be a matter of purely private significance: were it not that this happening—as was inevitable in one so constituted as she—had an effect upon her as a writer.

She was to write years afterwards, in a passage of her letters which will concern us later, that 'had she not known Love', the feeling of despair and hopelessness which had inspired her writing so far 'would have been her all'. But we hardly need her own plain statement to know that such a nature as hers would be deeply influenced by her love. Under the influence her work began to change. At first the readjustment was so confusing to her that she could not write at all. The bitterness and disillusion of her work so far were in conflict with her new experience: and only after many months emerged the story of *Something Childish but very Natural,* which is saturated with wistful and child-like idealism. This conflict between Love and Disillusion; Disillusion and Love which made its appearance at this time in Katherine Mansfield's life was to endure to the end. It is the ground pattern of her life and work.

I want to make clear the nature of this conflict. To understand it, is essential to an understanding of Katherine's genius; and an understanding of it enables us to grasp the singular likeness between the nature of Katherine and Keats to which I have already referred. What was the conflict? It was simply the conflict between the idealism of love and the bitterness of realising the cruelty of life—what Katherine called 'the snail under the leaf'. The conflict had begun before—there is not the faintest doubt. In those painful years concerning which she was so reticent, Katherine had stretched out eagerly to life: and she had been bitterly disappointed. The bitterness of which I have spoken—the savage and almost cynical realism of *In a German Pension* and *The Woman at the Store*—was the bitterness of a disappointed idealism. Now it had yielded before a new access of love: but after a year or two, partly through untoward circumstance, partly perhaps because of the character of her lover, but above all through the insidious encroachment of the war, the love again gradually gave way to disenchantment. In this particular realm we have a record of the process which was characteristic of Katherine, in a paragraph in her *Journal.*

> For a long time she said she did not want to change anything in him, and she meant it. Yet she hated things in him, and wished they were otherwise. Then she said she did not want to change anything in him, and she meant it. And the dark things that she had hated she now regarded with indifference. Then she said she did not want to change anything in him. But now she loved him so that even the dark things she loved, too. She wished them there; she was not indifferent. Still they were dark and strange, but she loved them. And it was for this that they had been waiting. They changed. They shed their darkness— the curse was lifted and they shone forth as Royal Princes once more, as creatures of light.

I quote that merely that we may have an authentic glimpse of the natural movement of Katherine Mansfield's soul. The reference is particular, but the movement itself is universal in her. In objective terms we may put it thus: she discovers and loves Beauty, then she discovers and hates the ugliness that seems to be inseparable from the Beauty—'the snail under the leaf'; then she becomes indifferent towards it; then, finally, she discovers and loves a new Beauty, in which the ugliness is included. This movement of the soul, which I have instanced in regard to her personal love, was exactly the same in the growth of her impersonal love—her love towards life itself. Love—disillusion—a new and more comprehensive love: that was the movement in the subject. Beauty—darkness—a new and more comprehensive Beauty: that was the reality in the object. She reveals essentially the same movement over and over again in her *Letters* and her *Journal*. Thus: 'Everything in life that we really accept *undergoes a change.* So suffering must become love. This is the mystery. This is what I must do. I must pass from personal to greater love.' And what was this impersonal love towards which she constantly strained? It was the power—to use the phrase of Keats—'of seeing Beauty *in all things'*. And to see the beauty of all things by the power of love was to see their truth. 'Why should one love?' she wrote. 'No reason; it's just a mystery. But it is like a light. I can see things truly, only in its rays.' Or again, 'Honesty (why?) is the only thing one seems to prize beyond life, love, death, everything. It alone remaineth. O those that come after me, will you believe it? At the end, *Truth* is the only thing *worth having*; it's more thrilling than love, more joyful and more passionate.' More thrilling (she means) than personal love, is the impersonal love that discovers the beauty of the total truth. It is hardly necessary to recall that this was precisely Keats's own final finding.

> Beauty is truth, truth beauty—that is all
> Ye know on earth, and all ye need to know.

Now, having laid as it were the groundwork of the pattern: before we consider in more detail how it was worked out in Katherine's life and writing, I will quote one simple example of the process at work, so to speak, in the very texture of her stories. I could choose any one of a dozen instances: but this one, for a good reason, is particularly dear to me:

> 'What are you looking at, my grandma? Why do you keep stopping and sort of staring at the wall?'
> Kezia and her grandmother were taking their siesta together. The little girl, wearing only her short drawers and her underbodice, her arms and legs bare, lay on one of the puffed-up pillows of her grandma's bed, and the old woman, in a white ruffled dressing-gown, sat in a rocker at the window, with a long piece of pink knitting in her lap. This room that they shared, like the other rooms of the bungalow, was of light varnished wood and the floor was bare. The furniture was of the shabbiest, the simplest. The dressing-table, for instance, was a packing-case in a sprigged muslin petticoat, and the mirror above was very strange; it was as though a little piece of forked lightning was imprisoned in it. On the table there stood a jar of sea-pinks, pressed so tightly together they looked more like a velvet pin-cushion, and a special shell which Kezia had given her grandma for a pin-tray, and another even more special which she had thought would make a very nice place for a watch to curl up in.
> 'Tell me, grandma,' said Kezia.

The old woman sighed, whipped the wool twice round her thumb and drew the bone needle through. She was casting on.

'I was thinking of your Uncle William, darling,' she said quietly.

'My Australian Uncle William?' said Kezia. She had another.

'Yes, of course.'

'The one I never saw?'

'That was the one.'

'Well, what happened to him?' Kezia knew perfectly well, but she wanted to be told again.

'He went to the mines, and he got a sunstroke there and died,' said old Mrs. Fairfield.

Kezia blinked and considered the picture again. . . . A little man fallen over like a tin soldier by the side of a big black hole.

'Does it make you sad to think about him, grandma?' she hated her grandma to be sad.

It was the old woman's turn to consider. Did it make her sad? To look back, back. To stare down the years, as Kezia had been her doing. To look after *them* as a woman does, long after *they* were out of sight. Did it make her sad? No, life was like that.

'No, Kezia.'

'But why?' asked Kezia. She lifted one bare arm and began to draw things in the air. 'Why did Uncle William have to die? He wasn't old.'

Mrs. Fairfield began counting the stitches in threes.

'It just happened,' she said in an absorbed voice.

'Does everybody have to die?' asked Kezia.

'Everybody!'

'*Me?*' Kezia sounded fearfully incredulous.

'Some day, my darling.'

'But, grandma.' Kezia waved her left leg and waggled the toes. They felt sandy. 'What if I just won't?'

The old woman sighed again and drew a long thread from the ball.

'We're not asked, Kezia,' she said sadly. 'It happens to all of us sooner or later.'

Kezia lay still thinking this over. She didn't want to die. It meant she would have to leave here, leave everywhere, for ever, leave—leave her grandma. She rolled over quickly.

'Grandma,' she said in a startled voice.

'What, my pet!'

'*You're* not to die.' Kezia was very decided.

'Ah, Kezia'—her grandma looked up and smiled and shook her head—'don't let's talk about it.'

'But you're not to. You couldn't leave me. You couldn't not be there.' This was awful. 'Promise me you won't ever do it, grandma,' pleaded Kezia.

The old woman went on knitting.

'Promise me! Say never!'

But still grandma was silent.

Kezia rolled off the bed; she couldn't bear it any longer, and lightly she leapt on to her grandma's knees; clasped her hands round the old woman's throat and began kissing her, under the chin, behind the ear, and blowing down her neck.

'Say never . . . say never . . . say never—'

She gasped between the kisses. And then she began, very softly and lightly, to tickle her grandma.

'Kezia!' The old woman dropped her knitting. She swung back in the rocker. She began to tickle Kezia. 'Say never, say never, say never,' gurgled Kezia, while they lay there laughing in each other's arms. 'Come, that's enough, my squirrel! That's enough, my wild pony!' said old Mrs. Fairfield, setting her cap straight. 'Pick up my knitting.'

Both of them had forgotten what the 'never' was about.

The simplicity of that is very subtle. The grandmother who looks back on the death of her son, and finds that the sadness has departed—she represents, instinctively, the discovery of the Beauty of the whole Truth: the acceptance of suffering and death and its change by acceptance into Beauty, seen by the Love which is true wisdom. It is not peculiar to writers of genius. It is the wisdom of Life itself. But it takes genius to express it: to convey to us the simple and surpassing truth that *'life is like that'*. But Kezia, on the other hand, represents the Innocence which has not yet discovered 'the snail under the leaf'. For one startled, frightened moment a glimpse of the grim fact that life is not eternal nor love enduring breaks in upon her: and her world almost breaks into pieces. But Innocence, so complete, eludes the impact of Experience; just as in the grandmother experience has passed beyond itself and become Innocence once more. And so the exquisite counterpoint is resolved. Wisdom and Innocence become one. 'Say never, say never, say never. Both of them had forgotten what the "never" was about.' The consciousness of life is gathered back again into the soft instinctive flow of life itself. To my mind the effortless perfection of this simplicity, containing in its transparent depths the jewel of a serene life-wisdom, is a masterpiece of art. It is for this, and things like this, that H. G. Wells deliberately placed Katherine Mansfield's stories at their highest as belonging to a world beyond the ordinary 'world of effort and compromise', in which even writers of genius are condemned to struggle.

There is an inexplicable element in true literary genius; and I do not pretend wholly to explain the genius of Katherine Mansfield. But there are also elements in it which are, I think, explicable: elements, further, which have meaning for our common humanity. That astonishing simplicity of hers by which she renders some of the most complex and evanescent conditions of the human soul, responsive to the truth and beauty of life—that simplicity was not (as it has often been represented to be) in the main a technical achievement. It could not be. It was the consequence of a moral or spiritual victory won at the end of a long travail of soul: a sustained effort at self-purgation, of self-refinement into a condition of 'crystal clarity' for which Katherine Mansfield unconsciously struggled and towards the end of her life consciously prayed.

A peculiar, a unique circumstance in Katherine Mansfield's progress was that a crucial moment in the progress towards this condition of inward clarity was intimately connected with her attitude towards her own country, New Zealand, and her memories of it. She had suffered in New Zealand, unconsciously and silently as a little child, consciously and resentfully as an adolescent girl. For many years her resentment against New Zealand became as it were the symbol of her resentment against life itself; into her feeling against what seemed to her in youth the stupidity and cruelty of her own country towards her, she concentrated much of her bitterness against the general cruelty of life: what she called 'the snail under the leaf'; 'Pas de nougat pour le Noël'. A moment came when all this was changed.

This moment came when the cruelty of life had dealt her a deadly blow. In the spring of 1915 her only brother had come from New Zealand to serve in the war. He was six years younger than she, and she felt towards him all the affectionate and protective tenderness which a little child feels towards a baby; and since Katherine Mansfield had left New Zealand to be educated in England when she was fourteen and her brother seven, their common memories were childish memories. And how they used to talk about them! I remember only too well, because I was sensitive and very much in love and felt very much out of it. 'Do you remember? . . . Do you remember?'

In October 1915 the brother's training ended. He sailed gaily and confidently for France.

> 'It's so curious—my absolute confidence that I'll come back. I feel it's as certain as this pear.'
> 'I feel that, too.'
> 'I couldn't not come back. You know that feeling. It's awfully mysterious.'

Within ten days a Mills bomb had exploded in his hands.

The shock to Katherine Mansfield was tremendous; but it was a shock of a peculiar kind. It was scarcely a personal grief to her: it was the occasion of a complete upheaval. Suddenly, all her values went into the melting-pot: and one alone emerged—that was Love. She felt an imperious need to shed all the bitterness and cynicism which she thought were still part of her. And this love which suddenly became her supreme value was at once personal and impersonal. Without Love, she suddenly knew, there was no Truth.

> Why should one love? No reason; it's just a mystery. But it is like a light. I can see things truly only in its rays.

But that was written afterwards, when the victory was won, and she knew the nature of her own discovery. For the moment her experience was that her early life in New Zealand appeared extraordinarily precious to her. Why, she hardly knew. Sometimes she thought it was something which she had preeminently shared with her brother. But, in fact, it was because it was some-thing which awakened Love in her. And the self which was utterly surrendered to this Love—this self which could live as it were only in the radiance of Love, was (she felt) a new Self. And so the act of writing *Prelude,* which she began at this time in the South of France, and which she felt could only be written out of this new Self, was itself one continual effort towards a spiritual rebirth.

Hence the inward struggle (of which we have so precious a record in the *Journal*) with which the writing of the first draft of *Prelude* was accompanied. 'You know how unhappy I have been lately'; she wrote as though to her dead brother on February 14, 1916. 'I almost felt: Perhaps "the new man" will not live. Perhaps I am not yet risen. . . . But now I do not doubt.' At that moment her brother was to her the counterpart and companion of her new, unseen, un-known self, whom she was struggling to bring to birth; but it was only for that moment. In the exclusive personal way which these remarkable pages of her *Journal* might suggest to the unadvised reader, her brother was not so supremely important to Katherine Mansfield. He was a symbol and a part of that world of Innocence and Truth and Beauty which only Love could appre-hend: and that world again was something far beyond the New Zealand which she was actually remembering. If she could overcome in herself her old resent-ment against her own country, if her bitterness against it could be dissolved 'in forgiveness of ancient injuries', if she could cease to feel that she personally had been wronged by New Zealand, then the truth and beauty of Life would emerge in it and through her.

It is not, perhaps, easy to explain; and perhaps I have failed in conveying the nature of a process which I believe I understand. Her brother's death was, at once, itself and more than itself. No doubt it was indeed his bitter ending, the mockery of his own triumphant confidence in his safe return from the war, which brought her up sharp and sudden against the bitterness of her own mem-ory of New Zealand, the elusive purpose of her own life, and the necessity of hastening on towards the goal she felt she must reach. The death of her brother was indeed a decisive event in Katherine Mansfield's life and art; but as an occa-sion, not as a cause. It brought to her a moment of profound self-knowledge.

From this moment onward her life was consciously directed towards the achievement of inward clarity—crystal clarity. It was not an uninterrupted as-cent: no human progress in this order can ever be. But the first great stage in the progress was indubitably the writing of the first draft of *Prelude.* The pu-rification of her memory of New Zealand, the purging of all resentment from her soul until that island could emerge, as from the waters of its own Pacific, with all the bloom and brightness of a new creation, was the outward and visi-ble sign of the inward and spiritual grace. To be worthy of her new vision of New Zealand was to be worthy in an absolute sense; it was to have achieved a new condition of being—to have recaptured the vision of Innocence. She after-wards described what she had tried to do, in *Prelude,* in these words:

In the early morning there I always remember feeling that this little island has dipped back into the dark blue sea during the night, only to rise again at the gleam of day, all hung with bright spangles and glittering drops. I tried to catch that moment—with something of its sparkle and flavour. And just as on those mornings white silky mists arise and uncover some beauty, then smother it again and again disclose it, I tried to lift that mist from my people and let them be seen and then to hide them again.... It's so difficult to describe all this, and it sounds perhaps overambitious and vain. But I don't feel anything but an intense longing to serve my subject as well as I can.

It really *was* difficult to describe. Katherine Mansfield was striving to make firm her hold upon a new kind of vision of which she was now visited by glimpses. To the full possession of this vision—which we may call indifferently the vision of Imagination or of Love—one achievement was absolutely necessary. There must be a complete abeyance of the Self.

Naturally, Katherine Mansfield had to feel her way towards expression of the nature of this inward necessity. Sometimes, as we have seen, the emphasis is on a sort of rebirth; in the passage I have quoted, written in October 1917, it is to be completely occupied to the exclusion of all other feeling by 'an intense longing to serve my subject as well as I can'; or it is 'to be made crystal clear' for the divine light to shine through; or it is 'to be simple as one would be simple before God'. She expresses it in many different ways: some artistic, some unmistakably religious: but they all have essentially the same meaning. And they all belong to that rare province of human experience where art and religion are veritably one. It is the authentic discovery of the necessity of self-effacement—the compulsion whereby the artist (if he is faithful to his calling) becomes, according to the doctrine of William Blake, the priest of the Everlasting Gospel.

What that Everlasting Gospel is cannot be simply expressed in words; or if in words, the words are so simple that they are easily misunderstood in spite, or because, of the depth of meaning with which they are burdened. The most famous statement of it is the lines of Keats, already quoted:

> Beauty is truth, truth beauty.

This power to see and feel the beauty of the truth is a rare power, though I suspect there are moments when we are all visited by it. It is what has been called the Divine Love—the Love in whose light alone, as Katherine Mansfield said, she could see things truly. But this was not and could not be a steady and continuous power. It was achieved through a continual and recurrent resolution of the conflict between Love and Disillusion.

In February 1918 she was ill and alone in the South of France. She began to write a long, beautiful and strange story *Je ne parle pas français*. In sending it to me she wrote to explain its nature.

I've two kick-offs in the writing game [she wrote in February 1918]. One is joy—real joy—the thing that made me write when we lived at Pauline, and that sort of writing I could only do in just that state of being in some perfectly blissful way at peace. Then something delicate and lovely seems to open before my eyes, like a flower without thought of a frost or a cold breath, knowing that all about it is warm and tender and 'ready'. And that I try, ever so humbly, to express.

The other kick-off is my old original one, and *had I not known love* it would have been my all. Not hate or destruction (both are beneath contempt as real motives) but an extremely deep sense of hopelessness, of everything doomed to disaster. There! I got it exactly—a cry against corruption—that is absolutely the nail on the head. Not a protest—a cry.

A week later came the first severe hæmorrhage, as she bounded out of bed to greet the morning sun: the first grim warning of the reality of her disease.

That passage from her *Letters* is vital to any true understanding of Katherine Mansfield. First we need to remember that the months at the Villa Pauline when she could, and did, write out of a state of being in some perfectly blissful way at peace—was the time when she was writing *Prelude*, and it was also the time when the unadvised reader of her *Journal* would imagine that she was sorrowing over the death of her brother. She was; nevertheless, in fact, it was a time of pure joy: of the self-effacement of love in writing and living.

But there was that other creative condition in Katherine Mansfield—what she calls an extremely deep sense of hopelessness: and this she says would have been her only creative condition, if she had not known love. The most astonishing examples of creation from this state are her stories *Je ne parle pas français* and the unduly neglected *A Married Man's Story*. There is nothing strained or forced in them: they spring naturally from a like attitude of self-effacement: only there is in them no joy.

These two conditions alternated incessantly in Katherine Mansfield. She goes out to the world in the self-abandonment of joy and love: or she withdraws into herself in despair and hopelessness. I do not think it is possible to choose between them, or to say that one more than the other is characteristic of Katherine Mansfield. It is the alternation itself which is characteristic of her: and above all characteristic of her letters.

But I think that as her work reached its final stage, before she gave up writing altogether, these two conditions became somehow blended together in her art. I have, myself, not much doubt that her two most perfect stories are two of her very last, written less than a year before her death: *The Doll's House* and *The Fly*. They are both very short: and they have, to my sense, an absolute finality about them. I can define their quality only in a phrase of Keats: they have in them 'a sorrow more beautiful than beauty's self'.

How was this achieved? I have tried to outline the movement of her mind and heart. I think it can only be understood as following some such pattern as this: (1) a sort of bitter revulsion from life—which is characteristic of her work prior to *Prelude*; (2) a joyous and loving acceptance of life—which finds its first complete expression in *Prelude*; (3) then a far more poignant disillusion with and revulsion from life—'nessum maggior dolore'—which found its first complete expression in *Bliss,* and gradually deepened through experience into the very profound sense of hopelessness which finds expression in *Je ne parle pas*; and, finally, (4) an acceptance even of this hopelessness: and out of this acceptance comes the last perfection of her work. This final change is the most difficult of them all to understand: but we get a glimpse of the nature of the metamorphosis in a letter which she wrote to me in 1920.

> And then bodily suffering such as I've known for three years. It has changed for ever everything—even the *appearance* of the world is not the same—there is something added. *Everything has its shadow.* Is it right to resist such suffering? Do you know I feel it has been an immense privilege. Yes, in spite of all. How blind we little creatures are! It's only the fairy tales we *really* live by. If we set out upon a journey, the more wonderful the treasure, the greater the temptations and perils to be overcome. And if someone rebels and says, Life isn't good enough on those terms, one can only say 'It is!' Don't misunderstand me. I don't mean a 'thorn in the flesh'—it's a million times more mysterious. It has taken me three years to understand this—to come to see this. We resist, we are terribly frightened. The little boat enters the dark fearful gulf and our only cry is to escape—'put me on land again'. But it's useless. Nobody listens. The shadowy figure rows on. One ought to sit still and uncover one's eyes.
>
> I believe the greatest failing of all is to be *frightened*. Perfect Love casteth out Fear. When I look back on my life all my mistakes have been because I was afraid. . . . Was that why I had to look on death? Would nothing less cure me? You know, one can't help wondering sometimes. . . . No, not a personal God. Much more likely—the soul's desperate choice.

'The soul's desperate choice'—those final words seem to me profound indeed: the inmost secret of an ultimate religion is in them.

What did she mean? She meant this: that an experiencing nature which obeys the compulsion of experience, which accepts experience truly for what it is, which does not turn the head away or avert the eyes, becomes ultimately the vehicle of a final wisdom. By this submission of the self to Life, the chosen nature finally becomes an instrument for the utterance of Life's secret. In the last resort, if we are not content with superficial understanding, Katherine Mansfield can only be comprehended, or the comprehension of her expressed, in some such terms as William Blake used to express his experience. His effort towards self-annihilation—the sole condition, as he believed, of the true, the Divine Imagination—was renewed in her. By 1921 it had become the burden of all her thinking on her purpose and herself. She had struggled through the abyss of despair that had overtaken her when she realised, in her illness and isolation in France in February 1918, that her dream of happy love on earth was to be denied her (as it was denied to Keats, and as he also realised it, and as he also struggled out of his despair). Now, in 1921, a bare eighteen months before her death, she was troubled with these things no longer. Her one concern was to be the pure vehicle of experience. 'Marks of earthly degradation still pursue me,' she wrote on July 16. 'I am not crystal clear.' Then, suddenly in her effort to write *At the Bay* she achieves the condition.

> There's my Grandmother, back in her chair with her pink knitting, there stalks my Uncle over the grass; I feel as I write, 'You are not dead, my darlings. All is remembered. I bow down to you. I efface myself so that you may live again through me in your richness and beauty.' And one is *possessed.*

The grandmother with her pink knitting—that is the passage which I quoted . . . : and now we see out of what a condition of soul that perfect and profound simplicity was created. There is the doctrine, there is the experience, there is Art. That in the last resort is what the supreme achievement of art is— the utterance of Life through a completely submissive being.

In scope Katherine Mansfield was a tiny artist; but because she was a perfectly pure, and perfectly submissive, artist she was a great one. In this order of artistic achievement, the small is veritably great, and the great no greater. In this order, achievement is absolute or not at all. There is Art, and there is not-Art; and between them is precisely the absolute difference which the philosophers of the Christian religion sought so often to express, between the descent of the divine grace and the utmost effort of the conscious personal being to achieve it. As Blake said—the great artist who was isolated because he knew the ultimate identity of Christianity and Art—'We in *ourselves* are nothing'. And Katherine herself wrote to my brother:

> About religion. Did you mean 'the study of life' or Christ's religion 'Come unto me all ye that labour and are heavy laden and I will give you rest'. The queer thing is that one does not seem to contradict the other, to me. *If I lose myself in the study of life, and give up Self, then I am at rest.* But the more I study the religion of Christ the more I marvel at it. (29.3.22.)

What may be the secret of this delicate and invincible integrity, no man dare say. It is perhaps enough that it should exist and that we should recognise and respond to it. But those who do recognise it see that it is manifest from the beginning in a strange compulsion to submit to experience. Between life and such natures the impact is not mitigated. It is naked all the while. Neither creed nor conception nor convention can interpose its comfortable medium. These natures are doomed, or privileged, to lead a life of 'sensations rather than of thoughts'. Such a life seemed, no doubt, good to Keats when he wrote those words, which after-generations have found it so easy to misunderstand; but he was to learn that as the joys of the immediate nature are incomparable, so are its sufferings; and that the time inevitably comes when the joy is suffering, and the suffering joy. For such natures, as though compelled by an inward law, return to the organic simplicity of the pre-conscious being; but in them that simplicity is enriched by all the subtleties of consciousness.

Of this simplicity in complexity—in life and art—Katherine Mansfield was a perfect example. She belonged, by birthright, to the 'experiencing natures'. They are sustained by some secret faith in life of which smaller souls are ignorant. They know what Blake meant when he proclaimed that 'the road of excess leads to the palace of wisdom'. They can take nothing in the matter of vital life-experience at second-hand. Always for them the truth must be proved as Keats said 'on their pulses'. And so, inevitably, in the eyes of the world they are not wise; for wisdom, in the world's eyes, consists precisely in refusing to expose ourselves to experience. The wise accept the report of others; of that great Other who is the worldly prudence of the race. They know that the Master of Life is a hard man, reaping where he did not sow, and they hide their talent in the earth. They take no risks with him.

And in this they *are* wise. But there is a greater wisdom than theirs. It is the wisdom which whispers 'Take the risk! If that is truly the urge of your secret soul, obey it. No matter what the cost, obey!' Or as D. H. Lawrence cried in his last and most lovely poem: 'Launch out, the fragile soul in the fragile ship of courage'. The same—identically the same image—that Katherine Mansfield used to express *her* final discovery, when she said 'The little boat enters the dark fearful gulf and our only cry is to escape—"put me on land again". But it's useless. Nobody listens. The shadowy figure rows on. One ought to sit still and uncover one's eyes'. Of what were these two friends speaking—in the same image? Of the same thing. Of the acceptance of Death and Suffering. Uncovering one's eyes before the final dark shadow of all existence—the supreme sadness—the type of all that pain and evil from which the soul seeks to avert its head. The death of the ideal, the death of love, the death that comes through the never-ending discovery of the snail under the leaf, the death of Bertha Young's happiness in *Bliss,* the death of Laura's happiness in *The Garden Party*—these are all variations of the one unending theme.

But out of death always the birth of a new life: a new life doomed in turn to die, but destined always to be re-born, until the final acceptance of a complete self-surrender. Then, as Katherine said, 'Everything for ever is changed'. It is the final entry into what Blake called the world of true Imagination, which is Spiritual Sensation—a world of sensation because it is a world of immediate experience; a spiritual world, because it is not discerned by the five senses or their ratio which is the Intellect. It is beyond all these; yet it does not deny all these. The world—one is driven back to the phrase—of the 'beauty of the truth'.

It seems to me [she wrote nine months before her death] that if Beauty were Absolute it would no longer be the kind of Beauty it is. Beauty triumphs

over ugliness in life. That's what I feel. And that marvellous *triumph* is what I
long to express. . . . I sit in a waiting-room where all is ugly, where it's dirty,
dull, dreadful, where sick people waiting with me to see the doctor are all
marked by suffering and sorrow. And a very poor workman comes in, takes off
his cap humbly, beautifully, walks on tiptoe, has a look as though he were in
church, has a look as though he believed that behind that doctor's door shone
the miracle of healing. *And all is changed, all is marvellous.* It's only then that one
sees for the first time what is happening. Life is, all at one and the same time, far
more mysterious and far simpler than we know. It's like religion in that. *If we
want to have faith, and without faith we die, we must learn to accept.* That's how it
seems to me.

And so it is that if I had to choose one adjective to describe the essential
quality of what she did and what she became, it would be the adjective
'serene'. And it seems to me that those who are responsive to her writing
recognise this serenity—the serenity of a rainbow that shines through tears—
and know that it comes from a heart at peace 'in spite of all'. Katherine could
look back on her life, with all its miseries and all its brevity, and declare that
'in spite of all' it was good: that 'in spite of all' suffering was a privilege, pain
the gateway to a deeper joy, sorrow the birth-pang of a new beauty. 'In spite of
all'—the phrase, mysterious and simple as life, contains the secret of herself
and her art. It is a phrase which more than any other echoes in my heart, with
the sweetness of a long familiar pain, when I think back on what she was, and
what she wrote from what she was. Beauty triumphs over Ugliness 'in spite of
all'. In spite of all, the little lamp glows gently and eternally in *The Doll's
House*; in spite of all, the sleeping face of the dead man in *The Garden Party*
murmurs that All is well; and though Ma Parker has nowhere to cry out her
misery, she is beautiful for ever, in spite of all.

# Katherine and Virginia, 1917–1923

## Antony Alpers

Neither had "arrived" when they met and both were concerned to do so, in order that their gifts might flourish and something permanent be created. It was the elder one, *apparently* much more secure, but cursed with a rival-complex, who feared that the younger might surpass her.

Virginia Woolf was already thirty-four when she first met Katherine Mansfield. All that she had to her own name then was *The Voyage Out,* a novel in traditional form which had taken her seven years to write and had cost her two breakdowns. Denouncing it herself as "long and dull," she was afraid it deserved to be condemned. She was now at work on the tedious *Night and Day,* but had not yet produced the short story "Kew Gardens"—her first departure from conventional narrative—whereas Katherine, a confident, healthy young woman of twenty-eight, had long since disavowed one book as "young and bad" and had lately begun to find new forms, in stories which Lytton thought "distinctly bright."

Both hurt by early wounds, both women were obliged to live behind some sort of mask. There was so much that neither could avow: in Virginia's case, the threat of insanity, brought nearer by her creative bouts. Publication of *The Voyage Out* has been followed by a harrowing breakdown of which Katherine knew nothing—screaming fits and violence, four mental nurses in attendance, her devoted husband scarcely seeing her for weeks. All that, Woolf covered up from the outside world.[1]

What Katherine saw when she went to Hogarth House was a woman secure in her husband and her home, with a room to write in, a background of relatives distinguished in the arts, and no need at all to repudiate her family or feel estranged by being creative. A Miss Beauchamp from Thorndon and a daughter of Sir Leslie Stephen did not begin as equals in the race, if race it had to be.

There was so much more unknown about the future. That Katherine would be dead before she reached the age of Virginia when they met, leaving only two more books that contained inferior work, Virginia could not know for her comfort; nor that she would then have eighteen good years in which to achieve what she hoped, with fame as well.

Reprinted from Antony Alpers, *The Life of Katherine Mansfield* (New York: Viking, c1980), 247–261.

The social barrier was of a kind that couldn't be removed. Virginia's family tree included Thackeray, John Addington Symonds, and even Ralph Vaughan Williams; as a girl she knew Henry James, and she and her sister grew up knowing the Cambridge conversation of brother's friends from Trinity—from among whom came both their husbands.

When Middleton Murry, the Oxford scholarship youth from Peckham, told Hal Beauchamp's daughter in 1913 that these Woolf people belonged to "a perfectly impotent Cambridge set," he implanted prejudice, no doubt—as did Strachey for Virginia two years later: "'Katherine Mansfield'—if that's her real name—I could never quite make sure. . . . decidedly an interesting creature. . . . wanted to make your acquaintance. . . . ugly impassive mask of a face. . . . sharp and slightly vulgarly fanciful intellect sitting behind it."

She has "dogged my footsteps for three years," Virginia had replied; and now the footsteps met. It is true that Virginia's one-time suitor Sydney Waterlow, who was fit to propose if not to be accepted, was Katherine's second cousin, and another intermediary. But *his* grandmother, the Australian one, as he once admitted to Virginia, was a ratcatcher's daughter ("which he profoundly regrets. And so do I"), and Virginia had since come to hold a low opinion of him,* which went still lower when, a few years later, he actually joined, by sharing Murry's house in Katherine's absence, what Virginia by that time called "the pigsty." Dogs, rats, pigs, the lot.

One other impediment existed. Woolf never liked Murry. He bore his sufferings in his own wife's illness with selfless dignity, and Murry's "strong Pecksniffian vein," as he called it, left him "irritated and revolted." He did like Katherine—"I don't think anyone has ever made me laugh more than she did in those days"—and he thought her a "very serious writer," who was in some way perverted and destroyed by Murry.[2]

There is no telling now what caused the first brush when they met, but by midsummer the two women had got to know each other well enough for Virginia to tell her sister that Katherine seemed to have "gone every sort of hog since she was 17," but had "a much better idea of writing than most." She also told Violet Dickinson that Katherine had had "every sort of experience, wandering about with travelling circuses over the moors of Scotland."[3] It sounds as though Katherine's confidences were either gaily inventive or not followed very closely.

A letter of Katherine's to Ottoline in July suggests how things stood then. Katherine had gathered that Virginia was "still *very* delicate," and seldom well enough to leave her own home and surroundings; she had dined with her last week and found her charming: "I do like her tremendously—but

---

*"By God! What a bore that man is! I don't know why exactly, but no one I've ever met seems to me more palpably second-rate and now the poor creature resigns himself to it, & proposes to live next door to us at Richmond, & there copulate day & night & produce six little Waterlows. His house for a long time stank to me of dried semen—And it's only a kind of mutton fat in his case."—V.W. to Lytton Strachey, 22 October 1915 (the Strachey Trust, London.) The remark about the ratcatcher is in the *Diary*, 22 August 1922.

I felt then for the first time the strange, trembling, glinting quality of her mind—and quite for the first time she seemed to me to be one of those Dostoievsky women whose 'innocence' has been hurt—Immediately I decided that I understood her completely—I wonder if you agree at all."[4]

In August, something happened which has not been brought to light before, and which now puts a different complexion on the relationship between the two women as writers.

When the Woolfs moved down to Asheham, their house in Sussex, Katherine was invited for a weekend. She was to take with her the typescript of *Prelude*, or as much as the typist had done of it, but neither she nor Virginia looked forward to the occasion with much eagerness, the reason being, on Virginia's side at least, that Clive Bell and Maynard Keynes had lately been spreading Bloomsbury gossip about Katherine, no doubt connecting her with Bertrand Russell. So it happened that on the Wednesday before the visit Virginia wrote to Lady Ottoline, having just read a letter from Katherine that seems to have set her teeth on edge:

> Katherine Mansfield describes your garden,* the rose leaves dying in the sun, the pool and long conversation between people wandering up and down in the moonlight. It calls out her romantic side; which I think rather a relief after the actresses, A.B.C.'s and paintpots.[5]

The letter from Katherine which prompted that has not survived—which is unusual, when the Woolfs were such meticulous keepers of her letters, and seem to have lost no others. By the same day's post, however, Lady Ottoline received one from the studio which almost alludes to it and must have resembled it. This is Katherine writing to Ottoline that same Wednesday (15 August 1917):

> Your glimpse of the garden—all flying green and gold made me wonder again *who* is going to write about that flower garden. It might be so wonderful, do you see *how* I mean? There would be people walking in the garden—several *pairs* of people—their conversation their slow pacing—their glances as they pass one another—the pauses as the flowers "come in" as it were—as a bright dazzle, an exquisite haunting scent, a shape so formal and fine, so much a "flower of the mind" that he who looks at it really is tempted for one bewildering moment to stoop & touch and make *sure*. The "pairs" of people must be very different and there must be a light touch of enchantment—some of them seeming so extraordinarily "odd" and separate from the flowers, but others quite related and at ease. A kind of musically speaking, conversation *set* to flowers. Do you like the idea? . . . Its full of possibilities. I must have a fling at it as soon as I have time.[6]

---

*Although the Morrells had been at Garsington for more than two years, the Woolfs had not yet been there. Because of Leonard's reluctance they had been putting it off. "A.B.C.'s a few lines lower, were the tea-rooms of the Aerated Bread Company, found all over London—tea-rooms of the common people, of *New Age* contributors and so on.

The emphasized "*who*" at the beginning shows Katherine thinking that someone else might write such a story, while the "again" suggests that she is somehow repeating herself.

On returning to London after the weekend with her *Prelude* typescript Katherine wrote Virginia a bread-and-butter letter containing a sentence that has often been cited as evidence in general terms of the literary relationship between the two: "We have got the same job, Virginia and it is really very curious and thrilling that we should both, quite apart from each other, be after so very nearly the same thing." But the letter also contained a much more specific piece of information. "Yes," it said, "your Flower Bed is *very* good. There's a still, quivering changing light over it all and a sense of those couples dissolving in the bright air which fascinates me."[7]

This means that Virginia had shown Katherine her story "Kew Gardens,"* in which four couples stroll among the flower beds in various states of enchantment, exactly as prescribed in the letter to Ottoline, and *possibly* as prescribed in the missing letter to Virginia. The pairs are symmetrically distributed: there are Eleanor and Simon; there is William, walking with another man; there are two elderly women "of the lower middle class," and a young man and young woman "in the prime of life." We do see their slow pacing, we see the "bright dazzle" of the tulips, and some insects; we hear snatches of conversation, and some of the people are indeed extraordinarily "odd." They are not at Garsington, since Virginia did not know that garden yet; but she did know Kew.

The resemblance of the story to the idea in the letter is so close that there must have been some connection. What was it? When was "Kew Gardens" written? Apart from the details given here there seems to be no evidence for dating it. Nothing on record suggests that it had been written previously. Mrs. Woolf's diary (which is full of Asheham insects in that week) says nothing anywhere about its writing, but does show that there was time for it to have been composed between the reading of the letter and Katherine's arrival late on Saturday. If it wasn't written then, and at Katherine's direct prompting, some extraordinary coincidence needs explaining.

Whatever *had* happened in that week, the question still remains why it was that Virginia, who had published one long novel when they met, but no short stories, soon afterwards wrote two important short pieces—"Kew Gardens" and "The Mark on the Wall"—of which one is an experiment in dialogue and is also her first departure from traditional ways of seeing. The evidence is very strong that Katherine Mansfield in some way helped Virginia Woolf to break out of the mould in which she had been working hitherto.

There followed some last revisions, no doubt, of *Prelude* in typescript, and then some more short stories. A *Journal* entry has Chekhov appearing in the role of

*So identified by Murry in a footnote, in the *Letters* of 1928.

a writer *confirming* Katherine's desire to write things of uneven length. It was a productive, fruitful autumn—the studio full of figs and quinces, and ideas. An invitation to Garsington was declined by Murry with the news that Katherine had disappeared into retreat in order to write some stories "which will be as good as the extraordinary achievement which she has handed over to the tender mercies of the Hogarth Press."[8]

"Tender mercies" meant something like this: faced with hand setting, from a newly acquired typecase, the seventeen thousand words of *Prelude* (their "Publication No. 2"), Woolf and Virginia made a start on returning to Richmond in October, and pulled a proof of one page which they invited Katherine to come and see. They then had the bright idea that Alix Sargant-Florence, aged twenty-two and just down from Newnham, might be the person to take on the tedious chore of setting. She accepted because she thought it would be "an introduction to literary work of some sort," and on going to Richmond, all ready to be literary with literary people, she was put on a stool in the top-floor room and shown how to pick up tiny pieces of metal, with forceps, and put them in "a metal frame," face up. Having shown her what to do (with forceps). Leonard and Virginia then went for a walk with their dog. They were surprised, on their return, to learn that Alix had decided she couldn't possibly do anything so boring. They were "very nice about it," so she packed up and left[9]—the first of a succession of intelligent young persons who were to discover, over the years, the extraordinary notions that Woolf and Virginia had of how to engage and treat employees. No doubt the Woolfs eventually learned, as they undertook corrections, what the forceps supplied with a typecase are meant for. After a while, a new apprentice was found in Barbara Hiles, a girl from the Slade with bobbed hair and a fringe, who for some weeks continued the setting of *Prelude.*

It happens that the week in which Katherine dined at Hogarth House and saw her page proof was also the week in which Virginia began a new volume of her diary—or rather, in its proper sense began the regular keeping of her diary as we know it. Thus the entry for 10 October 1917 records "the prospect of K. Mansfield to dinner, when many delicate things fall to be discussed." These were not in fact to do with *Prelude,* but with Clive Bell's gossip and its consequences.* Then on the following day:

---

*"I think these rumours that are put into motion, whether by Clive or the other Bloomsburies, too preposterous to be taken seriously."—Murry to Lady Ottoline, 15 September 1917. "Clive, that plump marrow, hiding under the leaves, and every leaf an ear, can't be taken seriously—do you think?"—K.M. to Lady Ottoline, 23 September. "All very odd, isn't it? And quite unimportant. Such people are not to be taken seriously."—Clive Bell to Vanessa Bell from Garsington, at about the same time,[10] the background to all of which is suggested in Katherine's letter to Virginia of 22 August (after the visit): "But don't let THEM persuade you that I spend any of my precious time swapping hats or committing adultery—I'm far too arrogant and proud." See also Virginia's diary for 27 October 1917. It should be recalled, perhaps, that Clive Bell's wife was living with Duncan Grant and he himself had an attachment to Mrs. St. John Hutchinson. Katherine's letter had therefore trodden rather heavily on family matters.

> The dinner last night went off: the delicate things were discussed. We could both wish that ones first impression of K.M. was not that she stinks like a—well civet cat that had taken to street walking. In truth, I'm a little shocked by her commonness at first sight; lines so hard & cheap. However, when this diminishes, she is so intelligent & inscrutable that she repays friendship.

This interesting passage has been rather freely interpreted by Leonard Woolf. Falling into a masculine error which Virginia herself did not commit, he has written, a little symmetrically perhaps, of Virginia's disliking Katherine's "cheap scent and cheap sentimentality."[11]

Katherine was fond of a rather expensive French perfume called Genêt Fleuri (it probably reminded her of Wellington's hills aflame with gorse). Whether this is what she was wearing on the night she went to Hogarth House, her biographer must not presume to say, but I think that anyone who has known her three sisters would declare with some vehemence that no Beauchamp, even the fallen Kathleen, could ever have worn "cheap scent." That it was a capital error to use scent at all when going to dine with Leonard and Virginia and look at page proofs is obvious, of course, and it may be that we have here discovered a whole new field for doctoral researches—Class and the Olfactory Symbol in Virginia Woolf. One simple fact remains, however:

> That perfume chaste
> Was but good taste
> Misplaced!

To Virginia, that evening, Katherine stank. But cheaply so? Or expensively so? Did Virginia dislike perfume altogether? Is there any in her novels? The Bond Street scene in *Mrs. Dalloway* contains a passing reference to "Atkinson's scent shop" which sounds distinctly slighting—but then what references to shops do not, in Virginia Woolf? Perhaps the question really turns upon a deeper difference between the two women, a larger issue altogether. Katherine, with a touch of Lawrence's "good animal" in her, did go in for the life of the senses, and Virginia shied away from it, which is why she had such curiosity in this regard. Katherine did love food and scents and colour and music (above all verbal music), with a passionate delight that ruled out *curiosity* altogether. And Virginia, though drawn by curiosity toward that side of her, at the same time found it somehow vulgar ("she seems to have gone every sort of hog since she was seventeen"); and this very distaste is a defect in her writing.

If Leonard Woolf was stretching the terms a little when he wrote of "cheap scent," then I think, with all respect, that Professor Quentin Bell is guilty of something similar when he writes, as it were on his aunt's behalf, that Katherine "dressed like a tart."[12] Mrs. Woolf doesn't say so in her diary; in fact she scarcely refers to Katherine's outward appearance or her dress (those "lines so hard and cheap" must refer to something else, since they diminished during the evening), whereas in other cases she is as generous with such information as Chaucer himself. That Katherine may have "behaved like a bitch" is for the family to say, and not for a mere biographer to question; but neither photographs nor reliable witnesses known to the present author have ever put Katherine Mansfield into clothes that would be suitable for duty in Leicester Square. "Dainty in appearance. . . . great charm in her femininity" (Anne Estelle Rice); "Exquisite in her person. . . . always scrupulously groomed" (Frieda Lawrence), and many similar accounts by word of mouth. Admittedly Lady Ottoline has described Katherine's dress as "rather a cheap taste, slightly Swan & Edgar," and the wife of Frank Harris is on record as calling her "no beauty," about five foot four in height, "and square everywhere," while Francis Carco seems to have known a dowdy phase.[13] But the further one tries to pursue this matter by authorities, the further certainty recedes. How a woman's dress strikes other women is one of the greater mysteries.

And so back to a scented dinner. Since Virginia was writing an article on Henry James which had to be ready two days later there was some discussion of him, a subject on which Katherine was "illuminating," Virginia thought. But then the doorbell rang. A "munition worker called Leslie Moor. . . . another of these females on the border land of propriety, & naturally inhabiting the underworld," had arrived to take Katherine back to Chelsea.

That is all the diary said of their talk next day. Although it often mentions the conversations Virginia had with Katherine, it seldom gives reports. However, Katherine too sat down at her desk, not with a notebook—for there is in all her notebooks not one word about her friendship with Virginia, at least avowedly—but to write to Brett. The long, informative letter which then went off to Scotland is almost certainly a record of that evening's talk, set off as it was by Henry James. For *Prelude,* she said, the Woolfs had served her up "so much praise in such a golden bowl that I couldn't help feeling gratified," and the whole letter seems an overflow from that:

> It seems to me so extraordinarily right that you should be painting Still Lives just now. What can one do, faced with this wonderful tumble of round bright fruits, but gather them and play with them—and *become them,* as it were. When I pass an apple stall I cannot help stopping and staring until I feel that I, myself, am changing into an apple, too, and that at any moment I can produce an apple, miraculously, out of my own being, like the conjuror produces the egg. . . . When you paint apples do you feel that your breasts and your knees become apples, too? Or do you think this the greatest nonsense. I don't. I am sure it is not. When I write about ducks I swear that I am a white duck with a round eye, floating on a pond fringed with yellow-blobs and taking an occasional dart at the other duck with the round eye, which floats upside down beneath me. . . . In fact the whole process of becoming the duck (what Lawrence would perhaps call this consummation with the duck or the apple!) is so thrilling that I can hardly breathe, only to think about it. For although that is as far as most people can get, it is really only the "prelude." There follows the moment when you are

*more* duck, *more* apple, and *more* Natasha than any of these objects could ever possibly be, and so you *create* them anew.

 *Brett* (switching off the instrument): "Katherine I *beg* of you to stop. You must tell us all about it at the Brotherhood Church one Sunday evening."[14]

There is not much doubt that the foregoing provides a sample of the sort of conversation with Katherine that Virginia valued.

How much it did mean to her is casually revealed by a mere three words slipped into the diary a few months later. One Saturday morning Virginia sat with her sister Vanessa and Duncan Grant in their studio, talking about art. Nessa and Duncan, unfavourably comparing a painter's life in England with that in France, said that there was no one worth considering as a painter in England, and no one like K.M., "or Forster even," with whom it was worth discussing one's business.[15] Forster by then had published all of his novels except *A Passage to India.*

There was still much delay in getting *Prelude* into type, and Katherine and Virginia seem not to have seen each other for some time—no doubt because of the Clive Bell episode. By January 1918, a sixth of the pages had been printed off and Virginia thought the rest would take five weeks, but it took five months. They were months, as it happened, in which Katherine's life was completely changed by illness. To that, the next chapter returns; but I think it will be easier for the reader if we follow the story of Katherine and Virginia to its end in this one.

By the end of June 1918, *Prelude* was ready to receive such publication as it got, Virginia's diary remarking that although it seemed "a little vapourish" and was freely watered with some of Katherine's "cheap realities," it had the living power of a work of art. Then her new story, *Bliss,* was published in the *English Review,* and Virginia threw it down with the exclamation, "She's done for!" Katherine's mind, after all, was very thin soil, and the story's whole conception was "poor, cheap, not the vision, however imperfect, of an interesting mind."

During the autumn, Virginia began visiting Katherine almost every week at the house which the Murrys by then had bought in Hampstead, and she found herself liking her more and more. Then, just after Christmas, she was puzzled, and as the *Diary* shows, very hurt, by the fact that Katherine seemed to have "dropped" her, and had not acknowledged some Christmas gifts which she had sent. She could never have known what agony on Katherine's side had caused this break—but it belongs in a later chapter.

Katherine's life then fell into the painful pattern of English summers and Mediterranean winters which disrupted her marriage, her friendships, and everything else, and Virginia watched the process with a sympathy which seems rather chilly at times.

It was in the spring and summer of 1919, after Murry had been appointed editor of the *Athenaeum,* that the two women had their best meetings and the longest diary passages were written, recording, for instance, on 22 March, Virginia's annoyance with "the inscrutable woman," but then, as well, "a sense of ease & interest, which is, I suppose, due to her caring so genuinely if so differently from the way I care, about our precious art." These passages are known by now; here is the other side, a letter of Katherine's to Lady Ottoline:

> I understand *exactly* what you say about Virginia—beautiful brilliant creature that she is and suddenly at the last moment, turning into a bird and flying up to a topmost bough and continuing the conversation from there . . . She delights in beauty as I imagine a bird does; she has a *bird's eye* for "that angular high step-ping green insect" that she writes about* and she is not *of* her subject—she hov-ers over, dips, skims, makes exquisite flights—sees the lovely reflections in water that a bird must see—but *not humanly.*[16]

It was possible for them in that summer to spend an hour together very happily. Virginia found herself really liking Katherine, and felt they had reached some kind of durable foundation. But, alas, there were rocks ahead.

In the autumn, Katherine went south to the Italian Riviera, from where she was reviewing novels for the *Athenaeum,* and Murry sent her *Night and Day* to review. Virginia had conceived that book as an "exercise in the conventional style" (the words are her own), perhaps as a recuperative work, after the terrors of *The Voyage Out.* Well knowing that it had not come from the best part of her mind, she even called it "that interminable *Night and Day.*"

Katherine, knowing none of this, and assuming, as one does, that a seri-ous writer's latest work puts her best foot forward, saw the novel as a pedes-trian affair; but there were also elements in it which she hated, and she dreaded the task of reviewing it. She was under great stress at the time, from her fear of death and other causes, but in sixteen days nine letters refer to her anxiety over the review. Her private opinion was that "it is a lie in the soul. The war never has been: that is what its message is. . . ." It reeked of intellec-tual snobbery, but she couldn't say so: "I tried my best to be friendly and erred on the side of kindness"—and so on.[17]

There is no doubt of the review's sincerity, or the serious thought that Katherine put into it.† As Quentin Bell says, it was perceptive and discreet, and by no means unfair to the novel. Unfortunately, in comparing the novel to a ship sailing serenely into port, the review had slipped into a hurtful phrase, occasioned by the fact that ships are feminine: "The strangeness lies in her aloofness, her air of quiet perfection, her lack of any sign that she has made a perilous voyage—the absence of any scars."

Virginia saw spite in the review, and so did Woolf, as the diary records. They had, after all, expected praise. They knew nothing of Katherine's dread-ful state in Italy just then.

---

*In "Kew Gardens." V.W.'s phrase is actually "the singular high-stepping angular green insect."
†It is printed in *Novels and Novelists.*

All questions of snobbery apart, there lay behind this episode a feeling of Katherine's which went beyond the personal: her conviction (of which she had spoken to Virginia in the week of the Armistice) that the novel must respond profoundly to the world's first total war. After telling Murry that *Night and Day* in effect denied the war, she went on:

> I don't want (G. forbid!) mobilisation and the violation of Belgium, but the novel can't just leave the war out. There *must* have been a change of heart. It is really fearful to see the "settling down" of human beings. I feel in the *profoundest* sense that nothing can ever be the same—that, as artists, we are traitors if we feel otherwise: we have to take it into account and find new expressions, new moulds for our new thoughts and feelings.[18]

Those closing words led, eventually, to her own little masterpiece, *The Fly.* A few days later she enlarged on what she meant about the post-war novel in general. The passage is important to an understanding of her own later work and cannot safely be condensed:

> I can't imagine how after the war these men can pick up the old threads as though it had never been. Speaking to *you* I'd say we have died and live again. How can that be the same life? It doesn't mean that life is the less precious or that "the common things of light and day" are gone. They are not gone, they are intensified, they are illumined. Now we know ourselves for what we are. In a way it's a tragic knowledge: it's as though, even while we live again, we face death. But *through Life:* that's the point. We see death in life as we see death in a flower that is fresh unfolded. Our hymn is to the flower's beauty: we would make that beauty immortal because we *know.* Do you feel like this—or otherwise—or how?
>
> But, of course, you don't imagine I mean by this knowledge let-us-eat-and-drink-ism. No, I mean "deserts of vast eternity." But the difference between you and me is (perhaps I'm wrong) I couldn't tell anybody *bang out* about those deserts: they are my secret. I might write about a boy eating strawberries or a woman combing her hair on a windy morning, and that is the only way I can ever mention them. But they *must* be there. Nothing less will do. They can advance and retreat, curtsey, caper to the most delicate airs they like,* but I am bored to Hell by it all. Virginia, *par exemple.*[19]

It seems a pity that neither Katherine nor Virginia could ever speak "bang out" about their deserts of vast eternity. One wants to show that letter to Virginia—even to show Virginia's later work to Katherine. Perhaps artists would be better not to live their lives until their biographies have been written.

---

*"Curtsey and retreat" was a phrase she had lately used in a letter to Murry of an *Athenaeum* article by Clive Bell. It perfectly describes his prose style, which makes much use of elegant inversion.

A winter passed with no correspondence between them, and when Katherine returned she seemed not anxious to meet again—but a fever was to blame. The *Diary* portrays her now as "of the cat kind: alien, composed, always solitary—observant." (Virginia never knew, of course, how much of Beauchamp or Dyer she was describing.) But then they fell into step, and Virginia found the other expressing *her* feelings as she never heard them expressed: to no one but Leonard could she speak in the same disembodied way about writing without altering her thought more than she altered it in the diary.[20]

More meetings occurred over the summer. Virginia went up to the house the Murrys had bought in Hampstead, to visit a Katherine who drew herself across the room "like some suffering animal." After a farewell visit, Virginia probed the strangeness of her emotions. Did she feel it as much as she ought to? Would Katherine mind their parting? She noted her own callousness, but then at once came "the blankness of not having her to talk to."

When *Bliss and Other Stories* was published in time for Christmas, and praised for a column in the *Times Literary Supplement,* Virginia saw the prospect of paeans to come, and felt a little nettle of jealousy growing in her, which she plucked by writing a little note to say how glad and proud she was. Katherine modestly said she didn't deserve the letter, and closed her reply with an odd note of finality: "I wonder if you know what your visits were to me—or how much I miss them. You are the only woman with whom I long to talk *work.* There will never be another. . . . Farewell, dear friend (may I call you that?)"[21]

It sounds as though Katherine had heard something she didn't like. At any rate, that letter of Katherine's was the end of the friendship, on her side at least. For, some weeks later, after hearing how ill and lonely she was at Menton, Virginia wrote again, but received no answer, and was hurt, as she later told Brett. Some "odious gossip" had assured her that this was Katherine's game, and so on; but she wished she had tried again, for Katherine had given her "something no one else can."[22]

In the meantime she had finished *Jacob's Room,* the novel in which new techniques, and experiments with the sense of time which probably owed something to her talks with Katherine, began to take her toward her future manner; the novel, as well, which repeatedly declares that human beings can never really know the truth about each other.

When Katherine died, Virginia confessed in her diary that Katherine's writing was "the only writing I have even been jealous of," and she later told Ottoline that while Katherine was alive she could never, from jealousy, read her books. No doubt we must look upon this jealousy as part of her illness, and not regard it in a moral light. Yet Katherine only envied what Virginia had (her home, and her security in her husband), whereas Virginia was jealous of what Katherine might attain. Perhaps that caused the guilt she also felt.

A diary entry made by Virginia within three weeks of Katherine's death[23] describes the feeling of melancholy that had been brooding over her for the past fortnight. She was alone now, with no competitor: cock of her walk, but a lonely one. She would go on writing, of course—"but into emptiness."

## *Notes*

1. Quentin Bell, *Virginia Woolf,* vol. II (1972), p. 28. Biographical facts about V.W. in this chapter, if not otherwise acknowledged, are owed to Professor Bell's work or to her diary.

2. Leonard Woolf, *Beginning Again* (1964), pp. 203–204.

3. V.W. to Vanessa Bell, 21 June 1917, NYPL. (All V.W./V.B. letters are quoted from that collection); and V.W. to Violet Dickinson, 10 June 1918, NYPL.

4. K.M. to O.M., "Tuesday" [3 July 1917], dated by reference to a letter of Murry's; TEXAS.

5. V.W. to O.M., "Aug. 15th" [1917], TEXAS.

6. K.M. to O.M. "Wednesday," TEXAS. Murry's dating, as of 1928, is clearly correct. The letter was written on 15 August.

7. K.M. to V.W., n.d. (assigned to 21 August by reference to the *Journal*), NYPL.

8. Murry to O.M., "Sunday" [possibly 7 October 1917], TEXAS.

9. Mrs. Alix Strachey in J. R. Noble, ed., *Recollections of Virginia Woolf* (1972); and her letter to Frances Partridge, 11 October 1971, made available by Mr. Stanley Olsen.

10. Murry to O.M., 15 September 1917, and K.M. to O.M., "Sunday night," TEXAS; Clive Bell to Vanessa Bell (CB/VB am I 40), KING'S.

11. The diary passage is in the *Diary,* vol. I, p. 58, and Woolf's comment is from his *Beginning Again,* p. 205. For K.M.'s use of *Genêt fleuri,* see her letters to Murry of 12 December 1915, 19 March 1918, and 13/14 October 1919.

12. Quentin Bell, vol. II (1972), p. 37.

13. Anne Estelle Rice, "Memories of Katherine Mansfield," in *ADAM* 300, 1963, p. 76; Frieda Lawrence's *Memoirs,* ed. E. W. Tedlock Jr. (1964), pp. 425–26; Lady Ottoline Morrell, quoted in *ADAM* nos. 370–75, 1972–73, p. 11; Helen Harris, MS. notes on K.M., n.d., TEXAS; Francis Carco, *Montmartre à vingt ans* (1938), p. 179.

14. K.M. to Brett, 11 October 1917, in *Letters* (1928), vol. I.

15. V.W.'s *Diary,* 2 March 1918.

16. K.M. to O.M., "Friday" ["27 June 1919"—J.M.M.], TEXAS.

17. K.M. to J.M.M., 10 November, 13 November, and 26 November 1919, ATL.

18. K.M. to J.M.M., 10 November 1919, ATL.

19. K.M. to J.M.M., 16 November 1919, ATL.

20. V.W.'s *Diary,* 31 May 1920, and 5 June 1920. The remark, quoted just below, about "some suffering animal," is from the *Diary,* 16 January 1920.

21. K.M. to V.W., 27 December 1920, typed copy, SUSSEX.

22. V.W. to Brett, 2 March 1923, CINCINNATI.

23. V.W.'s *Diary,* 28 January 1923.

# *Introduction to* The Critical Writings of Katherine Mansfield

## CLARE HANSON

'Not being an intellectual', Katherine Mansfield wrote to John Middleton Murry in 1920, 'I always seem to have to learn things at the risk of my life.' The remark suggests some of the dangers inherent in the enterprise of attempting to establish KM's reputation as a critic. She is alluding here, with some hostility, to Murry's book of critical essays *The Evolution of an Intellectual* (1920), and distancing herself from the kind of professional criticism produced by Murry, which did not often represent something learnt 'at the risk of [one's] life'. In an earlier letter she expressed her distaste for Murry's intellectual approach: a note of conviction is sustained rather than undermined by her admission of feelings of vulnerability in writing as a (relatively) uneducated woman and as a colonial—the 'little Colonial' from Karori.

> But this intellectual reasoning is never *the whole truth*. It's not *the artist's truth—* not *creative*. If man were an intellect it would do, but man ISN'T. Now I must be fair, I must be fair. Who am I to be certain that I understand? There's always Karori to shout after me. *Shout* it.[1]

From such a perspective KM's formal critical writings might be seen as anomalous: it could be argued that the reviews she wrote in 1919 and 1920 for the *Athenaeum,* in particular, were written against the grain, from a desire to placate Murry. Yet KM put 'her all' into these reviews, and devoted nearly two years of her short writing life to them, at the expense of her fiction. While we must acknowledge the reservations she felt about formal literary criticism and the English upper-middle-class male values embodied in it, we must recognise too that her critical writings represent a genuine attempt to take on the literary establishment on its own terms. KM wanted to 'preach',[2] to convert, and could and would take up the opposition's weapons in order to do this. The extent to which she at the same time subverted and undercut contemporary literary-critical forms must by the same token be recognised.

From *The Critical Writings of Katherine Mansfield,* ed. and introduced by Clare Hanson (New York: Macmillan, 1987), 1–20, 130–31. Reprinted by permission of the author.

KM's critical writings are not well known (unlike those of Virginia Woolf, for example), and it has been suggested that her finest critical insights came in an impromptu fashion, and were dashed off in moments of inspiration in letters and journals. This rather romantic view both fosters and depends on an over-emphasis on the immediately accessible 'personality' of the author, which, it is supposed, is reflected in all her writings. For the purpose of this introduction I would like to shift attention away from the attractive personality of 'Katherine Mansfield', back to the writing, in this case that body of critical work which lies so solidly across the path of the would-be KM reader or critic. What meaning, and what status, should we assign to it?

The difficulties of decision in this particular case are compounded by the presence of J. M. Murry in KM's life as in her work. Murry acted as KM's agent and took responsibility for the publication of her life and writings in a process of re-presentation which began years before her death. Antony Alpers has suggested that Murry introduced a kind of 'fuzziness' into the public picture of KM.[3] Certainly there is an unmistakable preference for the softer focus and rosier hue in Murry's view, as is suggested in Lytton Strachey's acid summing up of the discrepancy between the portrait of a lady produced for the public in Murry's 1927 *Journal,* and the woman he thought he had known: 'But why that foul-mouthed, virulent, brazen-faced broomstick of a creature should have got herself up as a pad of rose-scented cotton wool is beyond me', he wrote.[4]

For a variety of perfectly understandable reasons it would seem that Murry frequently miscast and misread KM both as a person and as a writer. At the very beginning of their relationship KM *wrote* to him (significantly) about her loathing of the role of 'wife':

> Yes, I hate hate *hate* doing these things that you accept just as all men accept of their women. I can only play the servant with a very bad grace indeed. It's all very well for females who have nothing else to do . . .[5]

Eight years later, still in the same vein, she wrote of Murry's refusal to accept the fact that for her, as for Virginia Woolf, the roles of 'wife' and 'writer' were—not just because of illness—incompatible:

> My only trouble is John. He ought to divorce me, marry a really young healthy creature, have children and ask me to be godmother. I shall never be a wife and I feel such a fraud when he believes that one day I shall turn into one.[6]

Murry's failures of vision affected important areas of professional life: it was while he was acting as KM's literary agent, for example, that he released what Antony Alpers calls the 'detested 1913 photograph' for publicity purposes. The photograph was rejected by KM not just because it gave a false picture of her as brimming with rude health, but because it gave a misleading picture of her *as a woman* and/or as a writer. KM complained too, when *Bliss, and Other Stories* was published, about what she perceived as a conflict inherent in the presentation of 'Katherine Mansfield' both as a woman and a writer. She felt threatened with silence specifically because of this conflict:

> Just while I'm on the subject I suppose you will think I am an egocentric to mind the way Constable has advertised my book and the paragraph that is on the paper cover. I'd like to say that I mind so terribly that there are no words for me. No—I'm DUMB!! I think it so insulting and disgusting and undignified that—well—there you are! It's no good suffering all over again. But the bit about 'Women will learn by heart and not repeat'. Gods! why didn't they have a photograph of me looking through a garter. But I was helpless here—too late to stop it—so now I *must* prove—no, convince people ce n'est pas moi. At least, if I'd known they were going to say that, no power on earth would have made me cut a word. I wish I hadn't. I was wrong—very wrong.[7]

To come down to more tangible textual matters, it is clear that Murry had a hand in the bowdlerisation of KM's fiction as well as of her letters and journals. In the quotation above, KM is referring to the fact that 'Je ne parle pas français' (one of the only two stories, she said in 1922, that satisfied her to any extent) had been adulterated for its publication by Constable. The original text, as published by the Heron Press in 1919, is far bolder—the story ends, for example, with two additional paragraphs:

> I must go. I must go. I reach down my coat and hat. Madame knows me. 'You haven't dined yet?' she smiles.
> 'No, not yet, Madame.' [Constable text ends here.]
> I'd rather like to dine with her. Even to sleep with her afterwards. Would she be pale like that all over?
> But no. She'd have large moles. They go with that kind of skin. And I can't bear them. They remind me somehow, disgustingly, of mushrooms.[8]

Many references to sexuality (important for the particular kind of 'corruption' KM was evoking here) have been cut for the Constable edition: KM felt she had 'picked the eyes out of [her] story', at Murry's and Michael Sadleir's instigation, to ensure its publication. Of course, she was responding to social pressures, not only to Murry, in doing this, and it would be wrong to suggest that Murry should take sole responsibility for the ways in which his wife's work and personality were presented to the public. It is unfair, I think, to take the line taken by Leonard Woolf, who claimed that Murry had a malevolent influence on KM which was in some way outside her control:

> I think that in some abstruse way Murry corrupted and perverted and destroyed Katherine both as a person and a writer. . . . She got enmeshed in the sticky sentimentality of Murry and wrote against the grain of her own nature.[9]

But Murry did certainly suggest, during KM's lifetime, that she should hide some of her cutting edge from the public, and after her death he ensured that her sharpness did not often appear. He was far more concerned than KM with the question of what it was decorous for a woman writer to say, and the effect of his editing of KM's life and works has undoubtedly been to obscure the clarity, the harshness and, I would suggest, the more 'masculine' qualities of her mind.

In KM's critical writings Murry's influence is directly detectable in certain turns of phrase and in a kind of portentousness which appears particularly in the earlier reviews. KM and Murry wrote enthusiastic manifesto articles together for *Rhythm* in 1912, and something of the Murry tone still lingers in the first reviews KM wrote for the *Athenaeum*—in the closing lines of a review of Maugham's *The Moon and Sixpence,* for example:

> But great artists are not drunken men; they are men who are divinely sober. They know that the moon can never be bought for sixpence, and that liberty is only a profound realisation of the greatness of the dangers in their midst.[10]

But KM quickly pulled herself up: she commented crisply when she pasted this review into her notebook, 'Shows traces of hurry & at the end, is pompous!'[11]

Her achievement was precisely to create her own voice—the least portentous of voices—while working within many constraints, both in the *Athenaeum* reviews and in her critical writing in letters and journals. Seen in this context, of an achieved critical point of view, Murry's influence (apart from specific questions of style or tone) is perhaps best seen as symbolic—he acts as a convenient scapegoat, a representative of many of the values of the contemporary literary establishment which KM wished to resist.

What KM really wanted to do in her criticism is explained in a letter of 1920 in which she admonished Murry regarding the *Athenaeum*:

> In my reckless way I would suggest all reviews were signed and all were put into the first person. I think that would give the whole paper an amazing lift-up. A paper that length must be *definite, personal* or die. It can't afford the 'we'— 'in our opinion'. To sign reviews, to put them in the 1st person stimulates curiosity, *makes for correspondence,* gives it (to be 19-eleventyish[12]) GUTS. You see it's a case of leaning out of a window with a board and a nail, *or* a bouquet, *or* a flag—administering whichever it is and retiring *sharp.* This seems to me essential.[13]

It is tempting to suggest that KM's dislike of the impersonal third-person style of contemporary reviewing is distinctively 'feminine', and on these grounds to align her with a writer such as Dorothy Richardson, who was a conscious campaigner against the rigid, impersonal, rule-bound qualities of 'male prose'. Yet this would be misleading and the adoption of such convenient distinctions might obscure the real complexity of KM's position as a woman writer at a particular point in time, writing for a particular audience. It does not take much reflection to see, for example, that KM's writing, both creative and critical, has qualities which, in such terms, would have to be considered 'masculine', though it is also true that it is very difficult to determine when she is consciously cultivating a 'masculine' tone for defensive purposes.

In broad terms, KM wanted her criticism to be more personal, and more concrete, very much as she wished her fiction to be 'personal'[14] and concretely affective, and she adopted rather similar strategies to achieve this. She sought the freedom of a tone in which she could be, as far as that was possible, 'most herself, and least personal', a tone achieved through placing of the self in a dramatic context and through the use of symbolism and indirect allusion rather than direct statement. She adopted a persona in her criticism just as she did in her fiction: a persona which is androgynous—tough, 'masculine' and fearless on the one hand, yet capable of the finest (feminine) judgements and discriminations on the other. A prevailing note of irony dissolves tensions between male and female, writer and work: we can see such irony in operation, defusing potentially disabling oppositions, in this extract from a review of M. Austen-Leigh's *Personal Aspects of Jane Austen*:

> It seems almost unkind to criticise a little book which has thrown on bonnet and shawl and tripped across the fields of criticism at so round a pace to defend its dear Jane Austen. . . . Can we picture Jane Austen caring—except in a delightfully wicked way which we are sure the author of this book would not allow—that people said she was no lady, was not fond of children, hated animals, did not care a pin for the poor, could not have written about foreign parts if she had tried, had no idea how a fox was killed, but rather thought it ran up a tree and hissed at the hound at the last—was, in short, cold, coarse, practically illiterate and without morality? Mightn't her reply have been, 'Ah, but what about my novels?'[15]

KM's criticism is also marked, like that of her modernist contemporaries Woolf and Eliot, by a striking and vivid use of metaphor. Such criticism is often called 'impressionistic'—the term has been applied particularly often to the sometimes flamboyant criticism of Virginia Woolf. Yet KM's literary criticism is the reverse of impressionistic in the derogatory sense of diffuse or vague. Through the use of metaphor she achieves two major objectives.

First, she enforces an extension of our critical capacity—we are led into an acknowledgement of relationships and suggestive analogies of whose existence we had previously been unaware. And it is important to note that in this context, of a discourse of persuasion, metaphor works very much as it does in some metaphysical poetry, to evoke and create very precise images and qualities.

Secondly, however, KM is able to exploit the 'luminous halo' surrounding the lighted core of any given metaphor: she is able to utilise the wider, less well defined attributes or associations of a particular image in order to suggest indirectly a point of view which she was unable openly to state. This kind of 'secondary' indirection is particularly important when we are considering the formal, and, in some respects, restrictive context in which the *Athenaeum* reviews were written. To take an example, in her review of Virginia Woolf's *Night and Day,* KM is able through her use of the metaphor of the ship for this novel to bring to our notice not only its solid, craftsman-like qualities and its seriousness (it is or it has been launched on the sea, which serves KM again and again as a metaphor for knowledge, consciousness and discovery), but also its heaviness and its rather unyielding aspects. These qualities of the ship are actually foregrounded by KM as she develops the metaphor:

> To us who love to linger down at the harbour, as it were, watching the new ships being built, the old ones returning, and the many putting out to sea, comes the strange sight of *Night and Day* sailing into port serene and resolute on a deliberate wind. The strangeness lies in her aloofness, her air of quiet perfection, her lack of any sign that she has made a perilous voyage—the absence of any scars. There she lies among the strange shipping—a tribute to civilisation for our admiration and wonder.[16]

KM similarly uses an extended metaphor in order briskly to dispose of Mrs Wharton:

> But what about us? What about her readers? Does Mrs Wharton expect us to grow warm in a gallery where the temperature is so sparkingly cool? We are looking at portraits—are we not? These are human beings, arranged for exhibition purposes, framed, glazed, and hung in the perfect light. They pale, they grow paler, they flush, they raise their 'clearest eyes', they hold out their arms to each other 'extended, but not rigid', and the voice is the voice of the portrait.[17]

KM's use of metaphor in her critical writings is thus not only a matter of personal preference in the sense that she was (or, rather, had become) a symbolist writer, delighting in obliquity and 'fine shades': it also served a very definite tactical purpose, enabling her to be 'definite and personal' in her criticism despite the constraints and conventions of her medium.

Other strategies employed by KM to subvert critical forms from within include the impassive retelling of a story simply in order to make it ridiculous. The tone of many of the novel reviews reminds us of Leonard Woolf's memorable picture of KM:

> I don't think anyone has ever made me laugh more than she did in those days. She would sit very upright on the edge of a chair or sofa and tell at immense length a kind of saga of her experiences as an actress or of how and why Koteliansky howled like a dog in the room at the top of the building in Southampton Row. There was not the shadow of a gleam of a smile on her mask

of a face, and the extraordinary funniness of the story was increased by the flashes of her astringent wit.[18]

Another tactic KM often adopts is the use of a rhetorical question to open a review, and then of a suspended conclusion—the effect is that of disclaiming responsibility for the criticism which has just been produced. An example is 'Anodyne', a withering account of a 'pastime novel', which opens with the bland question, 'What is a "sweetly pretty" novel?' and ends, 'though you would not doubt the issue of the fight, you cannot be absolutely certain how the victory will be obtained, and so—you read on'. At the end of the review KM is, as it were, like the cat which has neatly regained its balance after performing a superb trick—and then, like Kezia in 'Prelude', tiptoes away.

So KM, working flexibly within cultural and social restrictions and conventions, manages to a considerable extent to fit her own prescription and to be 'definite and personal' in her criticism. In looking more closely at this criticism it is useful, if rather artificial, to make a distinction between its general interest and value and its particular relevance for a consideration of KM's own fiction. In making high claims for her literary criticism, one is by implication inviting a reassessment of her creative work. I suggest that this is especially important in the case of KM, for in her work, as in that of many modernist writers, there is a particularly close connection between critical and creative writing. Modernist literature is by its nature oblique, allusive, formally experimental, and may exhibit a certain logical discontinuity. Most modernist writers have in consequence found it necessary to prepare and create the audience for their work, explaining their aims and techniques in critical manifestos which have acted as glosses on their work. Examples are T. S. Eliot's essays in the *Criterion,* or Virginia Woolf's early essays. I would suggest that the fiction of KM, too, would benefit from being read in the light of her expressed aesthetic aims, and that such a reading would lead to a fuller understanding and appreciation of her allusive and elusive art.

In order to understand KM's 'personal' aesthetic in this sense—her *particular* aims as a writer—we must focus predominantly on her technical and practical remarks on writing, more evident in the letters and journals, as we would expect, than in the formal reviews. The most important aspect of KM's aesthetic to emerge from such scrutiny is its symbolist[19] bias. KM was a symbolist writer in the sense that her work belongs to the post-Symbolist tradition in European literature. KM's earliest literary mentors were Arthur Symons and Oscar Wilde, the two most important representatives or 'translators' of the French Symbolist movement. KM's familiarity with the work of Symons, in particular, becomes clear from a study of her early—previously unpublished—notes on his work, printed in Appendix 1; Wilde too appears frequently in the early notebooks as a tutelary figure. The central idea which she took from these writers was the belief that in literature abstract states of mind or feeling should be conveyed through concrete images rather than described analytically. This view is expressed with remarkable clarity in an early notebook entry which appears among her annotations of Symons's *Studies in Prose and Verse*[20] (1904):

> The partisans of analysis describe minutely the state of the soul; the secret motive of every action as being of far greater importance than the action itself. The partisans of objectivity—give us the result of this evolution sans describing the secret processes. They describe the state of the soul through the slightest gesture—i.e. realise flesh covered bones—which is the artist's method for me—in as much as art seems to me *pure vision*—I am indeed a partisan of objectivity—[21]

It is a view to which KM held throughout her career. Compare, for example, this 1919 letter to Murry on her own indirect method in fiction (she is writing about the effect of the war on her contemporaries):

> I can't imagine how after the war these men can pick up the old threads as though it had never been. Speaking to *you* I'd say we have died and live again. How can that be the same life? It doesn't mean that life is the less precious or that the 'common things of light and day' are gone. They are not gone, they are intensified, they are illumined. Now we know ourselves for what we are. In a way it's a tragic knowledge. . . .
>
> But, of course, you don't imagine I mean by this knowledge let-us-eat-and-drinkism. No, I mean 'deserts of vast eternity'. But the difference between you and me is (perhaps I'm wrong) I couldn't tell anybody *bang out* about those deserts; they are my secret. I might write about a boy eating strawberries or a woman combing her hair on a windy morning, and that is the only way I can ever mention them. But they *must* be there. Nothing less will do.[22]

An abstract theme must be suggested through concrete images and symbols, and thus returned to its origin in concrete experience. Thus, in a Mansfield story, we might expect to find that most of the 'narrative' details work in this way, having a symbolic as well as a narrative function: in this respect her work may be closely linked with that of Joyce (of whom, incidentally, she could not conceivably have been aware in 1908, the date of the notebook entry on the revelation of the soul 'through the slightest gesture'). Both writers—independently—effected a revolution in the short-story form by introducing into it techniques of systematic allusion derived ultimately from French Symbolist poetry.

There is a limit, however, to the extent to which the all-purpose label 'symbolist' will fit KM. In one important respect her aesthetic differs from that of the symbolists: it is a difference that by its nature becomes clearer if we look beyond KM's letters and journal to her formal critical writing. A belief strongly expressed in the reviews is that art has an ethical *dimension,* if not an ethical function: KM did not in this respect assent to the symbolist belief in art as an entirely autotelic activity. While she did not suggest that the artist should in any crude sense set out to preach or prove a point, she did believe that the 'true' artist's work would make an ethical 'impression', and that it was the duty of the critic to register this impression and measure its depth and quality. This is a role which she plays, in the least abrasive manner, in much of her critical writing—for example, in a 1920 review of Galsworthy's *In Chancery*, in which she laments his inability to regard his characters 'from an eminence' both moral and intellectual:

> It is a very great gift for an author to be able to project himself into the hearts and minds of his characters—but more is needed to make a great creative artist: he must be able, with equal power, to withdraw, to survey what is happening— and from an eminence.[23]

While noting this 'ethical' aspect of KM's aesthetic, however, it is important too to observe the almost Jamesian distinctions which she herself made about the scope and function of the ethical element in art. She explains her position most clearly in a journal note on the philosophy of Vaihinger. Here she asserts the intrinsic identity of ethical and aesthetic ends ('the ideal') but suggests that this ideality can, paradoxically, only be achieved *within* the work of art itself, removed from *practical* use and function:

> Reality cannot become the ideal, the dream; and it is not the business of the artist to grind an axe, to try to impose his vision of life upon the existing world. Art is not an attempt of the artist to reconcile existence with his vision; it is an attempt to create his own world *in* this world.[24]

The second major aspect of KM's 'personal' aesthetic is her emphasis on memory, which she places at the centre of the artistic process. Memory is both selective, isolating the salient features of a particular event or experience, and synthetic, superimposing and juxtaposing remembered scenes and images so that in time (in the fullest sense) experience is literally reconstituted. This process is not mechanical but organic, and it too has an ethical[25] dimension which is rooted in the individual artist's temperament and disposition. These beliefs are expressed most forcefully in the review of Dorothy Richardson's *The Tunnel* which opened KM's series of reviews for the *Athenaeum*. Here, the moral and idealising aspects of memory are evoked through apocalyptic imagery:

> There is one who could not live in so tempestuous an environment as her mind—and he is Memory. She has no memory. It is true that Life is sometimes very swift and breathless, but not always. If we are to be truly alive there are large pauses in which we creep away into our caves of contemplation. And then it is, in the silence, that Memory mounts his throne and judges all that is in our minds—appointing each his separate place, high or low, rejecting this, select-

ing that—putting this one to shine in the light and throwing that one into the darkness.

We do not mean to say that those large, round biscuits might not be in the light, or the night in Spring be in the darkness. Only we feel that until these things are judged and given each its appointed place in the whole scheme, they have no meaning in the world of art.[26]

Memory idealises, in the fullest sense, and makes (ethical) judgements and discriminations; it is important to recognise this element in KM's richly worked and polished fiction, which is 'slight' or 'episodic' only in the most nominal technical sense.

Besides shedding light on KM's own aims and achievement in fiction, her criticism has an interest and value which extends far beyond particular insights into contemporary writers. The formal reviews written for the *Athenaeum* (as opposed to the working-notes found in letters and journals) constitute a formidable body of criticism, a framework of (sometimes veiled) polemic and advocacy. It has already been indicated that one of the important themes of KM's criticism is that of the effects of the First World War: this is partly a simple function of the timing of the reviewing-stint, but also stems from KM's clear belief that the war had, or should have, entirely changed man's perception of himself. She wrote to Murry that 'we have to face our war', the implication being that artists could not dismiss the war as the responsibility of other people, as many, she felt, wished to do. While illness made KM particularly susceptible to intimations of frailty and mortality associated with the war, one cannot deny the justice of her charge that for many artists the war simply had not been 'felt'. For most, direct personal suffering had been avoided, and the war had not brought a greater consciousness of man's inhumanity to man. When KM wrote that as a result of the war 'now we know ourselves for what we are', she was speaking, she felt, for a tiny minority—a minority which included most notably D. H. Lawrence (see KM's note on *Aaron's Rod,* 1922).

The major thrust of KM's polemic in the *Athenaeum* reviews is in an area related to her feelings about the war: she was concerned above all with 'seriousness in art', concerned that the literature of her day should, using whatever techniques were necessary, address the deeper issues of life—'nothing less will do'. She felt that much of the fiction she encountered was trivial, and consequently her attempts at definition of what is worthwhile in art occur as frequently in a context of denunciation (for instance, of the third-rate novels of Gilbert Cannan, or of the 'pastime novel') as in one of admiration and congratulation. Like all reviewers, KM was deluged with inferior novels: what makes her outstanding as a critic is the deft and deadly way in which she analyses the failures she so often encounters and, more rarely, illuminates the successful, achieved work of art.

It is important in this context to point out that KM was writing for the *Athenaeum* in a period which appeared a desert in terms of fiction: as Antony Alpers has remarked,[27] reading the *Athenaeum* reviews one comes fully to appreciate the climate of mingled dearth and expectation in which *The Garden Party, Jacob's Room* and *Ulysses* were so rapturously received. It was a desert more apparent than real, as Lawrence, Joyce, KM and Woolf were all writing in the years before 1922—but were not, for a variety of reasons, being published. Compared to the dramatic developments taking place in visual art at the same time, literature seemed to be lagging dully behind.

It is fortunate that KM was able with such frequency to turn reviews of novels which disappoint her into occasions for the exploration and celebration of those qualities which make for distinction. In a review of Joseph Hergesheimer's *Linda Condon,* for example, she uses the Yeatsian image of the tree to suggest the organic wholeness of the successful work of art—*not* achieved in this particular instance:

> If a novel is to have a central idea we imagine that central idea is a lusty growing stem from which the branches spring clothed with leaves, and the buds become flowers and fruits. We imagine that the author chooses with infinite deliberation the very air in which that tree shall be nourished, and that he is profoundly aware that its coming to perfection depends upon the strength with which the central idea supports its beautiful accumulations.[28]

The extended metaphor is one of the most often used tools through which she places, though often in negative terms, moral and aesthetic qualities. So, to register just a few, she uses metaphors for familiarity and change (the shallow and the deeper seas, the known and the unknown hotel); employs consumer metaphors for fictions which are no more than conventional confections or 'digestible snacks',[29] uses 'artful' metaphors for artful novels where the characters resemble portraits hanging in a gallery; or evokes in detail the atmosphere of the 'Garden City novel' with homes 'which seem to breathe white enamel and cork linoleum and the works of Freud and Jung'.[30]

As these allusions should make sufficiently clear, it is extremely difficult to disentangle ethical and aesthetic motives and beliefs in KM's literary criticism. It may be useful here to make a distinction between the 'ethical' and the 'moral': 'moral' might be used to refer to the practical sphere, to matters of action and conduct, while 'ethical' would denote a more disinterested ethical sense, rather like the 'undestroyed freshness' of Maisie in James's *What Maisie Knew,* which is, as it were, as much a matter of taste as of judgement. It is in this light—in relation to the 'ethical' in this sense—that we can perhaps best see KM's insistence on the relation between the ethical and the aesthetic, and on the relation between 'life' and 'art'. It is by no means a naïve insistence. In, for example, a review of *Mary Olivier: A Life* by May Sinclair, KM uses Blake's image of the 'bounding line' to suggest that widest possible ethical and aesthetic perspective which, she felt, should distinguish the great novel (and which was of course lacking in Sinclair's work):

> But if the Flood, the sky, the rainbow, or what Blake beautifully calls the bounding outline, be removed and if, further, no one thing is to be related to another thing, we do not see what is to prevent the whole of mankind turning author.

She goes on:

> Is it not the great abiding satisfaction of a work of art that the writer was master of the situation when he wrote it and at the mercy of nothing less mysterious than a greater work of art?[31]

The suggestion that the world of art and the world of 'fact' are analogous and conterminous (it is the world itself which is of course the greater work of art) reflects KM's very modernist feeling for the unreality and insubstantiality of any external world conceived of as existing outside the (involuntarily) creative mind of man.

To move now to—in relative terms—more specific issues, KM's criticism is of interest in relation to two questions much debated at the time: the influence of Russian literature in England between 1900 and 1920, and the contemporary debate over 'feminine prose'. KM was in a special position in relation to Russian literature. She felt passionately about it, as is indicated in this 1919 letter to Koteliansky:

> When you think that the english [sic] literary world is given up to sniggerers, dishonesty, sneering *dull, dull* giggling at Victorians in side-whiskers and here is this treasure—at the wharf only not unloaded . . . I feel that Art is like a sick person, left all alone in a house where they are having a jazz party downstairs and we have at least something of what that sick person needs to be well again. Can't we thieve up the back staircase and take it?[32]

She shares the general contemporary enthusiasm for Russian literature, and sense of its pre-eminence, but, perhaps because she worked intensively on translations from the Russian in collaboration with Koteliansky, she had a more acute, if sometimes frustrated, sense than most of the specificity of the achievement of the great Russian writers. Her method in translation was to work from Koteliansky's strange but literal translations, re-creating, in so far as she could, the sense of the original, and restoring harmony to the splintered fragments of Koteliansky's prose. The process taught her enough about the Russian language for her to feel confident in criticising Constance Garnett's (very influential) translations: she wrote in another 1919 letter to Koteliansky,

'She [Garnett] seems to take the nerve out of Chekhov before she starts work-ing on him, like the dentist takes the nerve from a tooth.'

The most intriguing question, in this context, is that of KM's reaction to the work of Chekhov, whose work she has so often been accused of plagiaris-ing. It is quite clear from an examination of KM's early notebooks that she had developed her method of obliquity and indirection quite independently of any study which she may have made of the works of Chekhov, and her attitude in her critical writings—formal and informal—is in every way consistent with this fact. Her attitude is one of joyful celebration, and there is no sign of the grudging or awkward praise which we would expect if she were dealing with an author towards whom she had an 'unholy' obligation.

There are two key reviews in relation to Chekhov. The first is the un-signed review of *The Cherry Orchard,* collected here for the first time. The re-view is remarkable more for its sensitivity to Chekhov's dramatic method, and its awareness of the implications of his work for the form of drama as a whole, than for its insight into the particular themes of this play. I would suggest that this fact, taken together with the way in which the review tails off into repeti-tion and generalisation, indicates that it was in fact written jointly (and hur-riedly) with Murry[33]—Murry finishing the review while KM had barely begun to make her points about the play.

The other review in which KM discusses Chekhov is that entitled 'Wanted, a New World' (25 June 1920). The books ostensibly under consider-ation here are three collections of 'short stories' or 'tales', as KM variously calls them. KM takes the opportunity that the contrasting failure of these stories afforded her to discuss the achievement of Chekhov. The review is significant because it is one of the very few in which she discusses directly the short-story form. In it she aligns herself with Chekhov as the pioneer of an art which she can only define negatively, *against* conventional terms and forms—'I am nei-ther a short story, nor a sketch, nor an impression, nor a tale', she writes. The missing term we might supply here is 'short fiction', to denote that kind of short prose fiction produced first by Chekhov and then by KM, in which ac-tion is less important than atmosphere and in which the process of language tends increasingly to become part of the subject as well as the agent of compo-sition (this type of short fiction has been developed most notably by Beckett in English fiction).

KM's relation to another contentious contemporary issue, that of 'femi-nine prose', is in itself contentious, or adversarial. Whether by design on Murry's part or not, KM did the bulk of the reviewing of novels by women during the period when she was with the *Athenaeum.* Her reviews thus offer an original response to the work of many women writers who are currently being reinstated in the literary canon: for example, May Sinclair, Rose Macaulay, Rhoda Broughton, Sheila Kaye-Smith. On the whole KM is more lenient with these writers than with their male counterparts (compare for ex-ample the review of Sheila Kaye-Smith's *Tamarisk Town* with that of Hugh

Walpole's *The Captives*); it is correspondingly true that by implication she takes male writers such as Walpole more seriously. Even more striking is the fact that she comes out very firmly against those women writers who were at this time attempting to pioneer a 'feminine prose'. I would suggest that, to some extent, her attacks on writers such as May Sinclair and Dorothy Richardson were defensive rather than offensive, and that her wariness of their fiction stems from the fact that it pointed to a whole area which was problematic and unresolved for her.

Elaine Showalter, in *A Literature of their Own,* sets the scene for a consideration of 'feminine prose'; she points out that by 1920 the debate over this issue was in full swing—R. Brimley Johnson, for example, had just produced a critical study in which he attempted to define the qualities of 'the new female version of realism'. He singled out May Sinclair's claim (in *The Creators,* 1910) that experience (in the sense of incident or adventure) can only hinder the woman writer: Showalter rightly links this with Sinclair's 'charmed' response to the work of Richardson—'Nothing happens. It just goes on and on', Sinclair wrote of *Pilgrimage.* Sinclair and Richardson were fascinated by the possibility that experience may be primarily, rather than ultimately or absolutely, indivisible and structureless.

The term 'feminine prose' is actually Richardson's: it comes from her introduction to the 1938 edition of *Pilgrimage:*

> Feminine prose, as Charles Dickens and James Joyce have delightfully shown themselves to be aware, should properly be unpunctuated, moving from point to point without formal obstructions. And the author of *Pilgrimage* must confess to an early habit of ignoring, while writing, the lesser of the stereotyped system of signs, and further when sprinkling in what appeared to be necessary, to a small unconscious departure from current usage.[34]

But, as has been indicated, Richardson was not alone in her beliefs: she was drawing on the work of many other women writers who, seeing language as inherently oppressive and male-centred, aimed to challenge it, and who saw the forms of fiction too as potentially restrictive and gender-bound. The work of Sinclair, Richardson and Gertrude Stein thus offers a particularly rich field for the study of the relations between gender, language and literary form: these women writers were by 1920 embarked on many of the projects which, after a lapse of nearly half a century, French feminist theory has recently republicised and redefined. In drawing attention to the arbitrary nature of language, Sinclair, Richardson and Stein identified what was to form the linchpin of linguistic structuralist theory; they wanted too to push against the antithetical nature of language and experience and to stress the seamless and undifferentiated nature of immediate experience (compare Julia Kristeva's notion of the pre-Oedipal, feminine, semiotic *chora,* as opposed to the over-differentiated and over-mediated language/experience of men).

Why did KM, and Virginia Woolf, find these projects distasteful, or simply wrong? Showalter argues that Virginia Woolf's 'flight into androgyny' was caused by a damaging inhibition of feelings of rage and frustration; she also offers a possible clue to KM's rejection of 'feminine prose' in noting the 'punitive' nature of her fiction.[35] Showalter is right about this punitive aspect of KM's art: in it, women who behave rather like KM herself are severely punished for their presumption in questioning conventional sexual roles. For example, the 'fast' and sexually ambiguous Mrs Kember of 'At the Bay' is punished by complete social ostracism and the faithlessness of her handsome husband. It is thus possible to liken KM's rejection of 'feminine prose' to that of Woolf, suggesting that KM too saw in feminine prose possibilities of exposure and subsequent retributive attack, rather than freedom. We might read KM's strictures on the undifferentiated worlds/words of Richardson and Sinclair as overreaction against something recognised and repressed in herself.

If we look at it in this light, the imagery KM uses in her reviews of Richardson and Sinclair is, to say the least, disconcerting: consider again, for example, that passage in the review of *The Tunnel* in which she describes the operations of a powerful, institutionalised, male memory, which has the power to judge what shall be allowed to 'shine' in the light of consciousness and what shall be consigned to unconsciousness and oblivion: 'And then it is, in the silence, that Memory mounts his throne and judges all that is in our minds— appointing each his separate place, high or low. . . .'[36] KM here seems to privilege male authority, and clarity, over feminine 'confusion' (compare also her *Night and Day* review, in which she comments acidly on Woolf's description of the 'confusion' of the 'finest prose').

There is a great deal of evidence from KM's early writings of her awareness of feminist issues, though it is also true that her response to these issues remained ambiguous. For example, an early notebook entry commenting enthusiastically on a novel by the feminist Elizabeth Robins is offset by an unpublished sketch in which KM dismisses feminists in a tone of quite awesome sentimentality:

> I longed to take them [the feminists] home and show them my babies and make their hair soft and fluffy, and put them in teagowns and then cuddle them—I think they would never go back to their Physical Culture, or the Society for the Promotion of women's Rights.[37]

An ambivalent attitude towards the opportunities afforded by feminism persisted throughout KM's life: like many of the characters in her fiction, she seems to have been torn between a desire to reject the conventional feminine role and a desire to accept it—to annihilate herself, as it were, by identifying completely with it. This ambivalence is clearly related to KM's bisexuality, itself a complex of forces and orientations which biography can only struggle to recover.[38] What is important for her writing is that this sexual ambivalence produced a fiction which is stronger, in feminist terms, than that of Virginia Woolf, who was of course shocked (and frightened?) by KM's exposure of the emptiness behind stereotypical female role-playing in the story 'Bliss'.[39]

I would suggest that KM's fiction is strong in feminist terms because her estrangement from, yet identification with, the feminine enabled her to see it as something learnt, not something given; something chosen, not necessarily determined by biological or psychological fact. In this context, I think it is thus reasonable to see KM's rejection of feminine prose as more than the self-protective strategy which Showalter describes: KM rejected the cultivation of 'the feminine', by such writers as Richardson, as something exclusive, inalienable and necessarily 'other' because this seemed to her untrue to the slippery and ambivalent nature of human sexual identity.

It is important too to see the wider context in which the movement towards 'feminine prose' can itself be seen as the product of particular cultural and historical forces, as can the sympathetic acceptance of its aims by recent French feminist critics such as Julia Kristeva and Hélène Cixous. As critics we are still emerging from the shadow of Jacques Lacan's theory of the 'Oedipal' moment of entry into the symbolic order of language, by means of which the feminine is necessarily defined in terms of lack. It is only comparatively recently that attempts have been made to theorise a positive rather than a negative entry into language for women. Feminist critics[40] are now drawing attention to the work of psychologists who have insisted that, *pace* Lacan, the entry into language is established prior to and independently of the Oedipal moment of repression. It may be, then, that we should now view Lacanian theory as a reflection *of* rather than a reflection *on* phallocratic values; his extraordinarily influential theory of language as by its nature patriarchal may perhaps itself be seen as symptomatic. If this is so, feminist criticism will have to focus again on questions of power, strength and authority in women's writing: this in turn may offer some vindication of the ways in which Katherine Mansfield held on firmly, in theoretical terms, to her own complex position of author-ity in language.

## Notes

The following abbreviations are used throughout:

ATL     Alexander Turnbull Library, Wellington, New Zealand
*Journal*   *The Journal of Katherine Mansfield*, ed. J. M. Murry (1954)
*LJMM*   *Katherine Mansfield's Letters to J. Middleton Murry*, ed. J. Middleton Murry (1951)
*NN*     Katherine Mansfield, *Novels and Novelists* (New York, 1930)

Books published in London unless otherwise indicated.

1. *LJMM*, p. 435 (8 Dec 1919).

2. Ibid., p. 283 (5 June 1918).

3. In conversation with the author, August 1983.

4. Michael Holroyd, *Lytton Strachey: A Critical Biography* (1968) II, 538.

5. *LJMM*, p. 4 (Summer 1913).

6. *The Letters and Journals of Katherine Mansfield*, ed. C. K. Stead (1977) p. 225 (June–July 1921).

7. *LJMM*, p. 614.

8. *Je ne parle pas français* (Hampstead: Heron Press, 1919).

9. Leonard Woolf, *Beginning Again: An Autobiography of the Years 1911–18* (1964) p. 204.

10. *NN*, p. 22.

11. ATL, MS Papers 119, Notebook 46.

12. The reference is to *Rhythm* (1911–13), which had for its slogan a phrase taken from Synge 'Before art can be human again it must learn to be brutal' (slightly misquoted from the Preface to Synge's *Poems and Translations*).

13. *LJMM*, pp. 612–13.

14. See *Journal*, p. 205, for a discussion of the artificial nature of 'the personal'.

15. *NN*, p. 314.

16. Ibid., pp. 112–13.

17. Ibid., p. 320.

18. Leonard Woolf, *Beginning Again*, p. 204.

19. A brief definition of terms: Symbolism capitalised is taken here to refer specifically to the Symbolist movement in French poetry towards the end of the nineteenth century; symbolism (lower-case) is used more broadly to describe the twentieth-century post-Symbolist movement in European Literature.

20. The notes in this section of ATL Notebook 2 have not previously been traced to Symons's *Studies in Prose and Verse*. Critics who have made brief references to them, e.g. Vincent O'Sullivan in 'The Magnetic Chain: Notes and Approaches to KM', *Landfall*, 114 (1975) 95–131, have assumed that they are KM's own comments, whereas in fact almost every entry, with the exception of that quoted here, is taken virtually verbatim from Symons. ATL Notebook 8 also contains notes from Symons's *Plays, Acting and Music* (see Appendix 1).

21. ATL Notebook 2, fo. 58.

22. *LJMM*, pp. 392–3.

23. *NN*, p. 317.

24. *Journal*, p. 273.

25. Cf. Wordsworth's almost mystical sense of the beneficent powers of memory in *The Prelude*.

26. *NN*, p. 6.

27. Antony Alpers, *The Life of Katherine Mansfield* (1980) p. 353.

28. *NN*, p. 236.

29. *NN*, p. 310.

30. *NN*, p. 178.

31. *NN*, pp. 44–5.

32. Letter of Katherine Mansfield to S. S. Koteliansky, British Library MS Add. 48970 (21 Aug 1919). The 'treasure' to which she refers is Russian literature in general, and, more specifically, the letters of Chekhov, which she and Koteliansky were currently translating.

33. The review (repr. in Ch. 2, pt II) has been accepted by KM scholars as being entirely by KM, but the internal evidence works strongly against this view.

34. Foreword to the 1938 edition of *Pilgrimage*, repr. in *Pilgrimage I* (Virago, 1979) p. 12.

35. Elaine Showalter, *A Literature of their Own* (1978) p. 246.

36. *NN*, p. 6.

37. Unpublished sketch, ATL Notebook 37, fos 8–14.

38. See, in this respect, Alpers, *The Life of Katherine Mansfield,* and C. A. Hankin, *The Confessional Stories of Katherine Mansfield* (1983).

39. Virginia Woolf's often cited hostile reaction to 'Bliss' should I think be referred to her own repressed feelings about lesbianism, and her unease over her perception of this theme in the story, in this respect more 'advanced' than anything she herself wrote.

40. See, for example, Sandra M. Gilbert and Susan Gubar (authors of *The Madwoman in the Attic,* 1979) in their article 'Sexual Linguistics: Gender, Language, Sexuality', *New Literary History,* 16.3 (Spring 1985) 515–43.

# Index

CHAPIN MEMORIAL LIBRARY
400 14TH AVENUE NORTH
MYRTLE BEACH, SC  29577
(803) 48-3338

9100 048 848 6

DATE DUE